USDA

United States
Department of
Agriculture

Forest Service

Forest
Products
Laboratory

Research
Paper
FPL–RP–637

U.S. Timber Production, Trade, Consumption, and Price Statistics 1965 to 2005

James L. Howard

Abstract

This report presents annual data but is published every 2 years. The data present current and historical information on the production, trade, consumption, and prices of timber products in the United States. The report focuses on national statistics, but includes some data for individual States and regions and for Canada. The data were collected from industry trade associations and government agencies. They are intended for use by forest land managers, forest industries, trade associations, forestry schools, renewable resource organizations, individuals in the major timber producing and consuming countries of the world, and the general public. A major use of the data is tracking industry production and consumption trends over time. One of the major shifts occurring in the wood using industry over the last 2 years is that both production and consumption of roundwood per capita have been increasing. The consumption of products per capita also increased over the last 2 years. Because of increased paper recycling and increased processing efficiency, the consumption per capita in roundwood equivalent has decreased since about 1987 from 83 ft^3 to 72 ft^3 per capita. In the 1960s and 1970s, consumption averaged 65 ft^3 per capita. Per capita consumption in 2004 increased to 71 ft^3 per capita before increasing further in 2005 to 72 ft^3 per capita. Another shift occurring during 2005 is increased emphasis on wood energy use, which has shown wide fluctuations over the last decade into 2005.

Keywords: production, consumption, import, export

Acknowledgments

This update required assistance from a very dedicated individual. Rebecca Westby, an Economic Assistant in the Timber Demand and Technology Assessment Project (FPL), created and updated computer files that will aid in future updates of this report. Rebecca helped with literature searches to locate much of the needed data and performed many of the statistical procedures such as changing base years and converting to required units. Rebecca also assisted in the overall report appearance by developing and updating figures and tables.

September 2007

Howard, James L. 2007. U.S. timber production, trade, consumption, and price statistics 1965 to 2005. Research Paper FPL-RP-637. Madison, WI: U.S. Department of Agriculture, Forest Service, Forest Products Laboratory. 91 p.

A limited number of free copies of this publication are available to the public from the Forest Products Laboratory, One Gifford Pinchot Drive, Madison, WI 53726–2398. This publication is also available online at www.fpl.fs.fed.us. Laboratory publications are sent to hundreds of libraries in the United States and elsewhere.

The Forest Products Laboratory is maintained in cooperation with the University of Wisconsin.

U.S. Timber Production, Trade, Consumption, and Price Statistics 1965 to 2005

James L. Howard
Forest Products Laboratory, Madison, Wisconsin

Preface

This report includes data for 1965 through 2005. Data for the years prior to 1965 can be found in earlier reports in the series. Since the last publication of this series in 2003 (data compiled through 2002), many agencies have discontinued the collection of various data. This change is indicated on the tables, where applicable. Some data were derived from mathematical calculations and some show conversions from different units of measurement. Throughout the tables and text, billion denotes 10^9. The references cited in the text and in the tables are listed separately. Text references are listed in literature cited. The sources for data in the tables are listed in an annotated bibliography, which is cross-referenced to the tables. This report is available through the Forest Products Laboratory web site (www.fpl.fs fed.us). Tables of conversion factors and a map of Forest Service Administrative regions follow. [Download Excel tables as .zip archive]

Factors for converting between metric and in-lb units of measure[a]

Unit	Conversion factor	Metric or in-lb unit
square foot	0.0929	square meter
cubic foot (log trade)	0.028317	cubic meter
short ton (chips)	0.0185	1,000 cubic feet
board foot (hardwood lumber)	0.00236	cubic meter
board foot (softwood lumber)	0.00170	cubic meter
board foot (lumber export and imports)	0.00236	cubic meter
board foot (logs)	0.00453	cubic meter
1,000 square feet (1/8-in. panels)	0.295	cubic meter
1,000 square feet (1/4-in. panels)	0.59	cubic meter
1,000 square feet (3/8-in. panels)	0.885	cubic meter
1,000 square feet (3/8-in. panels)	2.036	square foot (surface measure)
1,000 square feet (1/2-in. panels)	1.18	cubic meter
1,000 square feet (3/4-in. panels)	1.77	cubic meter
cubic meter[b]	0.0023	million square feet (surface measure)
square meter	10.7639	square foot (surface measure)
cord	2.27	cubic meter
cord	2.65	green ton
ton	0.0003	1,000 cords
ton (short ton)	0.907	metric ton
pound	0.453592	kilogram
inch	25.4	millimeter

[a]U.S. Department of Agriculture, Forest Service (20, 49).
[b]Based on square feet 3/8-in. panels.

Factors for converting standard units to short tons

Product	Standard unit	Weight of wood per standard unit (short tons)
Roundwood products		
Softwood	1,000 cubic feet	17.5 air dried
Hardwood	1,000 cubic feet	20.0 air dried
Softwood	cord (80 cubic feet)	1.4
Hardwood	cord (80 cubic feet)	1.6
Lumber		
Softwood	1,000 board feet	0.974
Hardwood	1,000 board feet	1.680
Laminated veneer lumber	1,000 cubic foot	17.5
Structural panels		
Softwood plywood	1,000 square feet, 3/8-in. basis	0.544
Waferboard and OSB[a]	1,000 square feet, 3/8-in. basis	0.866
Medium-density fiberboard	1,000 square feet, 3/4-in. basis	1.406
Nonstructural panels		
Hardboard	1,000 square feet, 1/8-in. basis	0.380
Insulation board	1,000 square feet, 1/2-in. basis	0.367
Particleboard	1,000 square feet, 3/4-in. basis	0.578
Hardwood plywood	1,000 square feet, 3/8-in. basis	0.657
Hardwood plywood	1,000 square feet, surface measure	0.2
Pulp, paper, and board	1,000 tons	1,000
Other industrial products	1,000 tons	16.5

[a]Oriented strandboard.

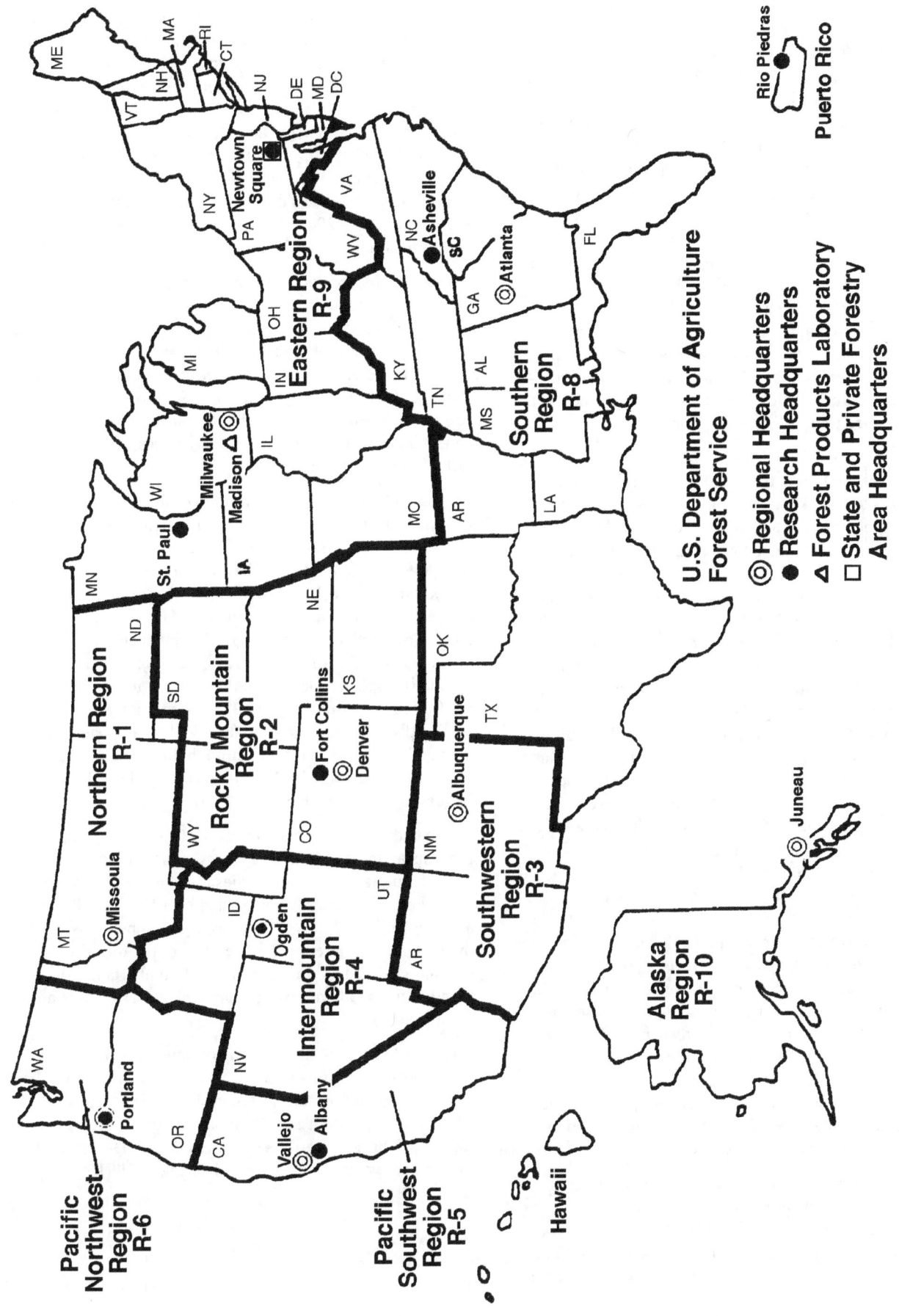

U.S. Department of Agriculture
Forest Service

◎ Regional Headquarters
● Research Headquarters
▲ Forest Products Laboratory
□ State and Private Forestry
   Area Headquarters

Northern Region
R-1

Rocky Mountain
Region
R-2

Eastern Region
R-9

Southern
Region
R-8

Southwestern
Region
R-3

Intermountain
Region
R-4

Pacific
Northwest
Region
R-6

Pacific
Southwest
Region
R-5

Alaska
Region
R-10

Puerto Rico

Rio Piedras

Asheville
SC

Atlanta

Newtown
Square

St. Paul

Milwaukee
Madison

Missoula

Ogden

Fort Collins
Denver

Albuquerque

Vallejo
Albany

Portland

Juneau

Hawaii

ME
NH
VT
MA
RI
CT
NY
PA
NJ
DE
MD
DC
VA
WV
NC
OH
IN
KY
TN
GA
AL
MS
LA
FL
AR
MO
NE
KS
OK
TX
NM
CO
UT
AZ
NV
CA
OR
WA
ID
WY
SD
ND
MN
WI
MI
IL
IA
MT

Highlights

Economic activity in most of the major timber products markets increased in 2005 and continued strong into the first half of 2006. New housing construction, which accounts for more than a third of the U.S. softwood lumber and structural panels consumed and for substantial volumes of other soft-wood and hardwood products, strengthened considerably in 2005 but declined steadily since July 2006. The consumption of oriented strandboard (OSB) during 2005 continued to exceed plywood consumption and should continue strong into 2006 as several new OSB mills and expansion of existing operations began to come online. The total industrial production index, an important demand determinant for pallet lumber, containerboard, and some grades of paper, rose 4.1% in 2005 (Table 1). Both private nonresidential construction expenditures and nonresidential fixed investment increased during 2005. Wood energy use in the United States continued to be volatile, declining during 2005 (Table 60).

The U.S. housing market remained strong during 2005, but some sectors did weaken. Sales of both new and previously occupied homes surged to record levels. More than 2.0 million new housing units were started, and more than $200 billion was spent to maintain and improve the existing housing stock. The single-family housing market was particularly strong, and the U.S. home-ownership rate climbed to a record high. Starts of conventionally built homes (excluding mobile homes) rose by 5.4% from a year earlier to 2.0 million units during 2005. A record high for home sales was also established during 2005 when 8.3 million units were sold. Of the 8.3 million units sold, 7.1 million units were previously occupied homes and 1.2 million were new units. In terms of market share within region, new homes sold were strongest in the South; 638,000 units were sold in 2005, which represented 50% of all new sales in the United States. Two of the indicators of demand for wood products declined slightly in 2005 relative to 2004. During 2005, the furniture and fixtures sector, as measured by industrial production, declined less than 1% from the 2004 level. The decline in furniture and fixtures output a determinant for pallet lumber, containerboard, and some grades of paper varied indirectly with durable goods production, which increased 6.2% in 2005 from 2004. The paper and products sector fell by 2.3%. Total industrial production rose in 2005, increasing by 4.1%, while production at utilities increased by 2.5%. Housing trends in 2005, along with the increase in economic growth, helped the lumber industry exceed production levels compared to a year earlier. U.S. softwood lumber production exceeded the previous year's levels by 3.9%.

U.S. consumption of wood and paper products required input to make products produced in the United States (for domestic consumption) plus roundwood required to make imported products. This consumption of roundwood to meet the needs of U.S. consumers (including fuelwood) increased 1.0% per year between 1965 and 1995, from 13.3 to 19.3 billion ft^3. This consumption declined to 19.1 billion ft^3 in 1997 and has since increased to 21.3 billion ft^3 in 2005. U.S. production of wood and paper products plus fuelwood use required roundwood harvest from U.S. forests, which also increased 1.0% per year from 1965 to 1995, from 12.2 to 17.6 billion ft3. In contrast to roundwood needed for U.S. product consumption, U.S. roundwood harvest needed for U.S. production has declined since 1995 from 17.6 to 17.1 billion ft^3 in 2005. Though, the 17.1 billion ft^3 marks the third straight year of production increases (Table 5a).

Along with record demand from the housing sector, which drove high demand in the lumber industry during 2005, U.S. National Forest sawlog stumpage prices increased in current dollars for Douglas Fir and Southern Pine in 2005, continuing the volatile price cycle over recent years. Southern Pine recovered modestly in the late 1990s but Douglas Fir continued downward. Increasing Canadian lumber imports contributed to the slump in softwood prices, while Western mill closures reflected the slump in prices.

During 2005, apparent consumption of most timber products increased over 1-year-ago levels. Although Western production of softwood lumber from the California redwood region was down 0.2%, Western softwood lumber production increased by 3.4%. Because of declining domestic markets for hardwood lumber, production decreased by 1.0% in 2005. The combined roundwood and forest chip production for pulp and OSB mills increased by 2.0% in 2005. Softwood plywood production continued its trend, falling 2.3% in 2005. The consumption of OSB for the first time exceeded plywood consumption during 1998 and has remained above plywood consumption through 2005. Shipments of particleboard declined 4.2% while MDF (MDF) shipments increased 3.5% for 2005.

Continued growth in U.S. imports of Chinese furniture presents an increasing problem for American furniture manufacturers and the companies that supply them with nonstructural panels such as particleboard and MDF as well as hardwood lumber. Not only has total lumber consumed by the U.S. furniture industry decreased, but the species mix has changed as well. Less red oak lumber and parts are being used and alternative species such as hard maple are being used.

The long-term outlook is one of continued growth in the demand for most timber products. Timber volumes supplied by the National Forest have fallen sharply in recent years. In 2005, valued at about $187 million, National Forest harvest totaled 1.3 billion board feet (bf) less than 2.0% of total U.S. timber harvest, down 75% from the peak in 1991.

Contents

U.S. Timber Production, Trade, Consumption, and Price Statistics 1965 to 2005

James L. Howard
Forest Products Laboratory, Madison, Wisconsin

General Economic Trends

> **Timber products markets stay strong during 2005—continued growth forecast for 2006**

The decade-long economic expansion came to a screeching halt in 2001 as the U.S. economy entered a brief downturn. The U.S. economy since 2001 has shifted from recovery to sustained expansion, having rebounded from the Gulf Coast hurricanes and large increases in energy prices in 2005. Economic activity, as measured by the Gross Domestic Product (GDP), rose at an annual rate of 2.7% in 2005 to $11,138.0 billion (1996 dollars). This was up from $10,841.3 billion (1996 dollars) during 2004. U.S. economic activity as measured by the GDP continued to increase in the first quarter 2006, increasing by 4.4%. Real GDP in private-service industries led the broad-based economic growth in 2005, increasing 4.1%. One of the leading contributors to this sector was the real estate, rental, and leasing industry group with a 2.5% growth in real GDP in 2005. The increase in real GDP growth of 4.0% in the manufacturing sector was due to durable goods manufacturing, which increased 5.7%. Information-communications-technology-producing industries experienced strong growth, increasing 11.9% in 2005. Prices paid by U.S. residents for goods and services, the price index for gross domestic purchases, increased 2.7% during the first quarter 2006 after increasing 3.7% during the fourth quarter 2005. This decrease was driven by lower energy and constant food prices. Growth in per capita personal income slowed during 2005 to 1.1%, down from 7.4% in 2004.

New housing construction, which accounts for more than a third of the U.S. annual consumption of softwood lumber and structural panels and for substantial volumes of other softwood and hardwood products, established new highs for 2005 (Tables 1 and 2, Fig. 1). Starts of single-family units led the increase and multi-family housing starts also increased by 2.3% during 2005. Housing starts for 2005 were 2,215,000 as sales of new houses set a new record in 2005 of 1,283,000 units. The home ownership rate reached 69% in 2005 equaling the all time high. Builders' expectations for housing starts in 2006 remain strong even though mortgage rates for the first 6 months of the year have increased slightly but remain at historically low levels. New housing,

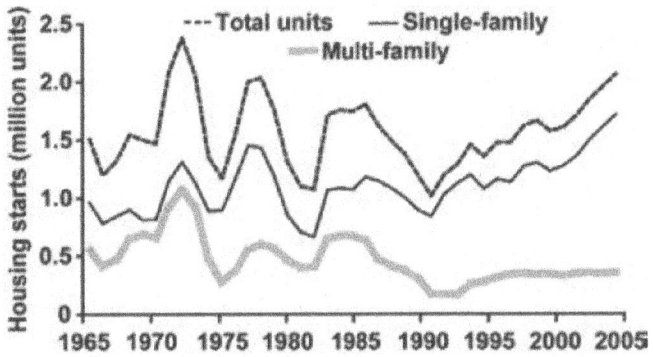

Figure 1. Housing starts by type of unit, 1965–2005.

and repair and remodeling continue to drive wood product demand. For the first 5 months ending in May 2006, starts were down slightly compared to 2005. Sales of new single-family homes fluctuated throughout the second quarter, after rising during the first quarter in 2006. Existing home sales were up in March and April before declining in May 2006 to 6,760,000 (down 2.1% from April). This shows that 2006 should be another strong year for home construction.

Shipments of manufactured housing increased during 2005 to 148,000 units, due partly to increased construction for hurricane relief. This was 16,000 units more than what was shipped a year ago. In the first 4 months of 2006, manufactured housing shipments were behind 2005 shipments for this period. The seasonally adjusted shipments for 2006 totaled 141,000 units.

Investment in residential repair and remodeling rose to $215.0 billion (current dollars) in 2005, increasing about 7.4% over 1 year ago. About two-thirds of the improvements were additions and alterations and the balance were replacements of major housing components such as roofs or heating systems. Total expenditures for maintenance and repairs to residential properties in 2005 amounted to an estimated $53.3 billion compared to $50.6 billion in 2004. Gross private domestic investment increased in 2005 for both residential and nonresidential housing units. Residential structures investment was stronger than the investment growth in nonresidential structures. Spending on new single family residential structures was $327 billion (1996 dollars) in 2005 compared to $253 billion for nonresidential structures.

Industrial production, an important demand determinant for pallet lumber, containerboard, and some grades of paper rose 4.2% in 2005 compared to 2004 (Table 1, Fig. 2). Output of the furniture and fixtures industry, a major market for hardwood lumber, plywood, veneer, particleboard, and hardboard, as measured by durable goods production, fell 0.3% in 2005. Further decreases are likely because of continued growth in China furniture imports. Paper and products decreased and the manufacturing sector increased slightly.

Timber Production, Prices, Trade, and Consumption

> **Total roundwood production grew for the second straight year.**

Total roundwood production increased to 17.2 billion ft³ in 2005, up slightly from the 16.8 billion ft³ of production of a year earlier (Fig. 3). This marks the second straight year of increased roundwood production. Roundwood has been on the decline since the mid-1990s. The high point for roundwood harvest was 1991 when total roundwood production was 18.8 billion ft³.

Lumber and the engineered wood products sector are the main contributors to the current volume level. The production of saw logs used in the domestic manufacture of lumber rose slightly in 2005 to 7.9 billion ft³. This represented about 51% of total industrial roundwood production. Softwood lumber production represented about 53% of softwood roundwood harvest and hardwood lumber made up 45% of hardwood roundwood harvest. Pulpwood, which composed about 37% of total industrial roundwood, increased 2.2% from a year earlier. Although roundwood pulpwood production has fallen since the late 1990s, during the 1990s pulpwood share of industrial roundwood production increased close to 1 billion ft³ since 1991. During that time, roundwood used to produce lumber increased slightly.

Lumber Production, Prices, Trade, and Consumption

Production—An estimated 52.3 billion bf (52.3×10^9 bf) of lumber (softwoods plus hardwoods) was produced in the United States in 2005 (Table 28). Since 1965, lumber production has generally trended upwards, except for periods of economic slowdown such as the mid-1970s and early 1980s. Many western mills dependent on federal timber were forced to dramatically reduce production or close entirely. This resulted in an overall decline in lumber production, shifts in production to other regions, and increased levels of foreign imports. These trends continued through 2005.

Softwood lumber production in 2005 was about 40.7×10^9 bf (Table 28, Fig. 4), 78% of total lumber production. Hardwood lumber production was about 11.6×10^9 bf. The overall decline in lumber production in the 1990s was entirely at the expense of softwood lumber. Softwood

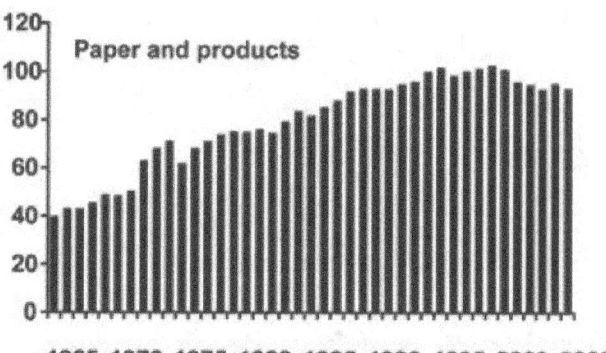

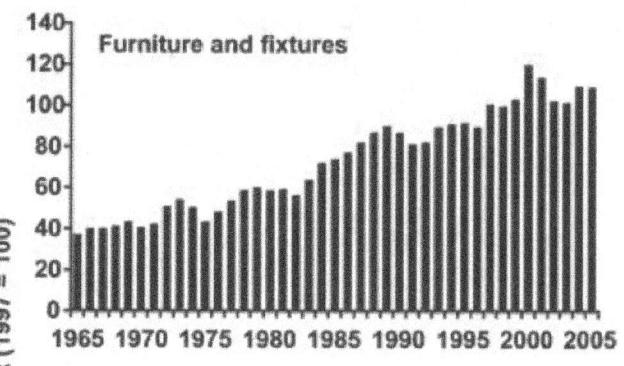

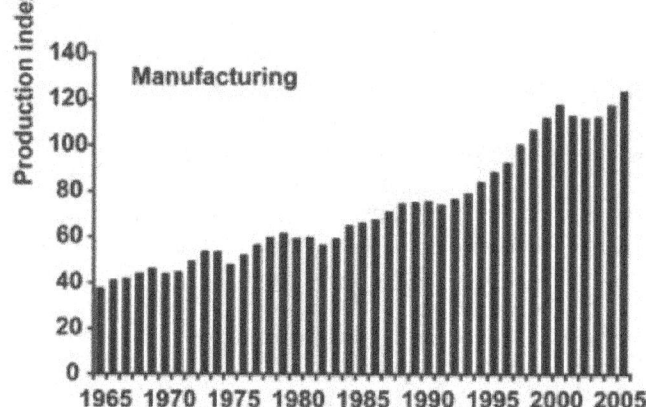

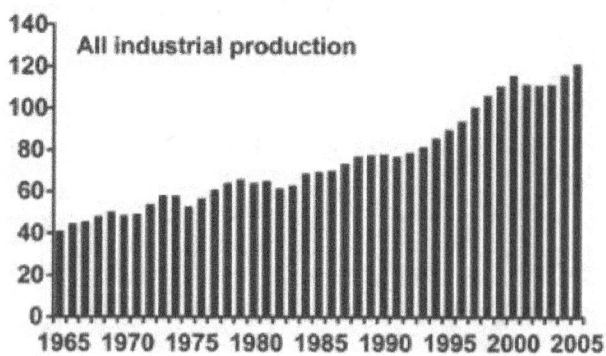

Figure 2. Economic activity in major industrial timber markets.

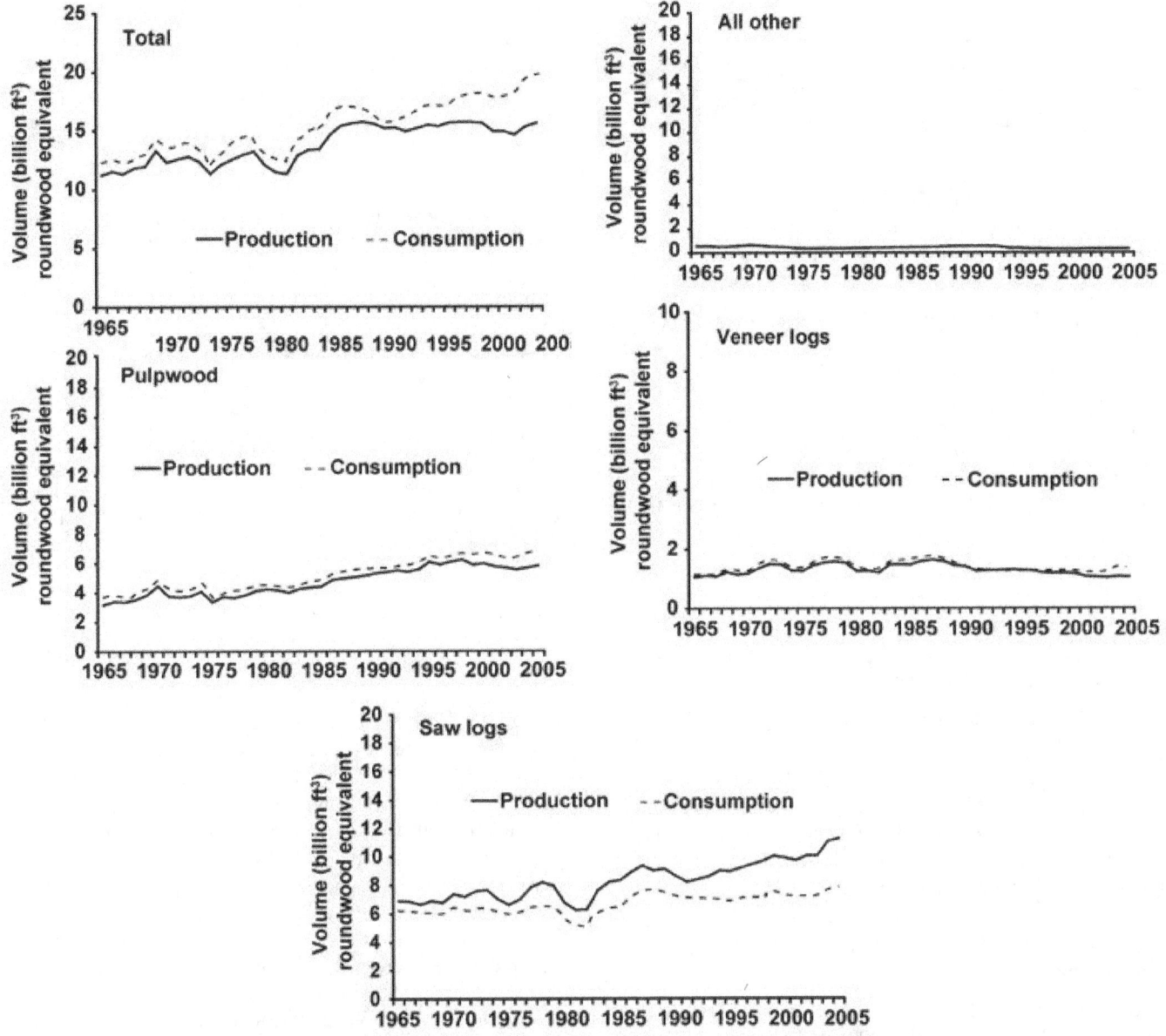

Figure 3. Production and consumption of timber products.

lumber production has had a bumpy ride over the first 3 years of this decade but generally trended toward record production levels, while hardwood lumber production has generally trended downward from the high production levels of the late 1990s.

In 2005, the South was the largest lumber-producing region in the United States at 22.8×10^9 bf (Table 29, Fig. 5). The West was the second largest region at 20.0×10^9 bf, followed by the North at 8.9×10^9 bf. The West, although second largest overall producing region, has traditionally been the largest softwood lumber producing region, with nearly 98% (19.5×10^9 bf) of its total production being softwood species. Softwood lumber production in the South was about 80% of its total production, nearly equal in volume to

that of the West. The North produced 2.4×10^9 bf softwood lumber in 2005.

Until recently the West had been the largest lumber-producing region in the United States. From 1966 until 1980 for example, more than half (55%) of all lumber produced in the United States came from the West. Much of this production came from old-growth timber on federally owned lands in the Pacific Coast region (Washington, Oregon, and California). Since the early 1980s, the proportion of lumber coming from the West has slowly decreased to just under half, due to declining levels of timber from public lands, and increasing levels of production in the South. In the late 1980s and early 1990s, large areas of federally owned land in the West were removed from harvest. This removal

3

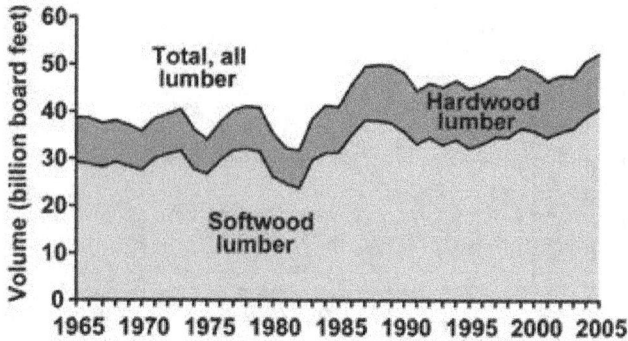

Figure 4. U.S. lumber production by wood type, 1965–2005.

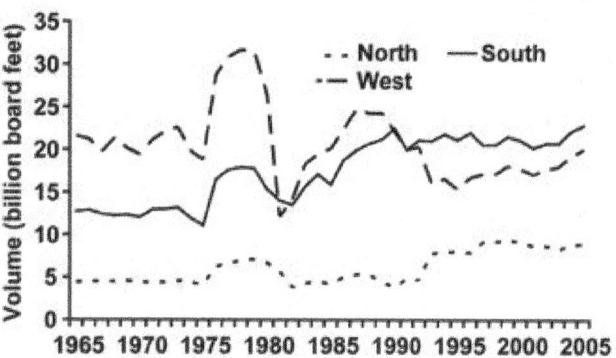

Figure 5. U.S. lumber production by region, 1965–2005.

further exacerbated the situation. In 1990, the South became the Nation's largest lumber-producing region, accounting for 35% of all softwood lumber and 80% of all hardwoods. During the late1990s, softwood lumber production in the South and West increased. Since 2000, softwood lumber production has increased in both the South and West while the West continued as the leading softwood lumber-producing region.

Total lumber production in the North remained fairly steady from 1965 through the early 1990s at about 4.5 × 10^9 bf per year (Table 29, Fig. 5). It then increased rapidly to 9.2 × 10^9 bf. Nearly all of this increase was in hardwood lumber production. Hardwood lumber production started to decline in 2000 brought on by the decline in the U.S. furniture manufacturing industry, which resulted from increased Chinese and other Asian imports. Also during this time, the shift in fashion trends away from red oak continued.

Imports and exports—In 2005, lumber imports to the United States from all countries totaled 25.7 × 10^9 bf, a record high (Tables 28 and 31). During the same year, exports from the United States to all countries totaled just 2.3 × 10^9 bf (Tables 28 and 32). The difference, 23.4 × 10^9 bf, was net foreign trade, and represented lumber consumption in the United States in excess of that which was produced domestically. Net foreign trade represented about one-fourth (31%) of total domestic lumber consumption in

2005. With few exceptions, lumber imports to the United States have grown steadily since 1965. Nearly all of the growth was in softwood lumber imports. In 1965, softwood lumber imports totaled 4.9 × 10^9 bf. By 2005, softwood lumber imports were 24.6 × 10^9 bf, an increase of 19.7 × 10^9 bf. In contrast, hardwood lumber imports were 0.3 × 10^9 bf in 1965 and 1.1× 10^9 bf in 2005.

Canada has always been the principal source of lumber imported into the United States (Table 31). In 2005, 85% of all imports were from Canada. Canada is the principal source of both softwood lumber and hardwood lumber imports to the United States. In 2005, nearly 87% of all softwood lumber and 44% of all hardwood lumber imported to the United States were from Canada. The percentage of softwood lumber from non-Canadian sources has been increasing in recent years. Hardwood imports from Canada as a percent of total hardwood imports fell fairly steadily from 1950 through the 1970s. Since then, Canada's share of the U.S. hardwood lumber import market has risen. Overall, the United States imported nearly 83% of Canadian lumber production

Lumber exports grew fairly steadily from 1965 through 1990, reaching a record high of nearly 4.6 × 10^9 bf in 1988 (Tables 28 and 32). Since 1990, lumber exports have fallen steadily to 2.3 × 10^9 bf in 2005. Numerous factors contributed to the decline in lumber exports in recent years. Some of these were reduced softwood sawtimber supplies, particularly from the Pacific Coast, changing economic conditions in the major importing countries, strength of the U.S. dollar in relation to other world currencies, and increased levels of exports from other major timber-producing countries. During the mid-1980s and early 1990s, Japan was by far the largest single market for U.S. exported lumber. In 1989, Japan purchased 1.6 × 10^9 bf of lumber (Table 32). Since then, exports to Japan have fallen to just one-tenth of their previous level. Canada is currently the largest single market for exported lumber, followed closely by the European Union (EU). They accounted for 28% and 15%, respectively, of all exports.

More than half (62%) of total exports in 1996 were softwood species, 1.8 × 10^9 bf (Table 32). In the late 1960s and early 1970s, softwood lumber accounted for about 85% of total exports. Since then, softwood lumber's share of total exports has fallen steadily from around 78% in the 1980s to just 38% currently. The most important softwood lumber export markets in 2005 were Canada, which accounted for about 25% of total softwood lumber exports, Japan at 5.5%, and the EU at 7.3%. All other countries accounted for the remaining exports. Canada and the EU were the two largest markets, respectively, for exported hardwood lumber from the United States in 2005.

Consumption—Lumber consumption in the United States in 2005 for all uses totaled 75.6 × 10^9 bf, continuing record consumption years through the early part of this decade

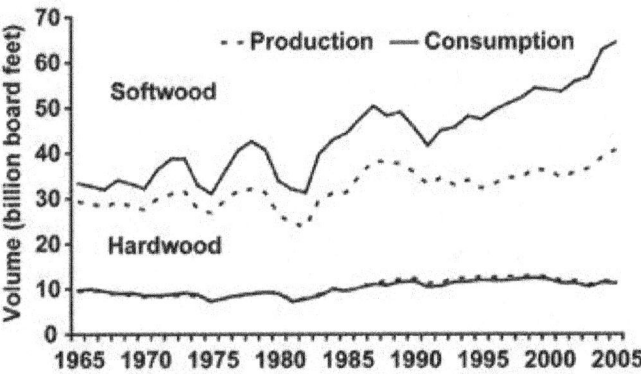

Figure 6. Lumber production and consumption by wood type, 1965–2005.

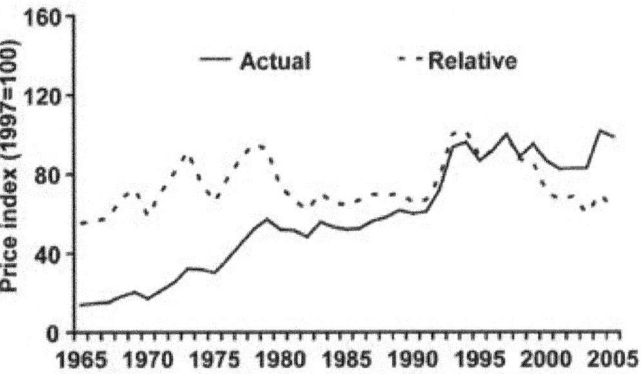

Figure 7. Price indexes for softwood lumber, 1965–2005.

(Table 28). Consumption in 2005 also exceeded levels in the early 1900s, when lumber was the most important raw material used in the United States for construction, manufactured products, and shipping.

Per capita consumption in 2005 was 255 bf, above the high of 253 bf set in 1987 (Table 28). However, per capita consumption was below averages for most years prior to 1965 and dramatically below the early 1900s when consumption exceeded 500 bf per person.

Overall, about 60% of the lumber consumed in 2005 was used for housing, with 35% used for the construction of new units, and 25% of consumption for the upkeep and improvement of existing units. New nonresidential construction (including railroads) accounted for about 7%. Manufacturing accounted for 12% of lumber consumption and shipping (pallets, containers and dunnage) for 10%. The remaining 11% was for all other uses. The "all other" category includes an unknown amount of lumber used for other construction purposes such as nonresidential upkeep and improvements.

In 2005, 64.4×10^9 of the 75.6×10^9 bf of lumber consumed in the United States was softwood species, or about 85% (Table 28, Fig. 6). Slight annual variations in the percentage of softwood and hardwood lumber used are common, and are a result of differing levels of activity in the various end use markets, and variations in species consumption between them. About 97% of the lumber used in new housing in 2005 was estimated to have been softwood species, up from 93% in 1962. In contrast, only 28% of the lumber used in shipping was softwood, down from 40% in 1962. The increase in percentage of softwood lumber used in housing was largely due to a decline in hardwood flooring use, and rapid increase in house size, which required larger amounts of softwood dimension lumber for framing. Increased use of engineered wood products in recent years, substituting for dimension lumber in both residential and nonresidential construction, tended to reduce the softwood percentage. Pallet recycling was another factor that reduced pallet lumber demand. The rapid and continued growth in the use of hardwood pallets for materials handling and transportation was the principal cause for the increased percentage use of hardwood lumber in shipping. Even with the variations caused by differences in end use markets, softwood lumber consumption as percent of total lumber consumption has remained around 80% since the 1960s.

Prices—Overall, softwood lumber prices in 2005 remained close to the record high set during the previous year. The actual producer price index for softwood lumber was 98.6 in 2005 (1997=100), up from 82.7 in 2002 and slightly below 1 year ago (Table 35, Fig. 7). Historically, the producer price index for lumber rose rapidly between 1965 and 1979, from 14.0 to 57.2. This represented an average increase of about 10.3% per year. A mild recession in the early to mid 1980s depressed lumber prices during the early years of the decade. It wasn't until late in the decade that prices again reached record levels. On average, lumber prices increased just 1.9% per year during the 1980s. The price index again began to move upward in the early 1990s due in part to the effect on the sawmill industry from timber harvest reductions in the West. Since 1995, the softwood lumber producer price index has fluctuated from a low of 86.5 in 1995 to a high of 101.6 in 2004. Overall, the softwood lumber producer price index increased at a rate of about 5.7% per year between 1965 and 1999, then 2.0% per year from 1999 into 2005.

Hardwood lumber prices, as measured by the hardwood lumber producer price index, have historically been much less volatile than softwood lumber. In 2005, the producer price index for hardwood lumber was 112.9, 1.6 points below the record high established a year earlier (Table 35, Fig. 8). Since 1965, hardwood lumber prices have increased at a rate of about 2.0% per year.

The relative producer price index for a given commodity measures the change in its price relative to all other commodities, and is calculated by dividing its producer price index by that for all commodities. If the relative price index is less than 100, then the given commodity is relatively less expensive than other commodities. If it is greater than 1,

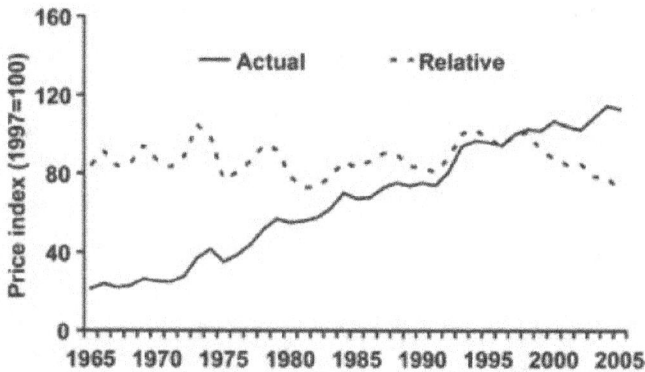

Figure 8. Price indexes for hardwood lumber, 1965–2005.

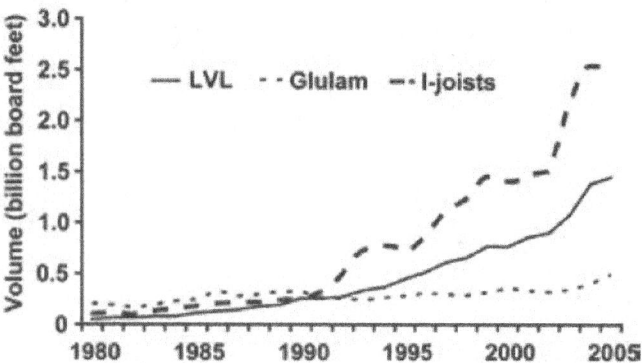

Figure 9. Production of glulam, I-joists, and laminated veneer, 1980–2005.

then it is relatively more expensive. In 2005, the relative price of softwood lumber was 62.6, down 6.7 points from 2004 (Table 35, Fig. 7). Since 1965, relative softwood lumber prices ranged from a low of 55.2 in 1965 to a high of 101.6 in 1994. The relative hardwood lumber price index in 2005 was 71.8, down from 102.4 in 1994 (Table 35, Fig. 8). Long-term hardwood price indexes have been more stable than those for softwood lumber, ranging from a low of 72.8 in 1981 to a high of 102.4 in 1994.

Engineered wood products production increased in 2005

Engineered wood products such as glulam, I-joists, and laminated veneer lumber (LVL) are still relatively new to the market and are forecast to increase steadily. Glulam production during 2005 was 491 million bf, up 1.8% from 2004 setting a record high (Table 34, Fig. 9). A little over one-half of U.S. glulam goes to new residential construction and remodeling uses. Nonresidential construction consumes the next largest proportion of glulam production.

LVL production during 2005 was 91 million ft^3, a record high, and I-joist production was 1,263 million linear feet, down slightly from 2004. The volume of LVL production

used for I-joist flanges has kept pace with I-joist production in recent years. In 2005, approximately 77% of I-joists were used in new residential floor construction and 6% in residential roofs and walls. Approximately 10% were used in remodeling and 7% in nonresidential construction. A small volume of I-joists is exported to Japan.

More recently, new hybrid products such as wood or natural fiber-plastic composites have also come on the market and now compete directly with traditional wood products. These new products are being used for decking, siding, roofing, and millwork. Production data for these new products are not available yet.

Woodpulp and Pulpwood Production, Prices, Trade, and Consumption

Pulpwood production in 2005 estimated at 89 million cords

Total woodpulp production in U.S. mills in 2005 is estimated to be 60.3 million tons based on data published by the American Forest & Paper Association (AF&PA) (Table 49). This is relatively unchanged from 2004 but 16% below the previous high produced in 1995. Most U.S. paper companies have experienced poor financial returns for nearly a decade. With the exception of a short-lived boom in 1995, the 1990s were a decade of low profitability. Plagued by overcapacity and low commodity prices, the industry failed to earn its cost of capital throughout most of the 1990s. The AF&PA's 2005–2007 capacity survey revealed that paper and paperboard capacity in the United States declined by 0.9% per year in the period between 2000 and 2005. The negative growth during 2001 and 2002 was the first time that capacity had ever declined for 2 years in a row during the 40 years that AF&PA and the American Paper Institute (API) have been compiling capacity data. Extending the downward trend that began in 2001, U.S. paper and paperboard capacity declined 0.8% in 2005, to 99.3 million tons. Paper and paperboard capacity declined 4.4% between 2000 and 2005.

On the basis of the above volumes, related data on pulpwood production published by the American Pulpwood Association (APA), which includes both roundwood and chips, shows an estimated 89 million cords in 2005 (Table 24, Fig. 10). This volume is about 1.9% above 2004 and 6.6% below the record high level established in 1994. The increase in pulpwood production reversed the downward trend that began in 1996, which coincided with the decline in woodpulp production. Mill shutdowns had a strong impact with nearly 3.7 million tons of paper and paperboard capacity removed between 1998 and 1999. Softwood roundwood and chip production in 2005 was 63.4 million cords, up 1.7% from 2004 (Table 24). The slowdown in pulpwood

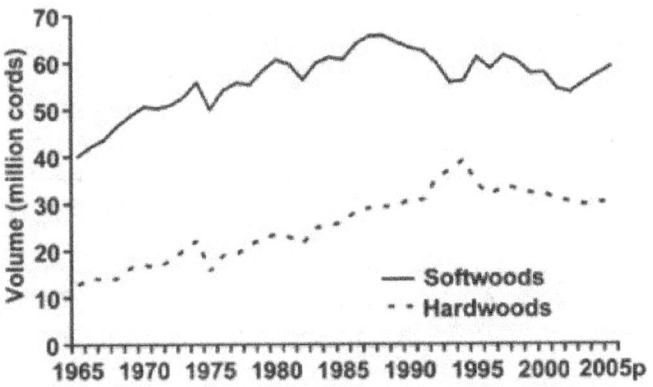

Figure 10. Pulpwood production by wood type, 1965–2004. p denotes preliminary data.

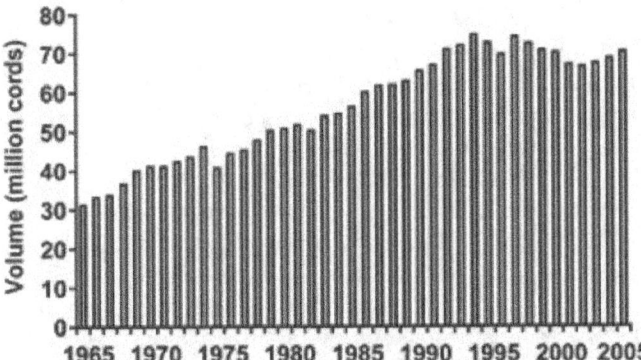

Figure 11. Pulpwood production in the U.S. South, 1965–2005. p denotes preliminary data.

production reversed in 2003 with the industry experiencing its third straight year of increased pulpwood production in 2005 (Table 24). Two of the three major producing regions in 2005 showed no change in output. In the West, production of softwood in 2005 was unchanged from 2004 at 3.8 million cords. Softwood output in the North remained constant at 5.5 million cords. Southern softwood roundwood production increased slightly in 2005, increasing by 3.4% to 49.7 million cords. About 84% of U.S. softwood roundwood pulpwood produced came from southern forests.

Output of hardwood roundwood and chips in 2005 was 30.3 million cords, similar to the 30.3 million cords in 2004. Although the output of hardwood pulpwood and chips was constant, the proportion of total round pulpwood and chips from hardwood species decreased. This continues the downward trend that started in 1994. Through the 1960s and early 1970s, hardwoods became an increasingly important source of round pulpwood, a reflection of changes in pulping technology, the types of pulp produced, and the relative price of different species. During 2005, hardwood pulpwood comprised 34% of total U.S. pulpwood production. This was down from 41% of pulpwood production at the high point in production during 1994. Further erosion in pulpwood demand is likely as capacity to produce paper and

paperboard continues a downward trend that began in 2001, and the percentage of recycled fiber inches higher.

> **Southern pulpwood production increased to 70.2 million cords in 2005**

Forest Resource Association data on pulpwood receipts indicate that pulpwood production in the south in 2005 was 70.2 million cords, up slightly from 2004 production but 6.0% below the high production year in 1994 when 74.7 million cords of pulpwood was produced (Table 25, Fig. 11).

The South has accounted for more than 65% of total U.S. pulpwood production in the past 10 years. During 2005, the South accounted for 79%. All of the 14 States in the South have contributed to the increase in pulpwood production noted above. However, this increase has been greatest in Georgia and Alabama, which together accounted for a third of the pulpwood output in this region. This is consistent with the location of the industry within the area. Of the total number of pulpmills in the South, some 30% are located in Alabama and Georgia.

About 71% of the 70.2 million cords of round pulpwood harvested in the South in 2005 was softwoods. This proportion was falling over the last decade, but the trend was reversed over the last 3 years into 2005. Southern softwood roundwood output has been increasing since 2003, while hardwoods have held fairly steady over the past 3 years. Between 2003 and 2005, for example, hardwood roundwood production declined by an average of .1 million cords per year while softwood roundwood increased on average by 1.1 million cords per year since 2003.

> **Production in the West has declined over the last decade**

Receipts of domestically produced pulpwood in the West leveled off after declining throughout the 1990s. Softwood production in the West has fallen in each year since 1988. Softwood production was 3.8 million cords in 2005, constant with 3.8 million cords since 2003, and down from 17.4 million cords of production in 1988 (Table 25, Fig. 12). Chips accounted for roughly the same percentage of pulpwood production in 2005 as it did in 2003, declining slightly over the last 3 years. Of the total production of pulpwood, roundwood, and chips, 76% was from softwood species. Production of hardwood roundwood has also held steady over the last 3 years.

> **Output in the North remains constant**

Data on domestically produced mill receipts indicate that pulpwood production in the North, roundwood plus chips, was 14.1 million cords

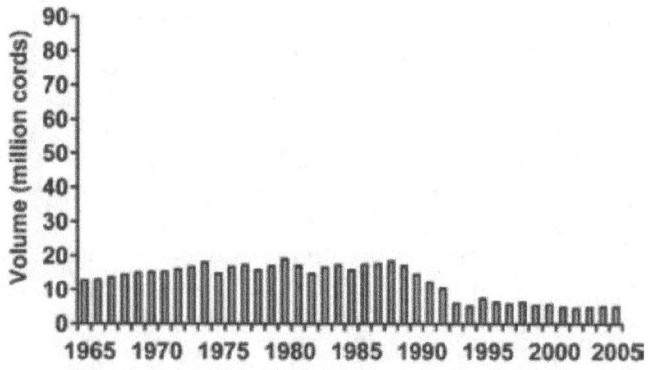

Figure 12. Pulpwood production in the U.S. West, 1965–2004. p denotes preliminary data.

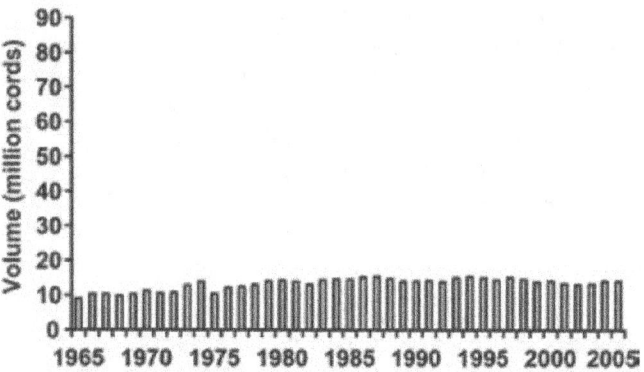

Figure 13. Pulpwood production in the U.S. North, 1965–2004. p denotes preliminary data.

in 2005, constant with 14.1 million cords in 2004 (Table 25, Fig. 13). About 61% of the total was from hardwood species, same as the proportion in 2004. About 72% of total pulpwood output in the North was from roundwood, about equal to the proportion for the South in 2005. The use of chip residues in the North has been declining steadily as in other U.S. regions.

Pulpwood prices depressed during 2005

Stumpage prices remain depressed in lower Louisiana and other areas in the South as clean-up from 2005 hurricane damage continues (Miller Freeman 2006). The decline in prices reflected also the recent contraction in both U.S. softwood and hardwood demand as more than a quarter of the country's 186 pulpmills shut down since 1996. With the market glutted with wood, pulpwood stumpage prices during 2005 remained lower than in 1999. Pine and hardwood pulpwood prices peaked in the South, the Nation's largest fiber market, during 1998 when the stumpage price for Louisiana pine was $28.8 per cord (1997 dollars), before falling to $14.9 per cord in 2005 (Table 26). Delivered pulpwood price for Southern Pine was $42.94 per cord in 2005, slightly higher than the $42.54 dollars per cord in 2004 (Table 27).

Pulpwood prices vary a great deal among species and regions. In general, prices were historically highest for softwoods, especially the long fiber northern species such as spruce and fir. In some areas in response to changes in pulping technology and pulpwood availability and quality, the relationship between hardwood and softwood prices has changed. For example, in Louisiana the softwood pulpwood price per cord stayed at a higher level than hardwoods during the 1990s for every year other than 1995 when the price of hardwood pulpwood exceeded the softwood price. Since 2001, the hardwood pulpwood price in Louisiana has exceeded the softwood pulpwood.

Pulpwood stumpage prices for most species followed the same trends as pulpwood prices and slowed during 1999 (Tables 26 and 27). In Louisiana for example, Southern Pine pulpwood stumpage increased from $12.87 (1997 dollars) in 2004 to $14.97 (1997 dollars) in 2005. In contrast to softwoods, Louisiana hardwood stumpage prices increased from 2004 to 2005, rising 15.5% as compared to a 14.0% increase for Southern Pine. Pulpwood and pulpwood stumpage prices have been quite volatile over the last 10 years. Most of the volatility has been due to falling capacity and industry restructuring, resulting in lowered demand. The U.S. pulp and paper industry has brought capital spending to levels well under depreciation and amortization, effectively pulling capital out of the industry. U.S. companies have also been consolidating their operations in response to increased global competition and poor financial returns. The result has been a rationalization of marginal mills, further reducing the capacity base.

Apparent pulpwood consumption in U.S. mills increased to 88.6 million cords in 2005

Apparent pulpwood consumption in U.S. mills in 2005 was an estimated 88.6 million cords (Table 24, Fig. 14). This was a small increase from the 86.9 million cords of consumption in 2004. In total, about 88.6 million cords of pulpwood domestic production plus net imports were required to meet the relatively flat demand for paper, paperboard, and pulp products in 2005. Wood requirements for exports amounted to an additional 1.2 million cords.

Plywood and Veneer Log Production, Prices, Trade and Consumption

Softwood plywood production in 2005 was estimated at 14.3 billion square feet (3/8-inch basis) based on data published by APA–The Engineered Wood Association (APA) (Table 37, Figs. 15 and 16). This is slightly below 1-year-ago softwood plywood production. The rise in production

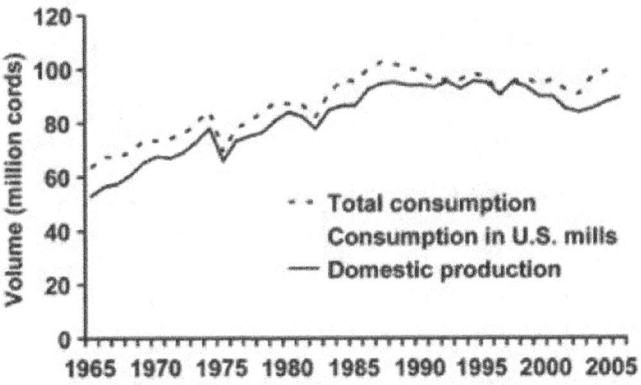

Figure 14. Total pulpwood consumption and production, 1965–2005.

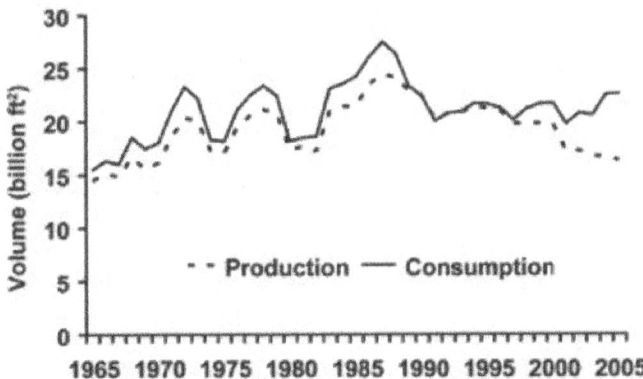

Figure 15. Total plywood production and consumption, 1965–2005.

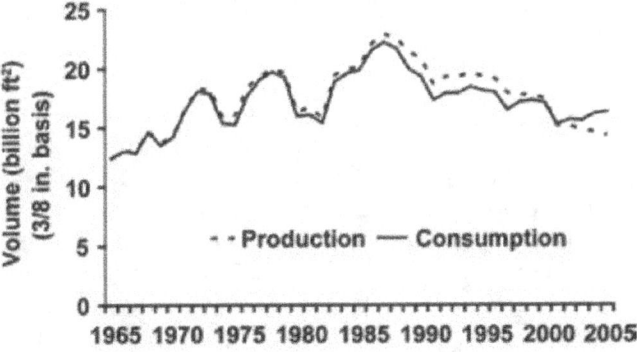

Figure 16. Softwood plywood production and consumption, 1965–2005.

during 2002 was short lived as OSB continued to increase its share of the market once dominated by plywood. For example, between 1994 and 2005, plywood production declined by 30%.

Historically, production of softwood plywood was concentrated in the West, chiefly in the Pacific Coast States of Washington, Oregon, and California. However, these three States during 2005 accounted for only 24% of plywood production. In the years since the first plywood plant began

production in the South, production in that region has grown to 67% of plywood production. For example, over the last 10 years from 1995 to 2005, production in the South has increased to 9.7 billion ft² (3/8-in. basis) in 2005 while falling to 3.4 million ft² in the West. Although the volume produced was down somewhat during the last 3 years in the South, the percent of total U.S. production from southern plants continued to increase.

About two-thirds of the softwood plywood manufactured in 2005 was from Southern Pine.

Production of hardwood plywood declined during 2005

Hardwood plywood production declined slightly from 1 year ago to an estimated 1.9 billion ft² in 2005 (3/8-in. basis) (Table 37, Fig. 17). This volume, the lowest since 1997, continues the recent trend of small annual decreases over the last 4 years. Weak demand from the furniture, cabinetry, and fixtures sector was the main factor fueling the percent decline in production. Stock hardwood plywood accounts for slightly more than half of all the hardwood plywood produced. Of this amount, eastern producers, with their proximity to the hardwood forest resource, produce 60% of hardwood plywood, while western producers account for 38% of production, with the Great Lakes States making up the remainder.

Hardwood plywood producers use a wide range of species for the face veneers of their products. Red oak remains the most popular species at 35% of the market, followed by birch at 29%, and maple at 17%. The cores used in the hardwood plywood industry vary from veneer plies at 63% of the market to MDF cores at 16%. The use of MDF and particleboard cores has increased steadily since 1991.

Softwood plywood prices remained strong in 2005.

Softwood plywood prices as measured by the actual producer price index rebounded in 2003 and have continued strong during 2005 (Table 42, Fig.18), reaching 143.1 in 2004 before falling to 127.5 in 2005, which is 15.6% below the high of 2004. The extent of the increase, particularly for the types and grades used in construction will depend primarily on continued strength in the housing markets and the market penetration of OSB. The relative softwood plywood price index in 2005 was 81.0 (Table 42, Fig.19). This was below the level of 1 year ago.

Hardwood plywood prices decrease in 2005.

Hardwood plywood prices have trended slowly upward since 1999 until 2003 when they began to decline (Table 42, Figs. 18 and 19). The

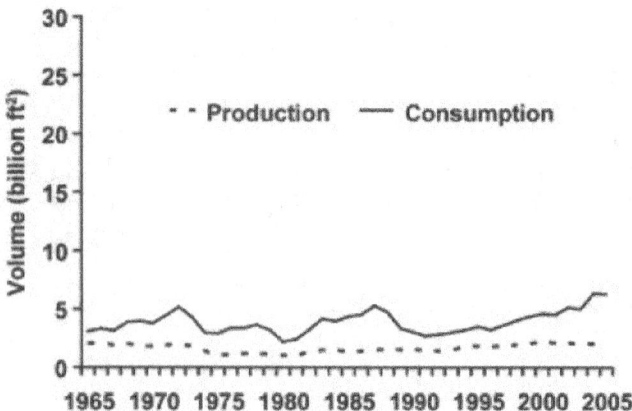

Figure 17. Hardwood plywood production and consumption, 1965–2005.

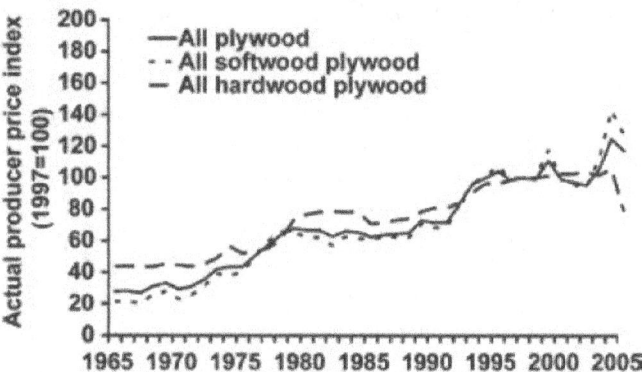

Figure 18. Actual producer price indexes for plywood, 1965–2005.

actual hardwood plywood price as indicated by the actual producer price index for 2005 was 78.7 (1997=100), below the 105.8 level registered 1 year earlier. The relative index also registered a decrease for 2005.

Softwood plywood imports and exports showed varying results in 2005

Imports of softwood plywood, about 2,421 million ft^2 (3/8-in. basis) in 2005, increased 16% over 2004 (Table 37). Imports of softwood plywood are small relative to overall U.S. plywood consumption. Exports of softwood plywood were estimated at about 411 million ft^2 in 2005. Exports in 2005 were 20% below exports in 2004. After declining since 1998, softwood plywood exports amounted to only 2.5% of production in 2005.

Softwood veneer imports were an estimated 3.5 billion ft^2 surface measure in 2005 (Table 40). This is 9.4% greater than the volume of imports compared to 1 year ago, composing about 61.1% of total veneer imports. Softwood veneer exports increased to 590.3 million ft^2 surface measure in 2005. This was a slight increase of 3.0% over 2004.

Hardwood plywood imports down 1.4% in 2005.

Hardwood plywood imports in 2005 were 4.5 billion ft^2 (3/8-in. basis), 1.4% below 1 year ago. The 4.6 billion ft^2 level in 2004 was the highest level of imports since 1988 when 3.2 billion ft^2 were imported. Although hardwood plywood imports were down in 2005, the current trend is one of import growth for hardwood plywood to the United States since 1997 (Table 37).

This changed over the past decade, with Canada, Brazil, Malaysia, and the Russian Federation becoming major sources of hardwood plywood imports. Asia is still the largest source of U.S. hardwood plywood imports, accounting for 66.8% of all hardwood plywood imported to the United States in 2005 (Table 39). Since 2003 China has become the largest single country source of U.S. hardwood plywood imports with 42% of total U.S. imports and 63% of all Asia imports to the U.S.

Imports of hardwood veneer, used chiefly in the manufacture of hardwood plywood in U.S. mills, totaled 2.2 billion ft^2 (surface measure) in 2005 (Table 40). This was 3.2% below 2004 and 24.4% below the peak import year of 1972. Since 1995, imports of hardwood veneer have fluctuated. Hardwood plywood exports in 2005 totaled 275 million ft^2 (3/8-in. basis) (Table 37). This was 5.8% below 2004 but the second highest level of exports since 1992. The increase in exports represents demand from the European and Canadian markets. Brazil, Indonesia, Malaysia, and the Russian Federation are the top four markets, representing nearly 71.4% of U.S. exports of these products. Hardwood veneer exports were an estimated 3.5 billion ft^2 (surface measure) in 2005, 4.7% below 2004.

Softwood plywood consumption up 1.0% in 2005 as OSB increases market share

Consumption of softwood plywood in 2005 was an estimated 16.3 billion ft^2 (3/8-in. basis) (Table 37, Fig. 20). This is 1.0% above consumption in 2004 and represented the second consecutive year that softwood plywood consumption has increased.

The small rise in consumption in 2005 occurred as OSB continued to erode softwood plywood market share. Since 1992 when OSB was certified to perform as well as softwood plywood, OSB has been rapidly eroding the market share of softwood plywood. This certification allows OSB to compete directly for the same markets while offering the consumer a lower cost product. However, certain applications are still dominated by the use of softwood plywood, such as underlayment for floors.

In the United States, there are 71 plywood-producing mills and 40 OSB mills (APA–The Engineered Wood Association 2007). Nearly 68% of all grades of softwood plywood are

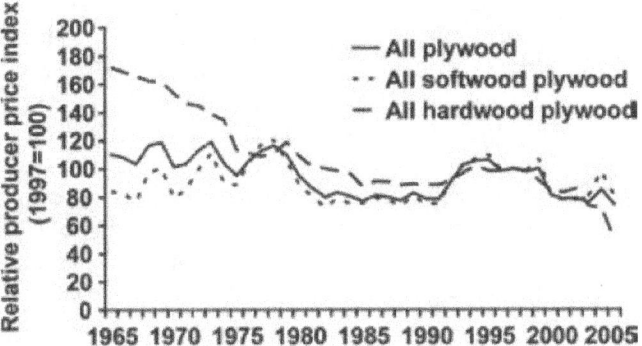

Figure 19. Relative producer price indexes for plywood, 1965–2005.

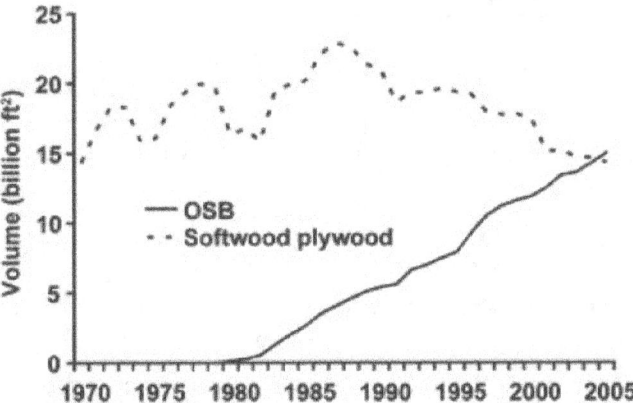

Figure 20. Softwood plywood and OSB production, 1970–2005.

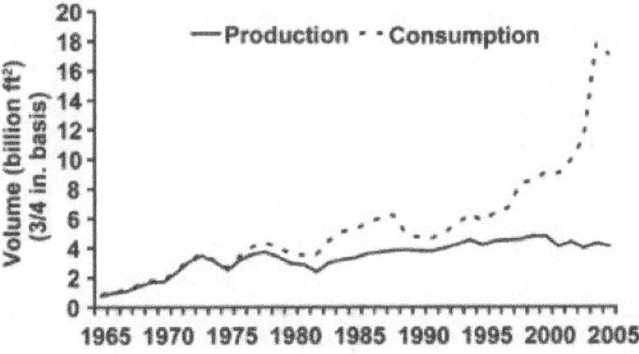

Figure 21. Particleboard consumption and production, 1965–2005.

produced in the South. The West, the traditional producer of softwood plywood, especially Douglas Fir plywood, is slowly adapting to serving niche markets because of the reduced timber supplies from public lands.

Although OSB is increasing its share in the previously dominated softwood plywood market, a strong residential construction market can explain some of the consumption increase for softwood plywood during 2005. Also important are nonresidential construction, manufacturing, and

maintenance, repair, and remodeling. The large proportion of single-family houses, which use more plywood per unit than multi-family structures, also contributed to the overall rise. These factors suggest that future changes in demand for softwood plywood will likely be closely related to changes in the volumes of residential construction and OSB production.

Consumption of hardwood plywood decreased less than 1.0%

Apparent consumption of hardwood plywood fell 0.7% in 2005 to an estimated 6.3 billion ft^2 (3/8-in. basis) (Table 37, Fig. 16). This was 47 million ft^2 less than in 2004, but it still represented a continuation of the rising trend since the past decade.

The continued strength in 2005 in part reflected the strong housing market, an important market for hardwood plywood for wall paneling, kitchen cabinets, and door skins. Mobile home output increased in 2005; mobile home production as well as furniture output contributed to the increase.

In 2005, 71.4% of the hardwood plywood consumed in the United States was supplied by imports (Table 37). This has been the trend throughout the 1990s and into 2005 as hardwood plywood imports consistently account for at least 60% of hardwood plywood consumption.

Log trade during 2005 remains mixed

Total softwood log exports decreased 6.0% during 2005 from 1 year ago (Table 18). However, softwood log exports from the western United States continued a downward trend as Douglas Fir log exports declined 14.1% in 2005 compared to 2004 and are down over 300% since 1988. Canada was the largest importer of logs from the United States; receiving 54% of U.S. softwood log exports. Japan was second, importing 26.6% from the United States, with South Korea being a distant third. During 2005, log imports from Canada continued strong and Canada remained the principal exporter of softwood logs to the United States. Softwood log imports accounted for 87% of all log imports (Table 16). Hardwood log imports from Canada decreased by 26% in 2005 as compared to 2004. Total hardwood log imports from all sources increased by 31.4% from 1 year earlier.

Particleboard, Hardboard, and Insulation Board Production, Prices, Trade, and Consumption

According to estimates of the National Particleboard Association, production of particleboard in 2005 totaled 4.1 billion ft^2 (3/4-in. basis), down from 4.3 billion ft^2 in 2004 (Table 53, Fig. 21). Particleboard is a generic term for a panel primarily composed of cellulose materials (usually wood), generally in the form of discrete pieces or particles. The cellulose materials are combined with a synthetic resin or another bonding system. Because of its uniformity, flatness, and dimensional stability, particleboard is used primarily for floor underlayment, kitchen counter underlayment, furniture components, and cabinet components.

Foreign trade in particleboard was insignificant before mid-1960 and very small through the early 1970s; however, both imports and exports experienced growth during the 1980s. Exports decreased by 35% to an estimated 57 million ft^2 (3/4-in. basis) in 2005. Imports of particleboard fell by 9.8% in 2005.

Apparent consumption of particleboard fell 4.2% during 2005 compared to 2004.

MDF output increasing

Production of MDF in 2005 was 1.8 billion ft^2 (3/4-in. basis). This is up from the 1.7 billion ft^2 of production in 2004. The major market for MDF at the present time is furniture and cabinetry applications because of its smoothness, dimensional stability, paintability, and the sharp lines that are left after a decorative cut is made on the panel.

Hardboard production rises as consumption rises

Hardboard production in 2005 was estimated to be 4.3 billion ft^2 (1/8-in. basis) (Table 56, Fig. 22). This was 10.7% above 1 year ago but well below the high in 1978. Hardboard production has been trending down since 1978 when hardboard production was 7.8 billion ft^2.

Imports of hardboard in 2005 amounted to 4.8 billion ft^2, 12.5% above 2004, continuing the upward trend of hardboard imports that started in 1993. Imports accounted for 60% of total U.S. hardboard consumption in 2005. Exports of hardboard, after a short-lived growth period during the mid-1990s, declined further in 2002. Exports of hardboard, although declining, still account for 25% of total production.

Consumption of hardboard in 2005 was 8.1 billion ft^2, 12.3% above 2004. This increase in consumption is partly a reflection of a strong housing sector. Hardboard is used primarily in the construction industry for exterior siding in new residential construction. In 2005, about one-fourth of all hardboard consumed was for residential exterior siding. Compressing wood fibers under extreme heat and pressure to form a panel produces hardboard.

Production of insulation board in 2005 was about 2.3 billion ft^2 (1/2-in. basis) or 857,000 tons (Tables 54 and 55, Fig. 23). Imports and exports of insulation board were relatively small, amounting to 112,000 and 62,000 tons, respectively.

Insulation board production remains flat in 2005

Production and trade of insulation board has been flat since 1993. The long-term outlook is one of no growth. Further developments of structural grades of particleboard at competitive prices could further accelerate particleboard demand for sheathing and other construction uses. MDF should also continue to provide increasing competition for the traditional board uses.

Miscellaneous Timber Products Production, Prices, Trade, and Consumption

Use of roundwood for miscellaneous industrial products holds steady

Production of miscellaneous industrial roundwood products, which includes cooperage logs, poles and piling, fenceposts, mine timbers, and an assortment of other products such as hewn ties and box bolts was estimated at 318 million ft^3 in 2005. This volume has been declining annually over the last 12 years (Table 5a).

Estimated round fuelwood production rises

Production of round fuelwood in 2005 was estimated at 1.6 billion ft^3, up slightly from 2004. Fuelwood consumption dropped sharply in the first five decades of the past century because of the substitution of oil, gas, coal, and electricity in home cooking, heating, and industrial uses. In recent years, however, substantial markets have developed for fireplace wood. Projected increases in income, population, and residential construction indicate this market will continue to grow.

Turpentine production continued to decline in 2005

Total domestic turpentine production fell to 22.0 million gallons in 2005 (Table 59). This continues the decline that began in 2003.

Total production in 2005 was composed of 100% sulphate turpentine. Historically, gum and steam distilled constituted about 15% of total turpentine production. But since 1985, the industry has declined and crude turpentine has dominated production. In the United States, the principal sources of turpentine are the longleaf and slash pine in the South. The substance obtained from these and other species of trees consists of 75% to 90% resin and 10% to 25% oil. Crude commercial turpentine is valuable mainly as a source of resins.

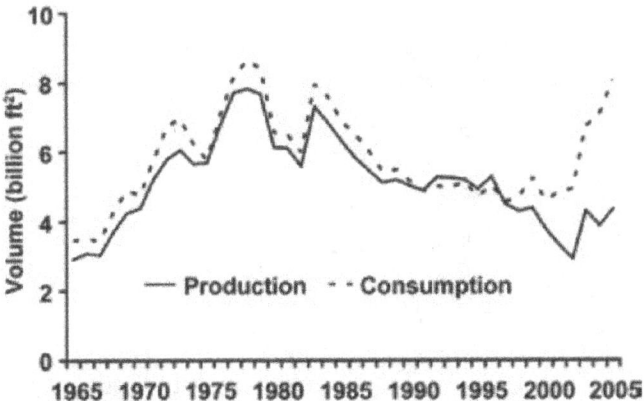

Figure 22. Hardboard consumption and production, 1965–2005.

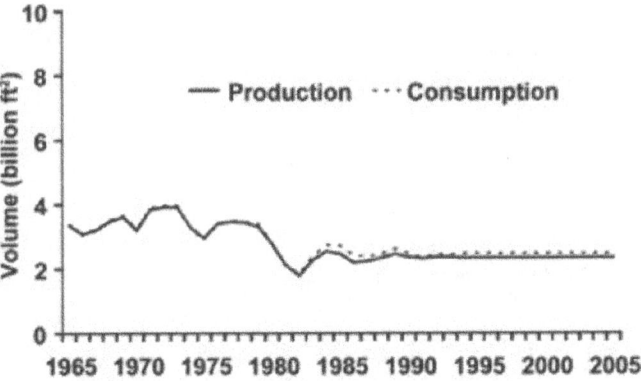

Figure 23. Insulation board consumption and production, 1965–2005.

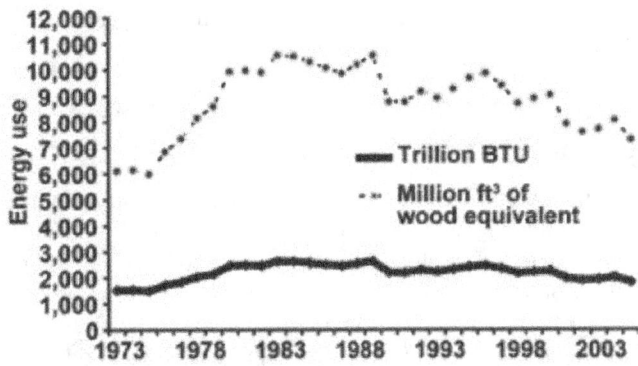

Figure 24. Wood energy use in the United States, 1973 to 2005.

Production of rosin shows continued volatility in 2005

Domestic production of rosin declined to 215 tons during 2005. Rosin production has fluctuated widely over the last decade. During 2005, rosin production was composed mainly of tall oil rosin. Historically gum and steam rosin composed about 15% of the industry. Since the mid-1980s, tall oil rosin has dominated the industry. Tall oil rosin is the rosin remaining after the removal of substantially all of the fatty acids from tall oil fractional distillation or other suitable means. The fatty acid content shall not exceed 5%.

Wood energy consumption declines in 2005

In 2005, wood energy use declined 10.4% from 1 year ago. Wood energy provided 1.8 quadrillion Btu of energy out of a total 99.9 quad consumed in the United States. This was equivalent to about 7.3 billion ft³ of wood (Table 60). Seventy percent was in industrial use, mostly in the form of wood residue and black liquor at pulp and paper mills. The remainder was for residential use (18%), electric

utilities (9%), and commercial buildings (2%). Total wood energy use has declined about 30% from a high in the early 1980s (Fig. 24). The decline was led by declines in industrial and residential use. Electric utility use has increased fairly steadily since the early 1990s.

Criteria and Indicators of Sustainable Forest Management

The Montreal criteria and indicators (C&I) of sustainable forest management (SFM) include 7 criteria and 67 indicators that measure the diverse sets of values that society places on forest resources (USDA Forest Service 2004). The support and development of the C&I for the United States reflects the evolution of forest policies and priorities in forest management among the diverse stewards of U.S. forest resources. Six of the 19 indicators under Criterion 6, maintenance and enhancement of long-term multiple socio-economic benefits to meet the needs of societies, assess the production and consumption of forest products. A subset of four of the six production and consumption indicators parallel and complement the standard measures in this report. These indicators are as follows:

- Value and volume of wood and wood products production, including value-added through downstream processing (indicator 29)

- Supply and consumption of wood and wood products, including consumption per capita (indicator 31)

- Value of wood and [nonwood products] production as a percentage of GDP (indicator 32)

- Degree of recycling of forest products (indicator 33)

Measures of production, consumption, and value are important to the goals underlying sustainable forest management. These types of measures reflect the importance of forest resources in supplying raw materials for manufacturing and the value that society places on the production of wood and wood products. Strategies to achieve sustainable forest management must reflect the role of forest resources in maintaining a dynamic and strong economy as a primary component of meeting the needs of society.

Volume and Value of Wood and Wood Products Production

The total volume of wood products production continues to grow, reflecting the value society places on wood raw materials. However, the mix of wood products reflects changing needs for specific types of products as well as technological change to accommodate increased competition for forest resources and to maintain an affordable supply of goods and services for consumers. The total volume of wood products (in roundwood equivalent inputs) in the United States, including fuelwood, has increased from 12 billion ft^3 in 1965 to 17.2 billion ft^3 in 2005 (Table 5a).

Of that production, approximately 67% and 33% was softwood and hardwood, respectively, in 2005, based on roundwood equivalent inputs (Tables 6a and 7a) (Howard 2003). The value of shipments for all wood furniture, wood products, and paper products production surpassed $364 billion in 2005 (Department of Commerce 2005) up from $350 billion in 2004. Value-added from all wood, furniture (including nonwood furniture) and paper products surpassed $163 billion in 2004 up from $152 billion in 2003(Department of Commerce 2005). Although lumber and wood products value-added accounted for 18% of total value-added or $43.7 billion, the highest value-added continues to come from the paper and allied products sector of forest products (Fig. 25). In 2004, this sector produced more than $74 billion of value-added, primarily by paper mills and paperboard containers and boxes. Furniture and fixtures (excluding nonwood furniture) represented 23% of valued-added, or more than $36 billion in 2004.

The total volume of sawnwood production has decreased in proportion to other wood products, from 51% of industrial roundwood production in 1965 to 46% in 2005 (Table 5a). Nevertheless, the volume of sawnwood production increased by 21% over the 40-year period between 1965 and 2005; the lowest volume was 5.1 billion ft^3 in 1982 and the highest volume was 7.9 billion ft^3 in 2005. On average, the value of sawnwood production has continued to increase in real terms (net of inflation) although in effect, still recovering from sharp declines in the early 1980s (Fig. 26). Meanwhile, the value-added by sawnwood production remained fairly stable during the 1990s at around $8 billion in real terms before increasing to $11 billion in 2004. The volume of sawnwood production increased by as much as 2.8 billion ft^3 from the low in 1982 to the current level of 7.9 billion ft^3 in 2005. Rising real lumber prices are important drivers in the introduction of new technologies to use more species, smaller dimension wood, and residues to make composite structural panels and engineered wood components such as OSB, I-beams, laminated beams, and truss framing.

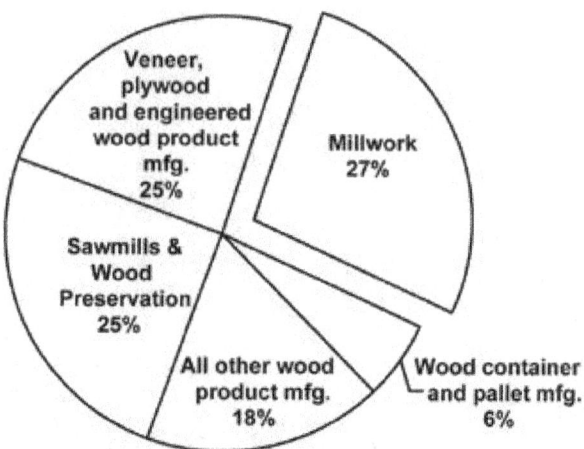

Lumber and wood product manufacturing
(22% of total value-added or $33 billion)

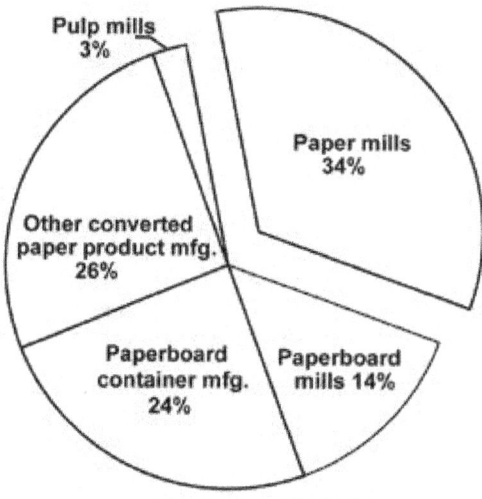

Paper manufacturing
(more than $74 billion of value-added)

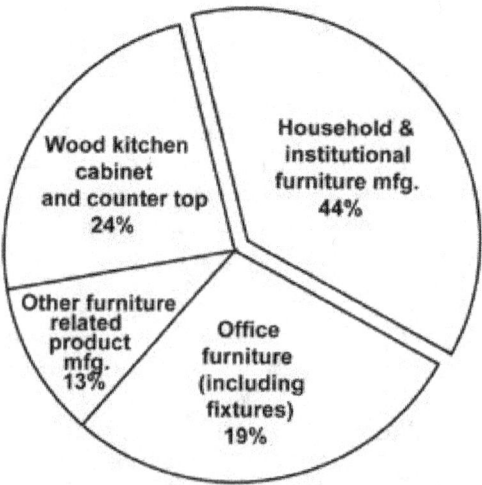

Furniture and related product manufacturing
(excluding nonwood)
(22% of value-added or $32 billion)

Figure 25. Value-added categories of wood and wood fiber products in 2004.

The production of plywood and veneer has declined in recent years, falling to the level produced in 1965. Other wood-based panels production has increased since 1965. Although current levels of plywood production are well below the peak level of 22.8 billion ft^2 (3/8-in. basis) in 1987 (Table 33), the total value of plywood shipments increased slightly to $10.8 billion in 2004 and made up more than 10% of the total value-added of all wood products (Department of Commerce 2005).

Pulp and paper products provide the highest value among wood commodities produced in the United States. The recent decrease in pulp and paper production reflects important linkages between decreased income and decreased demand for pulp and paper products. Paper and board products by weight increased more than 124% since 1965 (Table 43). The value-added of pulp and paper production has fluctuated widely during some periods, but was $74 billion in 2004 (Department of Commerce 2005). The decrease in pulp and paper volumes with somewhat falling values reflects advances in recycling as well as efficiency gains and lower production costs of foreign competitors.

Supply and Consumption of Wood and Wood Products

In addition to knowing the historical and current levels of production, we need to assess our ability to maintain, increase, or decrease levels of production in response to the changing needs of society. The rationale for this indicator is that we will know to what extent we have met and can continue to meet wood demands with our available supply. The additional information gained with this measure compared to the production and value indicators is that supply reflects all sources, domestic and international, of wood. However, no C&I variables directly measure the balance of trade in wood products; thus, potential dependence on outside sources (a possible indicator of management away from sustainable levels) is not evident.

The deficit in U.S. production compared to U.S. consumption of industrial wood products (in roundwood equivalents) increased net imports from just over 1 billion ft^3 in 1965 to almost 4.1 billion ft^3 in 2005 (Table 5a). This figure includes wood imports of more than 5.8 billion ft^3 and exports of 1.7 billion ft^3. Imports (in roundwood equivalents) constituted almost 30% of the volume consumed in 2005, compared to 12% in 1965 (Table 5a). Softwood lumber remains the primary import into the United States: approximately 61% or 3.6 billion ft^3 (in roundwood equivalent) of total wood imports in 2005 (Table 5a and 6a).

The roundwood equivalent of the total consumption of wood products in the United States has steadily increased over the last 37 years from 13.3 to 19.8 billion ft^3. Fluctuations in wood products flow reflects periods of economic downturns and recovery as the demand for wood and wood products

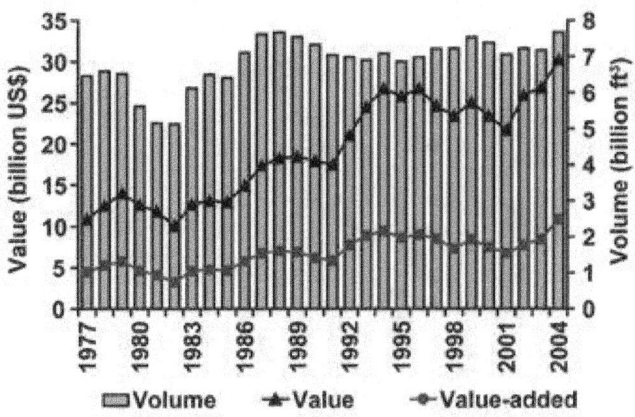

Figure 26. Volume, value, and value-added of U.S. sawn wood production, 1977–2004 (Howard 2003).

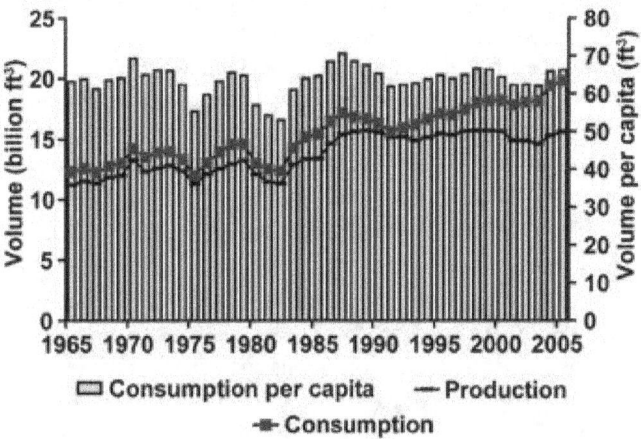

Figure 27. U.S. supply and consumption of roundwood, 1965–2005.

generally tracks basic macroeconomic indicators, such as those summarized in Table 1. Slower rates of increase in the consumption of wood products since 1990 have resulted in relatively stable trends in per capita wood consumption at about 75 ft^3 over the previous decade (Fig. 27). Per capita consumption by wood products sector shows a fairly stable proportion of individual consumption of most products, with slight decreases in plywood and veneer consumption (Fig. 28).

Value of Wood and Nonwood Production as a Percentage of GDP

The rationale for this indicator is that the percentage of production that an industry contributes to total domestic production reflects its value to society through contributions to national income and its competitiveness among other economic sectors. The value-added of wood production as a percentage of GDP has remained fairly stable at approximately 2% in real terms over the past three decades (USDA Forest Service 2004). The value-added by industry

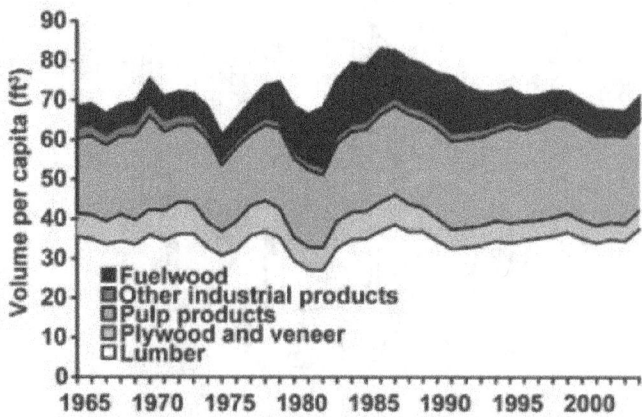

Figure 28. U.S. per capita consumption of wood products, 1965–2004.

wood and paper products as a percentage of GDP was 1.7% in 2004. Note that a simple measure of percentage of GDP might mask the move towards unsustainable levels of production if the resource is becoming scarce from overexploitation. If assessed relative to biophysical measures of land availability, rates of fragmentation, and timber productivity, this measure will provide a more comprehensive picture of sustainable forest management levels of production and consumption.

Recycling of Forest Products

The rationale for this indicator is that resource use and the conservation of forest resources are impacted by our re-use, recycling, and recovery of materials as well as direct consumption of resources. The value of a resource can be reflected in the level of recycling of products from that resource (USDA Forest Service 2004).

Traditionally, recovery and recycling in the forestry sector have been associated primarily with paper and paper products, namely newsprint and office waste paper. The majority of available data reflects these products. Recently, research and data on the recycling of solid wood materials from demolished structures, construction sites, and mill residues reflect the increasing value that society places on forest resources. Paper and paperboard recycling has increased steadily over the last few decades, with substantial increases in the 1990s. As of 2005, paper and paperboard was being recovered in the United States at a rate of 52%, up from 22% in 1970, while utilization of recovered paper exceeded 37%, up from 25% in 1965 (Tables 46 and 47) (American Forest & Paper Association 2005).

Literature Cited

American Forest & Paper Association. 2005. Wood pulp, recovered paper, and pulpwood. 45th annual survey. Washington, DC: American Forest & Paper Association.

APA–The Engineered Wood Association. 2007. Regional production and market outlook for structural panels and other engineered wood products. 2007–2012. Rep. E73. Tacoma, WA: APA–The Engineered Wood Association.

Department of Commerce. 2005. Statistics for industry groups and industries. Annual survey of manufacturers. M(AS–1). Washington, DC: U.S. Department of Commerce, Economics and Statistics Administration, Bureau of the Census. www.census.gov/prod/www/abs/industry.html

Howard, J.L. 2003. U.S. Timber Production, Trade, Consumption, and Price Statistics 1965–1999. FPL–RP–615. Madison, WI: U.S. Department of Agriculture, Forest Service, Forest Products Laboratory. 90 p.

Miller Freeman. 2006. International Woodfiber Report. 5(6).

USDA Forest Service. 2004. National report on sustainable forests –2003. FS–766. Washington, DC. 139p. www fs.fed. us/research/sustain

Annotated Bibliography

1. **Adams, D.** Timber assessment market model database. [unpublished]. Portland, OR: Oregon State University. *Hardwood and softwood lumber production.*

2. **American Forest & Paper Association.** Bilateral trade. [monthly] Washington, DC.

3. **American Forest & Paper Association.** Paper, paperboard, and wood pulp statistical summary. [monthly] Washington, DC. p. 3, 7, 9. *Production, imports, and exports of paper, paperboard, and wood pulp; pulpwood consumption; and related subjects.*

4. **American Forest & Paper Association**. Wood statistical roundup–statistical supplement. [monthly and quarterly]. Washington, DC. p. 2,4. *Lumber production, shipments, orders, stocks, trade, and other related subjects.*

5. **American Forest & Paper Association.** Statistics of paper, paperboard, and wood pulp. [annual—1977, 1982, 1985, 1990, 1995, 1998–2004]. Washington, DC. *Production, shipments, imports, and exports of paper, paperboard, and wood pulp; financial data on the paper industry and related subjects.*

6. **American Forest & Paper Association**. U.S. wood pulp data. [monthly]. Washington, DC. *U.S. and Canadian pulp production by grade, use, shipment, and inventory.*

7. **American Forest & Paper Association, Paper Recycling Group.** Statistical summary of recovered paper utilization; wood pulp, recovered paper, pulpwood fiber consumption. [annual–2004–2007] Washington, DC. p. 12, 80; *U.S. recovered paper usage by grade, region, and end use; quantitative data on consumption.*

8. **American Iron and Steel Institute.** Statistical report. [annual] Washington, DC. Table 10. Internet address: www.steel.org

9. **American Pulpwood Association.** Pulpwood summary. [monthly] New York.
Pulpwood consumption, domestic receipts, imports, and inventories by region and type of wood.

10. **American Pulpwood Association.** Pulpwood statistics. [annual] Washington, DC. Table 9.
Pulpwood consumption, receipts, and inventories by region, State, and type of pulpwood.

11. **APA–The Engineered Wood Association.** APA economics report. Curr. Pub. E67. Tacoma, WA. Table 7.
Quantitative data on demand for structural panel products in North America.

12. **APA–The Engineered Wood Association.** APA structural panel statistics. [weekly] Tacoma, WA.
Structural panel production, capacity, orders, and shipments.

13. **APA–The Engineered Wood Association.** Regional production and distribution patterns of the structural panel industry. [monthly].Tacoma, WA. Tables 1,6.
Structural panel production by major producing regions, shipments to major trading areas, description of market condition, and economic factors that affect production.

14. **Canadian Pulp and Paper Association.** Personal fax communication, June 1999. Montreal, Quebec, Canada.
Canadian exports of newsprint by destination; Canadian shipments of uncoated mechanical papers to the United States.

15. **Composite Panel Association.** Particleboard and MDF production and shipments. [annual] Silver Spring, MD.
Particleboard and MDF production, shipments, number of plants, value of shipments, and other related subjects.

16. **Conference Board.** Internet site that allows retrieval of business cycle indicators. Internet address: www.conference-board.org
Allows access to leading, coincident, lagging, and consumer confidence indices.

17. **Cornell University, Agricultural Experiment Station.** 1932. Wholesale prices for 213 years, 1720–1932. Memoir 142. Ithaca, NY.
Estimates of wholesale prices for various commodities,1720–1932.

18. **Forest Resources Association.** Pulpwood statistics. [annual–old 12]. Washington, DC.
Pulpwood consumption, receipts, and inventories by region, State, and type of pulpwood.

19. **Howard, James L.** 1997. U.S. timber production, trade, consumption, and price statistics. James Howard. FPL–GTR–98. Madison, WI: U.S. Department of Agriculture, Forest Service, Forest Products Laboratory.

20. **Ince, P.** 2000. Industrial wood productivity in the United States, 1900–1998. Res. Note FPL–RN–0272. Madison, WI: U.S. Department of Agriculture, Forest Service, Forest Products Laboratory. Internet address: www.fpl.fs fed. us/econ/Publications htm

21. **Ince, P., [and others].** Roundwood, residue, and recycled fiber equivalents of U.S. forest product production, consumption, and trade; 1982–1996. Madison, WI: U.S. Department of Agriculture, Forest Service, Forest Products Laboratory.

22. **Ingram, C.D.; Ince, P.J.; Mehlberg, R.L.** 1999. United States pulpwood receipts, softwood and hardwood, roundwood and residues, 1953–1996. Gen. Tech. Rep. FPL–GTR–115. Madison, WI: U.S. Department of Agriculture, Forest Service, Forest Products Laboratory.

23. **Louisiana Department of Agriculture, Office of Marketing.** Louisiana forest products market report. [quarterly] Baton Rouge, LA. Internet address: www.ldaf.state.la.us
Stumpage and delivered prices of saw logs and pulpwood for selected species and delivered prices of poles and pine stumps.

24. **Luppold, G.W.; and Dempsey, P.G.** 1989. New estimates of central and eastern U.S. hardwood lumber production. Northern Journal of Applied Forestry. 6(3).

25. **Manufactured Housing Institute.** Monthly manufactured home production and shipments (2001–2002). Internet address: www.mfghome.org/statistics/

26. **National Association of Home Builders.** Housing economics. [monthly] Washington, DC. p. 3.

27. **National Association of Home Builders.** Annual housing starts (1978–current year). Internet address: www nahb. org/

28. **Natural Resources Canada, Canadian Forest Service, Industry, Economics, and Programs Branch.** Selected forestry statistics Canada. [annual] Ottawa, ON.

29. **Naval Stores Review.** International yearbook. [annual]. New Orleans, LA.

30. **New Hampshire University, Cooperative Extension Service and New Hampshire Department of Resources and Economic Development.** Market pulse, NHTOA quarterly forest products market report, first, second, third, and fourth quarters.
Median and range of prices of species in North, Central, and South regions.

31. **Pine Chemicals Association, Inc.** Monthly summary. Atlanta, GA. Internet address: pinechemicals.org/

32. **Powell, D.S.; Faulkner, J.L.; Darr, D.R.; Zhu, Z; MacCleery, D.W.** 1993. Forest resources of the U.S., 1992. Gen. Tech. Rep. RM–GTR–234. (Revised, June 1994). Fort Collins, CO: U.S. Department of Agriculture, Forest Service, Rocky Mountain Forest and Range Experiment Station.

Data from periodic surveys of the forest resources by State and Forest Service region–land areas by class of land, timberland area by ownership, net volume of timber on timberland by class and species group, and related data.

33. **Statistics Canada, Industry Division.** Production, shipments, and stocks on hand of sawmills in British Columbia. [monthly]. Ottawa, ON.
Estimates of production, shipments (by destination), and stocks by species for interior and coast mills.

34. **Statistics Canada, Industry Division.** Production, shipments, and stocks on hand of sawmills east of the Rockies. [monthly]. Ottawa, ON.
Estimates of production, shipments (by destination), and stocks by species and providence (excluding Newfoundland and Prince Edward Island; price information for some species).

35. **Statistics Canada, Industry Division.** Wood industries. Census of manufacturers of wood industries. [annual]. Ottawa, ON.
Number of industries, employment, wages, shipments, material and supplies, and related subjects; figures on lumber production by Province.

36. **Timber Mart–South.** Daniel B. Warnell, School of Forest Resources, University of Georgia. [quarterly]. Athens, GA. Table: Yearly Summary Delivered *Timber. Internet address: www.tmartsouth.com/tmart/contact.html*
A brief, easy-to-read, quarterly report of the market prices for timber products of the Southeast.

37. **United Nations, Food and Agriculture Organization, Economic Commission for Europe.** European timber trends and prospects: into the 21st Century. Geneva timber and forest study papers, No. 11 [annual]. Geneva, Switzerland.
Projections of European supply, demand, and trade for timber products.

38. **United Nations, Food and Agriculture Organization.** Forestry database: FAOSTAT. Internet address: www fao.org
Historical data to 1998 on production and trade of pulp and paper products, and other wood products.

39. **U.S. Council of Economic Advisors.** Economic indicators. [monthly]. Washington, DC: Superintendent of Documents, U.S. Government Printing Office. p. 1, 2, 6, 10, 23, 30, 35.
Output, income, and spending; employment, unemployment, and wages; production and business activity; prices; money, credit, and security markets; Federal finance; and other related subjects.

40. **U.S. Council of Economic Advisors.** Economic Report of the President. [annual]. Washington, DC: Superintendent of Documents, U.S. Government Printing Office.
Detailed description of the economic situation at the beginning of each year; comprehensive series of

historical statistics on national income, population, employment, wages, productivity, business activity, prices, money supply, finance, corporate profits, agriculture, international trade, and other related subjects.

41. **U.S. Department of Agriculture, Forest Service.** Bulletin of hardwood market statistics: first, second, and third quarters [quarterly]. Princeton, WV.

42. **U.S. Department of Agriculture, Forest Service.** Production, prices, employment, and trade in Northwest forest industries. [quarterly]. Portland, OR: Pacific Northwest Forest and Range Experiment Station.
Current information on the timber situation in the West; data on log, lumber and plywood production, and prices; employment in the forest industries; international trade in logs and lumber; volume and average prices of stumpage sold by public agencies; and related subjects.

43. **U.S. Department of Agriculture, Forest Service.** Pulpwood prices in the Mid-South. Res. Note SO. [annual]. New Orleans, LA: U.S. Department of Agriculture, Forest Service, Southern Forest Experiment Station.
Pulpwood prices in U.S. Mid-South, by wood type (hardwoods and softwoods) and purchase point.

44. **U.S. Department of Agriculture, Forest Service.** Pulpwood production in the North Central region by county. [annual]. St. Paul, MN: North Central Forest Experiment Station.
Pulpwood production in the Lake and Central States by State, county, and species.

45. **U.S. Department of Agriculture, Forest Service.** Pulpwood production in the Northeast. [annual]. Radnor, PA: Northeastern Forest Experiment Station. *Pulpwood production by State and species group, wood pulp production, and location and name of pulp producers in the Northeast.*

46. **U.S. Department of Agriculture, Forest Service.** Southern pulpwood production. [annual]. Asheville, NC: Southern Forest Experiment Station, and New Orleans, LA: Southern Forest Experiment Station.
Pulpwood production in 12 southern States by species, group, State, and county.

47. **U.S. Department of Agriculture, Forest Service.** Volume and value of sawtimber stumpage sold from National Forests, by selected species and region. [quarterly and annual]. Washington, DC.
Stumpage prices of timber sold from National Forests by selected species and region.

48. **U.S. Department of Agriculture, Forest Service.** The demand and price situation for forest products, 1964. Misc. Pub. 983. Washington, DC: Superintendent of Documents, U.S. Government Printing Office.
Historical data on U.S. timber production, trade, consumption, and prices.

49. U.S. Department of Agriculture, Forest Service. 1989. An analysis of the timber situation in the United States 1952–2040. GTR–RM–199. Washington, DC. p. 262, Table B-7.
Comprehensive survey and analysis of present and prospective timber demand, supply, and prices in the United States.

50. U.S. Department of Agriculture, Forest Service. Forest resources of the United States, 1997 & 2002. NC–GTR–219. St. Paul, MN: North Central Research Station. Table 39.
Current National Forest resource statistics by ownership, region, or State. Providing information on forest area, volume, mortality, growth, removals, and timber products output.

51. U.S. Department of Agriculture, Forest Service. 2004. National report on sustainable forests–2003. FS–766. Washington, DC. 139 p.

52. U.S. Department of Commerce, Bureau of the Census. Manuf. & Constr. Div. Curr. Ind. Rep. MQ327D. [quarterly and annual]. Washington, DC. Table 1.
Production and shipments of clay construction products.

53. U.S. Department of Commerce, Bureau of the Census. Hardwood plywood. Curr. Ind. Rep. Ser. MA321T. Washington, DC.
Production and shipments of hardwood plywood by type of plywood, geographic division, and face species.

54. U.S. Department of Commerce, Bureau of the Census. Manuf. & Constr. Div. Tables Q6 and "Selected characteristics of new manufactured homes placed for residential use, by region. Washington, DC." Internet address: www.census.gov/const/www/index.html
Manufacturing, mining, and construction statistics.

55. U.S. Department of Commerce, Bureau of the Census. Housing completions. Constr. Rep. C 22. [monthly] Washington, DC. Superintendent of Documents, U.S. Government Printing Office.
Number of houses completed in the United States by structure type, ownership, region, and metropolitan statistical area.

56. U.S. Department of Commerce, Bureau of the Census. Housing starts. Constr. Rep. C 20. [monthly]. Washington, DC: Superintendent of Documents, U.S. Government Printing Office.
Number of houses started in the United States by structure type, ownership, region, and metropolitan statistical area; information on shipments of mobile homes.

57. U.S. Department of Commerce, Bureau of the Census. Lumber production and mill stocks. Curr. Ind. Rep. Ser. MA24T & MA–321T. [annual]. Washington, DC.
Lumber production by major species, producing region, and State.

58. U.S. Department of Commerce, Bureau of the Census. New one-family houses sold and for sale. Constr. Rep. C 25. [monthly and annual]. Washington, DC: Superintendent of Documents, U.S. Government Printing Office.
Number of privately owned, one-family homes sold and for sale in the United States by stage of construction and sale price.

59. U.S. Department of Commerce, Bureau of the Census. Particleboard. Curr. Ind. Rep. Ser. MA–24L. [annual]. Washington, DC.
Production of particleboard by State, production by type, shipments, and resin consumption.

60. U.S. Department of Commerce, Bureau of the Census. Population characteristics. Curr. Pop. Rep. Ser. P-20-537. [monthly]. Washington, DC. Superintendent of Documents, U.S. Government Printing Office.
Estimates of households, families, marital status, fertility, and related data.

61. U.S. Department of Commerce, Bureau of the Census. Population estimates and projections. Curr. Pop. Rep. Ser. P–25. [monthly]. Washington, DC: Superintendent of Documents, U.S. Government Printing Office.
Estimates of U.S. population by type and month.

62. U.S. Department of Commerce, Bureau of the Census. Pulp, paper, and board. Curr. Ind. Rep. Ser. MA–26A. [annual]. Washington, DC.
Pulpwood receipts, consumption, and inventories; wood pulp production, transfers, and inventories; paper and board shipments by grades; and other subjects.

63. U.S. Department of Commerce, Bureau of the Census. Residential alterations and repairs. Constr. Rep. C 50. [quarterly and annual]. Washington, DC: Superintendent of Documents, U.S. Government Printing Office. Table 2. Internet address: www.census.gov/const/www/c50index.html
Regional data on expenditures for additions, alterations, maintenance, repairs, and replacements for all residential units and for owner occupants of one-housing unit properties.

64. U.S. Department of Commerce, Bureau of the Census. Softwood plywood. Curr. Ind. Rep. Ser. MA–24H. [annual]. Washington, DC.
Production of softwood plywood and veneer and consumption of softwood veneer logs.

65. U.S. Department of Commerce, Bureau of the Census. Statistics for industry groups and industries. M (AS–1). Washington, DC.
Internet address: www.census.gov/prod/www/abs/industry.html

66. U.S. Department of Commerce, Bureau of the Census. U.S. exports/schedule E commodity by country. FT 410. [monthly]. Washington, DC: Superintendent of Documents, U.S. Government Printing Office.

Volume and value of exports by product and country of destination. Exports of lumber are broken down by major species and grade.

67. **U.S. Department of Commerce, Bureau of the Census.** U.S. imports for consumption and general imports/ TSUSA commodity by country of origin. FT 246. [annual]. Washington, DC: Superintendent of Documents, U.S. Government Printing Office.
Volume and value of imports by product and country of origin. Imports of lumber are broken down by major species and grade.

68. **U.S. Department of Commerce, Bureau of the Census.** Value of new construction put in place. Constr. Rep. C 30. [monthly]. Washington, DC: Superintendent of Documents, U.S. Government Printing Office. Table 1.
Value of new construction put in place by type of construction.

69. **U.S. Department of Commerce, Bureau of the Census, and U.S. Department of Housing and Urban Development.** Characteristics of new housing. [annual]. Constr. Rep. C 25. Washington, DC: Superintendent of Documents, U.S. Government Printing Office.
Housing completions by type of structure and location.

70. **U.S. Department of Commerce, Bureau of Economic Analysis.** Survey of current business. [monthly]. Washington, DC: Superintendent of Documents, U.S. Government Printing Office.
Gross national product, national income, personal income and outlays, foreign transactions, and other national subjects.

71. **U.S. Department of Commerce, Bureau of Industrial Economics.** Constr. Rev. [monthly]. Washington, DC: Superintendent of Documents, U.S. Government Printing Office, Washington, DC.
Volume of construction, costs, employment, and related subjects.

72. **U.S. Department of Energy, Energy Information Administration**
Monthly energy review. Internet address: www.eia.doe.gov/ emeu/mer/renew.html

73. **U.S. Department of Labor, Bureau of Labor Statistics.** Employment and earnings, United States.
Internet address: www.bls.gov/ces/
Employment and earnings of individual nonagricultural industries in the United States.

74. **U.S. Department of Labor, Bureau of Labor Statistics.** Producer prices and price indexes. [monthly and annual]. Washington, DC.
Prices and price indexes of several hundred commodities, including selected lumber items of important commercial species and of plywood, pulp, and paper items.

75. **U.S. Department of Labor, Bureau of Labor Statistics.** The CPI detailed report. [monthly]. Washington, DC: Superintendent of Documents, U.S. Government Printing Office. Internet address: www.bls.gov/ces/
Consumer price indexes for goods and services usually bought by all urban consumers and by urban wage earners and clerical workers.

76. **U.S. Department of Labor, Bureau of Labor Statistics.** 1979. Employment and earnings, United States, 1909–78 and supplements. Washington, DC: Superintendent of Documents, U.S. Government Printing Office.
Employment and earnings of individual nonagricultural industries in the United States.

77. **U.S. Federal Reserve System, Board of Governors.** Federal Reserve Bulletin. [monthly and annual]. Curr. Pub. G.5A (405). Washington, DC. Internet address: www.federalreserve.gov/rnd.htm
Interest rates; security prices; Federal and business finances; selected indexes on business activity, and wholesale and consumer prices; sales, profits, and dividends of large manufacturing corporations; and related subjects.

78. **U.S. Federal Reserve System, Board of Governors.** Industrial production. [monthly]. Washington, DC.
Indexes of industrial production by market and industry.

79. **U.S. Geological Survey.** Mineral commodity summaries. [annual]. Reston, VA. p. 44. Internet address: minerals. usgs.gov

80. **U.S. International Trade Commission.** Interactive tariff and trade data web. Internet address: dataweb.usitc.gov/
Interactive database containing Department of Commerce data on imports and exports of commodities identified by trade code.

81. **U.S. International Trade Commission.** U.S. trade shifts in selected industries. [annual].
Volume and value data on imports and exports of timber products.

82. **Western Wood Products Association.** Western lumber facts. [weekly]. Portland, OR.
Softwood lumber production, orders, shipments, stocks, and realization value in the western woods region by major species.

83. **Western Wood Products Association.** Lumber track. [monthly] Portland, OR. Dec. issue.
Review of North American lumber statistics, including trade highlights and key markets.

84. **Wood Markets.** International Solid Wood Report. [monthly]. Curr. Pub. Dec.–Jan. Table 2. Vancouver, BC, Canada: International Wood Markets Research Inc. Internet address: www.woodmarkets.com
Special report: U.S./Canada lumber outlook.

85. **Wood Preservers Institute.** The 1996 wood preserving
industry production statistical report. [annual]. Fairfax, VA.
*Volume and value of wood preservatives and wood
products treated with preservatives.*

86. **Wood Technology.** North American fact book. Panel
review [annual].
*Data published by APA, Statistics Canada, National
Particleboard Association, and the American
Hardboard Association.*

87. **U.S. Department of Energy, Energy Information
Administration**
Monthly energy review. Internet address: www.eia.doe.gov/
emeu/mer/renew.html [Table 47 cites 88 as an AF&PA pub]

Table 1—Measures of economic growth, population, and prices, 1965–2005

Year	Gross domestic product[a] Billion current dollars	Gross domestic product[a] Billion 1996 dollars	Disposable personal income[a] Billion current dollars	Disposable personal income[a] Billion 1996 dollars	Expenditures for new construction[b] Billion current dollars	Expenditures for new construction[b] Billion 1996 dollars	Non-residential fixed investment[b] Billion 1996 dollars	Number of housing starts[a,c] Thousand units	Mobile homes[d] Thousand units	Population[a] Millions	Total industrial production[a,e] 1997=100	Manufac-turing[a,e] 1997=100	Furniture and fixtures[e] 1997=100	Paper and products[e] 1997=100	Producer price index all commodities[e] 1997=100	Consumer price index all items[a] 1997=100
1965	719.1	2,998.7	493.9	2,059.6	81.9	341.5	226.7	1,473	217	194.3	40.3	37.3	36.6	39.4	25.3	19.6
1966	787.8	3,193.4	533.7	2,163.4	85.8	347.8	255.0	1,165	217	196.6	43.9	40.7	39.4	42.5	26.1	20.2
1967	833.6	3,278.0	571.9	2,248.9	87.2	342.9	251.5	1,292	240	198.7	44.8	41.4	39.4	42.5	26.2	20.8
1968	910.6	3,432.3	621.4	2,342.3	96.8	364.9	262.5	1,508	318	200.7	47.3	43.8	40.8	45.0	26.8	21.7
1969	982.2	3,531.8	668.4	2,403.5	104.9	377.2	282.4	1,467	413	202.7	49.5	45.7	42.7	48.4	27.9	22.9
1970	1,035.6	3,535.7	727.1	2,482.4	105.9	361.6	280.8	1,434	401	205.1	47.9	43.6	40.0	47.9	28.9	24.2
1971	1,125.4	3,650.3	790.2	2,563.1	122.4	397.0	280.6	2,052	497	207.7	48.5	44.3	41.6	50.0	29.9	25.2
1972	1,237.3	3,844.6	855.3	2,657.9	139.1	432.3	306.1	2,357	576	209.9	53.2	48.9	50.2	62.5	31.2	26.1
1973	1,382.6	4,064.1	965.0	2,836.6	153.8	452.1	350.7	2,045	567	211.9	57.5	53.3	53.5	67.7	35.3	27.7
1974	1,496.9	4,050.1	1,054.2	2,852.3	155.2	419.9	353.5	1,338	329	213.9	57.2	53.1	49.8	70.8	41.9	30.7
1975	1,630.6	4,039.1	1,159.2	2,871.4	152.6	378.0	318.4	1,160	213	216.0	52.0	47.5	42.6	61.3	45.8	33.6
1976	1,819.0	4,251.0	1,273.0	2,975.0	172.1	402.2	334.1	1,538	246	218.0	56.0	51.7	47.6	67.7	47.9	35.6
1977	2,026.9	4,445.9	1,401.4	3,073.9	200.5	439.8	371.6	1,987	277	220.2	60.1	56.1	53.2	70.6	50.9	37.8
1978	2,291.4	4,700.3	1,580.1	3,241.2	239.9	492.1	424.1	2,020	276	222.6	63.4	59.5	58.1	73.6	54.8	40.7
1979	2,557.5	4,852.9	1,769.5	3,357.7	272.9	517.8	466.6	1,745	277	225.1	65.3	61.2	59.5	74.8	61.7	45.2
1980	2,784.2	4,852.2	1,973.3	3,439.0	273.9	477.3	466.3	1,292	222	227.7	63.5	58.9	58.0	74.6	70.4	51.3
1981	3,115.9	4,969.5	2,200.2	3,509.1	289.1	461.1	492.6	1,084	241	230.0	64.3	59.5	58.5	75.7	76.8	56.7
1982	3,242.1	4,874.6	2,347.3	3,529.2	279.3	419.9	474.2	1,062	240	232.2	60.9	56.2	55.7	74.3	78.4	60.1
1983	3,514.5	5,075.8	2,522.4	3,643.0	311.6	450.0	469.4	1,703	296	234.3	62.5	58.8	63.0	79.0	79.4	62.1
1984	3,902.4	5,435.1	2,810.0	3,913.6	369.0	513.9	552.0	1,750	295	236.3	68.1	64.6	71.5	83.2	81.3	64.8
1985	4,180.7	5,645.8	3,002.0	4,054.0	401.4	542.1	589.0	1,742	284	238.5	68.8	65.7	73.5	81.4	80.9	67.1
1986	4,422.2	5,844.8	3,187.6	4,213.1	429.9	568.2	573.1	1,805	244	240.7	69.5	67.1	76.6	84.8	78.5	68.3
1987	4,692.3	6,028.1	3,363.1	4,320.5	441.6	567.3	572.5	1,621	233	242.8	72.8	70.7	81.4	87.7	80.6	70.8
1988	5,049.6	6,275.9	3,640.8	4,525.0	455.6	566.2	603.6	1,488	218	245.0	76.3	74.3	86.4	91.3	83.8	73.7
1989	5,438.7	6,508.7	3,894.5	4,660.7	469.8	562.2	637.0	1,376	198	247.3	77.0	74.8	89.5	92.5	87.9	77.3
1990	5,743.8	6,615.6	4,166.8	4,798.8	468.5	539.6	641.7	1,193	188	249.9	77.6	75.2	86.3	92.4	91.1	81.5
1991	5,916.9	6,599.0	4,343.7	4,844.6	424.2	473.1	610.1	1,014	171	252.7	76.3	73.7	80.8	92.3	91.3	84.9
1992	6,244.4	6,799.2	4,613.7	5,023.6	452.1	492.3	630.6	1,200	211	255.4	78.3	76.3	81.6	94.5	91.8	87.4
1993	6,553.0	6,967.6	4,790.2	5,093.2	482.7	513.2	683.6	1,288	254	258.1	80.9	78.9	89.0	95.5	93.2	90.1
1994	6,935.7	7,223.9	5,021.7	5,230.4	519.5	541.1	744.6	1,457	304	260.7	85.2	83.7	90.5	99.7	94.4	92.4
1995	7,253.8	7,394.3	5,320.8	5,423.9	538.1	548.5	817.5	1,354	340	263.0	89.3	88.1	91.1	101.4	97.7	95.0
1996	7,575.9	7,575.9	5,588.5	5,588.5	583.6	583.6	899.4	1,475	363	265.5	93.2	92.2	88.9	98.0	100.1	97.8
1997	8,110.9	7,955.8	5,886.6	5,854.5	618.2	606.4	1,009.3	1,474	354	267.9	100.0	100.0	100.0	100.0	100.0	100.0
1998	8,511.0	8,247.1	6,027.8	6,168.6	655.4	635.1	1,135.5	1,617	373	270.3	105.6	106.5	99.1	101.0	97.5	101.6
1999[r]	9,274.3	8,858.8	6,639.2	6,328.4	765.9	731.6	1,228.4	1,641	349	273.2	110.1	111.8	102.7	102.2	98.4	103.8
2000	9,824.6	9,191.3	7,120.2	6,630.3	820.3	767.5	1,324.2	1,569	251	282.1	115.3	117.4	119.4	100.5	104.0	107.3
2001	10,082.2	9,214.2	7,393.2	6,748.0	842.5	770.0	1,255.1	1,603	193	284.8	111.2	112.6	113.2	95.3	105.2	110.3
2002	10,445.6	9,440.2	7,829.1	7,049.8	846.1	764.6	1,183.4	1,705	168	287.5	110.5	111.5	101.7	94.3	102.7	112.1
2003	10,971.2	9,915.2	8,159.9	7,374.5	915.7	827.6	1,301.6	1,848	131	291.1	110.9	112.2	101.0	92.3	108.2	114.6
2004	11,734.3	10,841.3	8,622.8	7,966.6	999.6	923.5	1,423.6	1,956	131	294.0	115.5	117.2	108.9	94.8	115.0	117.7
2005	12,487.1	11,138.0	9,031.3	8,055.5	1,120.6	999.6	1,544.6	2,068	147	296.7	120.5	123.3	108.6	92.7	123.4	121.7

[a] U.S. Council of Economic Advisors (39,40).
[b] U.S. Department of Commerce, Bureau of the Census (68).
[c] U.S. Council of Economic Advisors (39); series (1965-1999)
[d] U.S. Department of Commerce, Bureau of the Census (54); National Association of Home Builders (26, 27); Manufactured Housing Institute (25).
[e] U.S. Federal Reserve System, Board of Governors (78).
[f] U.S. Department of Labor, Bureau of Labor Statistics (75).
[r] Revised.

Table 2—Number of households and housing market indicators, 1965–2005

				New housing units								Expenditures for residential upkeep and improvements[f]	
	Number of house-holds[a]	New home mortgage interest rates[b]	Total units	New housing starts					Mobile homes				
				Total starts[c,d]	One family		Multifamily		Number shipments[c]	Floor area[e]			
					Number starts[c]	Floor area[e]	Number starts[c,d]	Floor area[e]					
Year	Millions	Average percent	Thousand units	Thousand units	Thousand units	Average square feet	Thousand units	Average square feet	Thousand units	Average square feet		Million current dollars	Million 1996 dollars
1965	57.4	5.81	1,727	1,510	965	1,498	545	1,053	217	650		11,442	52,009
1966	58.4	6.25	1,413	1,196	780	1,544	416	1,076	217	660		11,691	50,830
1967	59.2	6.46	1,562	1,322	845	1,585	477	1,094	240	670		11,687	49,312
1968	60.8	6.97	1,863	1,545	900	1,642	645	1,123	318	670		12,703	50,812
1969	62.2	7.81	1,913	1,500	811	1,616	689	1,095	413	684		13,535	50,504
1970	63.4	8.45	1,870	1,469	815	1,482	654	995	401	732		14,770	52,007
1971	64.8	7.74	2,582	2,085	1,153	1,520	932	1,011	497	780		16,299	53,792
1972	66.7	7.60	2,955	2,379	1,311	1,555	1,068	1,035	576	780		17,498	54,342
1973	68.3	7.96	2,625	2,058	1,133	1,660	925	1,031	567	882		18,512	52,891
1974	69.9	8.92	1,682	1,353	889	1,695	464	1,021	329	910		21,114	53,184
1975	71.1	9.00	1,384	1,171	896	1,645	275	1,000	213	952		25,239	58,154
1976	72.9	9.00	1,794	1,548	1,166	1,700	382	940	246	966		29,034	63,811
1977	74.1	9.02	2,279	2,002	1,451	1,720	551	938	277	1,000		31,280	63,707
1978	76.0	9.56	2,312	2,036	1,433	1,755	603	902	276	1,010		37,461	68,610
1979	77.3	10.78	2,037	1,760	1,194	1,760	566	938	277	1,050		42,231	69,119
1980	80.8	12.66	1,535	1,313	852	1,740	461	979	222	1,050		46,338	68,345
1981	82.4	14.70	1,341	1,100	705	1,720	395	980	241	1,015		46,351	63,582
1982	83.5	15.14	1,312	1,072	663	1,710	409	990	240	1,000		45,291	59,830
1983	83.9	12.57	2,009	1,713	1,068	1,725	645	942	296	1,035		49,295	63,936
1984	85.4	12.38	2,051	1,756	1,084	1,780	672	914	295	1,060		70,597	105,369
1985	86.8	11.55	2,029	1,745	1,072	1,785	673	922	284	1,080		82,127	120,245
1986	88.5	10.17	2,049	1,805	1,179	1,825	626	911	244	1,110		94,329	132,113
1987	89.5	9.31	1,854	1,621	1,146	1,905	475	980	233	1,140		98,413	131,744
1988	91.1	9.19	1,706	1,488	1,081	1,995	407	990	218	1,175		106,864	137,534
1989	92.8	10.13	1,574	1,376	1,003	2,035	373	1,000	198	1,195		108,054	133,730
1990	93.3	10.05	1,381	1,193	895	2,080	298	1,005	188	1,205		115,432	138,408
1991	94.3	9.32	1,185	1,014	840	2,075	174	1,020	171	1,225		107,692	128,052
1992	94.6	8.24	1,411	1,200	1,030	2,095	170	1,040	211	1,255		115,569	134,696
1993	95.3	7.20	1,542	1,288	1,126	2,095	162	1,065	254	1,295		121,899	135,443
1994	96.0	7.49	1,761	1,457	1,198	2,100	259	1,035	304	1,330		130,625	138,963
1995	97.3	7.87	1,694	1,354	1,076	2,095	278	1,080	340	1,355		124,971	127,391
1996	98.7	7.80	1,838	1,475	1,161	2,120	314	1,070	363	1,380		131,362	131,362
1997	99.9	7.71	1,828	1,474	1,134	2,150	340	1,095	354	1,420		133,577	129,812
1998	101.0	7.07	1,990	1,617	1,271	2,190	346	1,065	373	1,450		133,693	126,603
1999[r]	103.9	7.04	2,012	1,663	1,303	2,223	341	1,104	349	1,465		142,900	129,438
2000	104.7	7.52	1,824	1,573	1,231	2,266	342	1,114	251	1,505		152,975	132,561
2001	108.2	7.00	1,796	1,603	1,273	2,324	330	1,171	193	1,540		157,765	131,911
2002	109.3	6.43	1,874	1,706	1,359	2,320	347	1,166	168	1,595		173,324	141,374
2003	111.3	5.80	1,979	1,848	1,499	2,330	349	1,173	131	1,570		176,899	143,703
2004	112.0	5.77	2,087	1,956	1,611	2,349	345	1,243	131	1,625		198,557	171,170
2005	112 0[p]	5.94	2,215	2,068	1,716	2,462	353	1,288	147	1,625		215,030	180,006

[a] U.S. Department of Commerce, Bureau of he Census (60).

[b] U.S. Council of Economic Advisors (39).

[c] U.S. Department of Commerce, Bureau of he Census (53, 55, 65); U.S. Department of Commerce,
U.S Department of Commerce, Bureau of the Census and U.S. Department of Housing and Urban Development (69);
National Association of Home Builders (26,27).

[d] Data for privately owned housing starts from 1986 to present.

[e] U.S. Department of Agriculture, Forest Service estimates based on data from the Manufactured Housing Institute; U.S. Department of Commerce,
U.S. Department of Commerce, Bureau of he Census (54,55); U.S. Department of Commerce, Bureau of the Census and U.S. Department of Housing and
Urban Development (69); Manufactured Housing Ins itute (25).

[f] U.S. Department of Commerce, Bureau of he Census (63).

[r] Revised

[p] Preliminary

Table 3—Average hourly earnings[a] in timber-based industries and all manufacturing in the United States, 1972–2005[b]

Year	Lumber and wood products except furniture		Logging camps and logging contractors		Sawmills and planing mills		Millwork, plywood, and structural members		Paper and allied products		Furniture and fixtures		Manufacturing	
	U.S. dollars	Index 1996=100	U.S. dollars	Index 1996=100	U.S. dollars	Index 1996=100	U.S. dollars	Index 1996=100	U.S. dollars	Index 1996=100	U.S. dollars	Index 1996=100	U.S. dollars	Index 1996=100
1972	3.33	31.9	4.25	36.1	3.29	31.1	3.37	35.5	3.95	26.9	3.08	30.3	3.82	29.9
1973	3.61	34.6	4.56	38.8	3.62	34.2	3.62	34.4	4.20	28.6	3.29	32.4	4.09	32.0
1974	3.89	37.3	4.91	41.8	3.88	36.6	3.91	37.2	4.53	30.9	3.53	34.8	4.42	34.6
1975	4.26	40.8	5.28	44.9	4.34	41.0	4.26	40.5	5.01	34.1	3.78	37.2	4.83	37.8
1976	4.72	45.2	6.03	51.3	4.86	45.9	4.67	44.4	5.47	37.3	4.34	42.8	5.68	44.4
1977	5.10	48.9	6.58	56.0	5.28	49.9	5.04	48.0	5.96	40.6	4.34	42.8	5.68	44.4
1978	5.60	53.6	7.25	61.6	5.83	55.1	5.55	52.8	6.52	44.4	4.68	46.1	6.17	48.3
1979	6.07	58.1	7.97	67.8	6.32	59.7	5.95	56.6	7.13	48.6	5.06	49.9	6.70	52.4
1980	6.55	62.7	8.64	73.5	6.70	63.3	6.41	61.0	7.84	53.4	5.49	54.1	7.27	56.9
1981	6.99	67.0	9.11	77.5	7.19	67.9	6.89	65.6	8.60	58.6	5.91	58.2	7.99	62.5
1982	7.43	71.2	9.79	83.2	7.73	73.0	7.33	69.7	9.32	63.5	6.31	62.2	8.49	66.4
1983	7.80	74.7	10.17	86.5	8.20	77.4	7.64	72.7	9.93	67.6	6.62	65.2	8.83	69.1
1984	8.03	76.9	10.70	91.0	8.42	79.5	7.81	74.3	10.41	70.9	6.84	67.4	9.19	71.9
1985	8.22	78.7	10.92	92.9	8.52	80.5	8.06	76.7	10.83	73.8	7.17	70.6	9.54	74.6
1986	8.34	79.9	10.82	92.0	8.58	81.0	8.23	78.3	11.18	76.2	7.46	73.5	9.73	76.1
1987	8.40	80.5	10.68	90.8	8.58	81.0	8.35	79.4	11.43	77.9	7.67	75.6	9.91	77.5
1988	8.61	82.5	10.78	91.7	8.75	82.6	8.55	81.4	11.69	79.6	7.94	78.2	10.18	79.7
1989	8.84	84.7	11.13	94.6	9.03	85.3	8.73	83.1	11.96	81.5	8.25	81.3	10.48	82.0
1990	9.08	87.0	11.22	95.4	9.22	87.1	9.04	86.0	12.31	83.9	8.52	83.9	10.83	84.7
1991	9.24	88.5	11.06	94.0	9.37	88.5	9.28	88.3	12.72	86.6	5.76	56.7	11.18	87.5
1992	9.44	90.4	11.17	95.0	9.59	90.6	9.48	90.2	13.07	89.0	9.01	88.8	11.46	89.7
1993	9.61	92.0	11.37	96.7	9.78	92.4	9.65	91.8	13.42	91.4	9.27	91.3	11.74	91.9
1994	9.84	94.3	11.44	97.3	10.05	94.9	9.89	94.1	13.77	93.8	9.55	94.1	12.06	94.4
1995	10.12	96.9	11.64	99.0	10.31	97.4	10.12	96.3	14.23	96.9	9.82	96.7	12.37	96.8
1996	10.44	100.0	11.76	100.0	10.59	100.0	10.51	100.0	14.68	100.0	10.15	100.0	12.78	100.0
1997	10.76	103.1	12.16	103.4	10.85	102.5	10.89	103.6	15.06	102.6	10.55	103.9	13.17	103.1
1998	11.10	106.3	12.48	106.1	11.12	105.0	11.25	107.0	15.51	105.7	10.90	107.4	13.49	105.6
1999	11.46	109.8	13.24	112.6	11.40	107.6	11.59	110.3	15.97	108.8	11.23	110.6	13.91	108.8
2000	11.94	114.4	13.70	116.5	11.90	112.4	12.08	114.9	16.25	110.7	11.74	115.7	14.37	112.4
2001	12.26	117.4	14.40	122.4	12.19	115.1	12.45	118.5	16.87	114.9	12.24	120.6	14.83	116.0
2002	12.50	119.7	14.76	125.5	12.42	117.3	12.60	119.9	17.50	119.2	12.61	124.2	15.29	119.6
2003[c]	12.71	121.7	14.95	127.1	13.84	130.7	12.60	119.9	17.32	118.0	12.98	127.9	15.74	123.2
2004	13.03	124.8	15.03	127.8	14.05	132.7	13.20	125.6	17.90	121.9	13.16	129.7	16.14	126.3
2005	13.16	126.1	15.74	133.8	13.97	131.9	13.48	128.3	17.98	122.5	13.44	132.4	16.56	129.6

[a]For production or nonsupervisory workers.
[b]U.S Department of Commerce, Bureau of Economic Analysis (70); U.S. Department of Labor, Bureau of Labor Statistics (74).
[c]Changed from SIC to NAICS in 2003

Table 4—Average employment in lumber-producing and lumber-dependent industries in the United States, in thousand people, 1972–2005[a]

	Lumber producing				Lumber dependent							
Year	Logging	Sawmills and planning mills, general[q]	Millwork	Wood kitchen cabinets[q]	Wood containers[q]	Wood buildings and mobile homes[q]	Misc. wood products[q]	Lumber, plywood, and millwork	Lumber and other building materials	Residential building construction	Operative builders[q]	Special trade contractors
1972	69.0	182.0	78.5	38.1	45.8	110.5	86.3	z	268.3	577.6	93.6	1,950.6
1973	75.9	185.9	83.3	41.9	47.5	115.0	91.1	z	286.1	594.2	101.8	2,086.7
1974	80.7	191.3	75.1	38.5	46.3	82.2	90.0	z	287.6	576.0	92.1	2,029.0
1975	73.5	169.6	67.6	31.5	38.9	63.1	78.1	z	267.9	479.9	68.3	1,778.8
1976	81.5	184.4	75.2	36.9	41.2	71.4	84.5	z	283.4	513.8	67.2	1,805.8
1977	84.2	189.3	80.8	44.2	42.0	82.1	87.0	z	302.1	578.1	75.4	1,982.7
1978	84.8	192.3	85.5	50.0	44.4	87.3	91.3	z	325.5	637.3	81.9	2,172.6
1979	88.5	196.4	84.5	54.1	46.9	83.4	92.7	z	337.5	625.1	83.3	2,292.6
1980	87.5	178.2	76.3	48.4	42.5	65.6	87.9	z	325.3	554.3	66.6	2,278.3
1981	82.1	168.4	74.8	47.0	41.2	66.7	87.5	z	315.1	508.1	59.7	2,228.6
1982	75.4	148.1	70.4	42.0	37.6	60.0	78.9	77.2	298.3	446.9	47.9	2,119.2
1983	82.9	160.3	81.1	48.7	37.8	69.3	81.2	83.1	320.9	492.9	54.8	2,173.6
1984	87.5	166.5	90.3	57.0	41.0	73.5	84.4	92.9	346.8	578.9	57.9	2,461.7
1985	84.4	160.2	95.0	60.4	40.9	72.0	83.3	97.2	363.2	622.6	58.4	2,652.2
1986	84.1	158.3	100.9	65.4	40.8	69.4	84.2	100.1	380.4	665.4	57.0	2,770.6
1987	85.4	163.7	109.0	70.8	41.9	69.0	87.4	106.5	412.8	692.3	53.5	2,901.4
1988	88.0	165.8	111.7	72.7	43.8	68.0	89.8	116.2	436.6	710.6	46.6	3,005.2
1989	86.9	163.2	109.6	73.6	44.7	64.4	87.3	119.4	441.0	680.9	41.9	3,072.1
1990	84.6	160.1	106.6	72.3	45.1	59.4	84.8	117.9	432.8	642.8	38.0	3,051.0
1991	78.7	148.0	97.9	64.6	44.0	54.1	80.2	109.7	417.1	553.7	30.7	2,783.3
1992	78.7	144.6	100.3	65.7	43.5	56.4	80.8	110.1	429.3	528.2	27.2	2,704.1
1993	81.1	145.2	103.3	68.8	45.9	64.2	83.8	113.1	450.6	560.8	27.2	2,835.6
1994	82.1	150.3	110.2	74.7	49.3	73.5	87.7	119.5	491.9	604.7	27.9	3,058.4
1995	82.5	148.0	111.4	76.0	51.2	81.4	87.8	123.5	512.6	608.8	26.6	3,201.1
1996	80.7	143.5	113.9	78.4	52.4	89.1	88.6	126.0	535.2	642.0	26.2	3,383.6
1997	82.2	144.6	117.4	81.4	54.5	93.4	89.1	130.0	562.6	672.5	26.6	3,582.3
1998	80.0	144.1	121.4	87.6	55.8	99.7	87.6	134.3	576.7	706.1	27.5	3,803.6
1999	79.0	141.7	124.8	95.6	56.8	102.9	85.4	142.2	612.3	767.3	29.9	4,084.2
2000	79.0	142.2	126.5	103.1	58.4	90.3	83.5	145.4	643.4	798.4	32.0	4,251.2
2001	73.5	134.1	123.2	103.6	56.2	76.9	79.5	137.8	680.5	753.4	33.0	4,300.5
2002	69.1	131.7	122.3	107.2	55.1	70.7	75.2	138.6	709.2	773.9	32.8	4,194.2
2003	69.4	117.1	150.3	153.5	59.2	44.2	96.9	114.1	537.6	837.9	28.9	4,255.7
2004	67.8	117.5	156.0	161.2	60.8	43.9	96.8	117.3	548.4	894.1	28.6	4,429.7
2005	64.2	119.3	157.6	169.7	57.0	45.7	98.2	122.9	554.9	948.7	31.2	4,629.1

[a]U.S. Department of Commerce, Bureau of Economic Analysis (70); U.S. Department of Labor, Bureau of Labor Statistics (74).

[q]Changes in topics cause data changes after 2003 when SIC changed to NAICS

[z] Change from SIC to NAICS causes change in data in 2003 and after

Table 5a—Production, imports, exports, and consumption of timber products, by major product, 1965–2005 (million cubic feet, roundwood equivalent)[a]

Year	All products: Production	All products: Consumption	All products: Imports	All products: Exports	Total (Industrial roundwood use): Production	Total: Consumption	Total: Imports	Total: Exports	Lumber: Production	Lumber: Imports	Lumber: Exports	Lumber: Consumption	Plywood and veneer: Production	Plywood and veneer: Imports	Plywood and veneer: Exports	Plywood and veneer: Consumption	Pulpwood-based products: Production	Pulpwood-based products: Imports[b]	Pulpwood-based products: Exports[b]	Pulpwood-based products: Consumption	Other industrial products, production and consumption[c]	Logs[e]: Imports	Logs[e]: Exports	Pulpwood chip[d]: Imports	Pulpwood chip[d]: Exports	Fuelwood production and consumption[d]
1965	12,276	13,325	1,610	554	11,230	12,287	1,610	554	6,233	829	148	6,914	1,070	69	3	1,137	3,176	701	213	3,665	560	11	191	z	7	1,038
1966	12,578	13,598	1,679	641	11,520	12,558	1,679	641	6,222	826	182	6,867	1,118	82	4	1,196	3,392	755	232	3,915	565	15	223	z	17	1,040
1967	12,445	13,245	1,619	772	11,332	12,179	1,619	772	6,037	816	197	6,655	1,100	81	7	1,175	3,365	709	253	3,822	515	12	315	z	47	1,066
1968	13,013	13,851	1,816	877	11,814	12,753	1,816	877	6,112	975	181	6,906	1,238	124	6	1,355	3,539	705	280	3,964	515	13	411	z	101	1,098
1969	13,208	14,106	1,945	901	11,963	13,006	1,945	901	5,965	1,001	182	6,784	1,153	138	16	1,276	3,861	792	320	4,334	600	13	383	z	146	1,100
1970	14,702	15,487	2,019	1,084	13,287	14,222	2,019	1,084	6,511	1,089	221	7,379	1,197	133	12	1,318	4,488	773	413	4,849	652	23	438	z	150	1,265
1971	13,656	14,744	2,105	894	12,300	13,511	2,105	894	6,182	1,201	184	7,199	1,378	166	8	1,535	3,773	725	336	4,162	602	13	366	z	123	1,233
1972	13,994	15,162	2,394	1,070	12,567	13,892	2,394	1,070	6,339	1,492	232	7,598	1,512	206	18	1,700	3,698	690	317	4,071	517	6	502	z	157	1,270
1973	14,213	15,209	2,416	1,204	12,795	14,007	2,416	1,204	6,490	1,516	327	7,679	1,496	165	34	1,628	3,775	729	305	4,200	495	5	538	z	216	1,202
1974	13,909	14,662	2,169	1,175	12,352	13,346	2,169	1,175	6,114	1,228	314	7,028	1,287	107	45	1,349	4,100	822	393	4,529	428	12	423	z	240	1,316
1975	12,774	13,233	1,747	1,090	11,317	11,974	1,747	1,090	5,884	1,036	285	6,635	1,277	125	64	1,338	3,345	572	314	3,602	385	14	427	z	198	1,259
1976	13,580	14,263	2,121	1,193	12,102	13,031	2,121	1,193	6,026	1,298	295	7,029	1,466	154	59	1,562	3,715	655	319	4,052	375	13	520	z	245	1,232
1977	14,218	15,382	2,513	1,089	12,529	13,954	2,513	1,089	6,461	1,692	268	7,885	1,551	148	26	1,674	3,641	648	304	3,985	385	25	491	z	261	1,428
1978	15,012	16,448	2,843	1,183	12,930	14,591	2,843	1,183	6,586	1,925	304	8,207	1,587	167	25	1,729	3,817	735	309	4,244	395	15	545	z	225	1,857
1979	15,730	16,828	2,758	1,380	13,221	14,599	2,758	1,380	6,516	1,808	366	7,958	1,541	137	32	1,646	4,136	792	359	4,569	405	21	623	z	280	2,230
1980	14,998	15,641	2,390	1,469	12,074	12,996	2,390	1,469	5,623	1,524	407	6,739	1,265	81	30	1,316	4,250	765	510	4,505	415	20	522	z	278	2,645
1981	14,495	15,314	2,345	1,306	11,458	12,497	2,345	1,306	5,158	1,497	397	6,258	1,275	99	53	1,321	4,195	734	451	4,477	425	16	405	z	220	2,817
1982	15,037	15,868	2,317	1,309	11,320	12,328	2,317	1,309	5,133	1,478	332	6,279	1,220	122	35	1,307	4,019	698	428	4,288	435	19	513	z	178	3,540
1983	16,433	17,717	2,872	1,432	12,879	14,319	2,872	1,432	6,121	1,902	384	7,638	1,483	179	44	1,618	4,270	766	444	4,592	445	26	560	z	156	3,397
1984	17,138	18,789	3,144	1,349	13,368	15,164	3,144	1,349	6,491	2,080	350	8,220	1,493	161	28	1,627	4,370	880	412	4,838	455	24	559	z	145	3,626
1985	16,999	18,882	3,404	1,376	13,400	15,428	3,404	1,376	6,404	2,275	317	8,362	1,485	194	28	1,654	4,432	918	419	4,931	465	16	615	z	144	3,454
1986	18,328	20,017	3,379	1,538	14,644	16,484	3,379	1,538	7,105	2,196	394	8,907	1,598	199	45	1,751	4,881	972	514	5,338	475	13	585	z	151	3,533
1987	18,472	20,087	3,528	1,755	15,385	17,158	3,528	1,755	7,611	2,263	510	9,364	1,639	240	57	1,823	4,982	1,012	530	5,463	495	13	657	z	158	2,929
1988	18,736	19,691	3,279	2,106	15,618	16,791	3,279	2,106	7,667	2,045	704	9,009	1,598	201	72	1,728	5,075	1,021	563	5,533	510	11	767	z	218	2,901
1989	18,572	19,566	3,376	2,382	15,722	16,716	3,376	2,382	7,541	2,225	655	9,112	1,454	114	97	1,471	5,149	1,022	607	5,565	555	6	753	z	271	2,850
1990	18,477	19,215	3,044	2,306	15,577	16,315	3,044	2,306	7,317	1,905	589	8,633	1,423	97	109	1,410	5,313	1,038	645	5,705	562	4	674	z	288	2,900
1991	18,823	19,269	2,864	2,419	15,187	15,633	2,864	2,419	7,039	1,810	646	8,203	1,267	83	95	1,255	5,397	969	745	5,621	551	2	602	z	332	3,636
1992	18,065	18,777	3,056	2,343	15,215	15,927	3,056	2,343	6,982	1,955	561	8,376	1,294	100	106	1,288	5,516	992	800	5,707	546	7	524	2	351	2,850
1993	17,358	18,638	3,423	2,142	14,914	16,194	3,423	2,142	6,894	2,238	533	8,599	1,293	94	86	1,328	5,423	1,065	723	5,765	517	15	460	5	326	2,444
1994	17,365	18,862	3,636	2,140	15,164	16,661	3,636	2,140	7,085	2,409	514	8,979	1,320	94	86	1,328	5,576	1,102	757	5,921	401	18	429	14	354	2,201
1995	17,604	19,249	3,929	2,284	15,454	17,099	3,929	2,284	6,857	2,545	462	8,939	1,303	107	89	1,321	6,079	1,245	904	6,420	387	13	451	19	377	2,150
1996	17,268	18,934	3,935	2,269	15,344	17,010	3,935	2,269	6,975	2,664	454	9,185	1,281	97	87	1,291	5,908	1,144	890	6,161	342	18	422	12	416	1,924
1997	17,362	19,128	4,063	2,297	15,662	17,428	4,063	2,297	7,210	2,675	457	9,428	1,213	114	103	1,224	6,101	1,250	929	6,422	330	20	384	4	424	1,700
1998[f]	17,319	19,645	4,284	1,957	15,687	18,013	4,284	1,957	7,222	2,791	354	9,658	1,201	131	55	1,277	6,230	1,353	818	6,738	305	30	316	7	414	1,632
1999	17,308	19,800	4,427	1,935	15,683	18,175	4,427	1,935	7,533	2,884	410	10,007	1,208	151	55	1,304	5,910	1,343	735	6,518	298	47	326	2	409	1,625
2000	17,253	19,836	4,622	2,039	15,631	18,214	4,622	2,039	7,384	2,943	435	9,892	1,187	154	51	1,290	5,983	1,451	776	6,658	300	72	422	2	355	1,622
2001	16,528	19,421	4,700	1,807	14,907	17,800	4,700	1,807	7,052	3,007	359	9,699	1,088	176	39	1,225	5,780	1,443	742	6,481	320	73	403	1	265	1,621
2002[f]	16,398	19,536	4,877	1,738	14,878	18,016	4,877	1,738	7,217	3,154	359	10,012	1,067	223	34	1,256	5,699	1,412	768	6,343	317	86	388	1	188	1,520
2003	16,129	19,658	5,064	1,535	14,614	18,143	5,064	1,535	7,177	3,193	347	10,023	1,052	240	35	1,257	5,557	1,547	643	6,462	318	80	356	4	155	1,515
2004	16,836	20,978	5,744	1,602	15,296	19,438	5,744	1,602	7,671	3,704	348	11,028	1,082	354	43	1,393	5,692	1,608	678	6,622	318	73	366	5	168	1,540
2005	17,015	21,172	5,802	1,646	15,465	19,622	5,802	1,646	7,889	3,737	389	11,237	1,068	373	37	1,403	5,679	1,570	708	6,541	318	114	345	9	166	1,550

[a] U.S. Department of Agriculture, Forest Service (21); U.S. Geological Survey (79); Data may not add to totals because of rounding. Data have been revised.
[b] Includes pulpwood and the pulpwood equivalent of wood pulp and paper and board.
[c] Includes cooperage logs, poles and piling, fence posts, hewn ties, round mine timbers, box bolts, excelsior bolts, chemical wood, shingle bolts, and miscellaneous items.
[d] Prior to 1989, pulpwood chips are not included in total production.
[e] Prior to 2000, Pulpwood logs are not included in logs.
z Not available.
[p] Preliminary
[r] Revised

Table 5b—Production, imports, exports, and consumption of timber products, by major product, 1965–2005 (thousand cubic meters, roundwood equivalent)[a]

Year	All products Production	All products Consumption	Total Production	Total Imports	Total Exports	Total Consumption	Lumber Production	Lumber Imports	Lumber Exports	Lumber Consumption	Plywood and veneer Production	Plywood and veneer Imports	Plywood and veneer Exports	Plywood and veneer Consumption	Pulpwood-based products Production	Pulpwood-based products Imports[b]	Pulpwood-based products Exports[b]	Pulpwood-based products Consumption	Other industrial products, production and consumption[c]	Logs[d] Imports	Logs[d] Exports	Pulpwood chip[e] Imports	Pulpwood chip[e] Exports	Fuelwood production and consumption[d]
1965	347,613	377,313	318,010	45,577	15,688	347,920	176,489	23,473	4,185	195,777	30,305	1,941	74	32,194	89,947	19,655	6,018	103,784	15,658	308	5,413	z	209	29,393
1966	356,161	385,067	326,221	47,542	18,150	355,617	176,197	23,402	5,149	194,450	31,672	2,318	117	33,878	96,051	21,389	6,583	110,857	15,999	433	6,301	z	491	29,450
1967	352,413	375,067	320,898	45,836	21,874	344,882	170,941	23,101	5,592	188,450	31,153	2,300	196	33,278	95,287	20,087	7,153	108,221	14,583	349	8,933	z	1,329	30,186
1968	368,480	392,210	334,537	51,437	24,844	361,118	173,064	27,605	5,118	195,551	35,044	3,498	161	38,368	100,213	19,977	7,933	112,257	14,583	358	11,632	z	2,850	31,092
1969	374,021	399,445	338,743	55,065	25,522	368,297	168,918	28,336	5,150	192,105	32,646	3,916	453	36,119	109,334	22,441	9,063	122,712	16,990	371	10,855	z	4,129	31,149
1970	416,319	438,537	376,240	57,160	30,700	402,716	184,380	30,829	6,250	208,959	33,884	3,778	349	37,328	127,099	21,899	11,686	137,312	18,463	654	12,415	z	4,257	35,821
1971	388,711	417,517	348,312	59,594	25,320	382,603	175,057	34,001	5,208	203,850	39,010	4,692	238	43,479	106,831	20,520	9,506	117,845	17,047	380	10,367	z	3,484	34,915
1972	396,276	429,332	355,869	67,780	30,290	393,399	179,490	42,236	6,565	215,162	42,805	5,831	519	48,125	104,705	19,536	8,977	115,264	14,640	178	14,229	z	4,444	35,963
1973	402,482	430,656	362,316	68,406	34,104	396,619	183,771	42,938	9,273	217,436	42,371	4,678	949	46,101	106,910	20,639	8,635	118,913	14,017	152	15,247	z	6,128	34,037
1974	393,850	415,179	349,779	61,425	33,282	377,914	173,140	34,767	8,894	199,013	36,442	3,039	1,281	38,193	116,108	23,272	11,138	128,242	12,120	347	11,969	z	6,806	37,265
1975	361,710	374,728	320,465	49,480	30,863	339,077	166,608	29,345	8,069	187,884	36,163	3,551	1,812	37,897	94,712	16,197	8,903	102,006	10,902	387	12,080	z	5,594	35,651
1976	384,533	403,872	342,698	60,065	33,791	368,986	170,639	36,768	8,364	199,042	41,515	4,369	1,681	44,217	105,204	18,559	9,026	114,738	10,619	370	14,721	z	6,949	34,887
1977	402,613	435,574	354,796	71,162	30,843	395,134	182,953	47,914	7,581	223,287	43,933	4,194	748	47,398	103,103	18,354	8,610	112,847	10,902	700	13,904	z	7,377	40,440
1978	425,104	465,751	366,145	80,507	33,495	413,161	186,505	54,521	8,616	232,410	44,926	4,729	694	48,965	108,088	20,818	8,743	120,163	11,185	439	15,442	z	6,369	52,590
1979	445,438	476,523	374,381	78,090	39,093	413,386	184,521	51,187	10,366	225,343	43,630	3,873	903	46,607	117,110	22,428	10,172	129,365	11,468	602	17,652	z	7,920	63,137
1980	424,693	442,903	341,899	67,679	41,590	367,993	159,213	43,162	11,536	190,839	35,815	2,285	847	37,257	120,349	21,654	14,436	127,567	11,752	578	14,770	z	7,884	74,910
1981	410,460	433,630	324,444	66,410	37,003	353,858	146,058	42,386	11,242	177,202	36,094	2,793	1,492	37,403	118,778	20,772	12,790	126,760	12,035	458	11,479	z	6,243	79,773
1982	425,817	449,324	320,538	65,618	37,060	349,080	145,341	41,863	9,405	177,799	34,554	3,464	989	37,013	113,793	19,761	12,134	121,419	12,318	530	14,531	z	5,035	100,244
1983	465,336	501,675	364,708	81,339	40,561	405,474	173,314	53,846	10,888	216,272	42,007	5,067	1,233	45,828	120,923	21,679	12,577	130,025	12,601	747	15,663	z	4,426	96,202
1984	485,301	532,052	378,538	89,034	38,209	429,383	183,798	58,887	9,905	232,779	42,286	4,559	797	46,070	123,739	24,923	11,677	136,985	12,884	665	15,830	z	4,094	102,669
1985	481,347	534,688	379,447	96,377	38,955	436,669	181,337	64,425	8,968	236,793	42,040	5,500	701	46,839	125,496	26,003	11,878	139,621	13,167	450	17,408	z	4,081	97,818
1986	518,982	566,820	414,662	95,678	43,565	466,776	201,204	62,180	11,156	252,227	45,242	5,626	1,282	49,585	138,208	27,517	14,568	151,157	13,451	356	16,558	z	4,275	100,044
1987	523,073	568,796	430,647	99,901	49,695	485,853	215,532	64,072	14,451	265,153	46,423	6,802	1,605	51,620	141,062	28,653	15,026	154,689	14,017	374	18,613	z	4,483	82,944
1988	530,553	557,585	442,251	92,840	59,640	475,450	217,114	57,908	19,922	255,100	45,262	5,703	2,042	48,923	143,700	28,921	15,944	156,676	14,442	309	21,733	z	6,167	82,135
1989	525,916	554,016	445,213	95,586	67,486	473,313	213,540	63,005	18,534	258,011	41,164	3,242	2,755	41,650	145,805	28,952	17,208	157,549	15,716	178	21,316	z	7,672	80,703
1990	523,213	544,485	441,094	86,198	65,326	461,996	207,204	53,945	16,689	244,460	40,292	2,733	3,093	39,933	150,436	29,391	18,297	161,530	15,914	105	19,083	z	8,165	82,119
1991	533,020	545,608	430,059	81,104	68,516	442,648	199,322	51,250	18,286	232,286	35,885	2,344	2,681	35,548	152,827	27,437	21,126	159,138	15,603	62	17,035	64	9,387	102,961
1992	511,534	531,690	430,830	86,541	66,384	450,987	197,700	55,366	15,888	237,178	36,485	2,832	3,001	36,147	156,204	28,081	22,695	161,590	15,472	197	14,852	150	9,949	80,703
1993	491,517	527,752	422,311	96,924	60,689	458,545	195,211	63,361	15,085	243,487	36,628	2,827	2,837	36,618	153,560	30,160	20,499	163,221	14,643	425	13,028	390	9,240	69,207
1994	491,734	534,083	429,408	102,965	60,616	471,757	200,618	68,203	14,552	253,288	37,378	2,657	2,436	37,599	157,887	31,215	21,457	167,645	11,355	500	12,155	534	10,015	62,326
1995	498,482	545,043	437,601	111,259	64,698	484,162	194,168	72,065	13,094	253,139	36,883	3,035	2,515	37,403	172,136	35,261	25,634	181,763	10,959	364	12,773	341	10,682	60,882
1996	488,966	536,153	434,484	111,439	64,252	481,671	197,505	75,443	12,845	260,103	36,275	2,752	2,458	36,570	167,291	32,383	25,222	174,452	9,684	521	11,938	101	11,789	54,482
1997	491,641	541,625	443,502	115,042	65,058	493,486	204,169	75,744	12,950	266,964	34,357	3,234	2,930	34,660	172,776	35,385	26,322	181,839	9,345	578	10,662	186	11,994	48,139
1998	490,420	556,578	444,207	122,058	55,901	510,365	204,493	79,022	10,036	273,478	33,999	3,700	1,553	36,147	176,409	38,313	23,642	191,078	8,637	839	8,958	45	11,711	46,213
1999	490,118	560,904	444,103	125,345	55,199	514,899	213,317	81,653	11,602	283,368	34,199	4,277	1,563	36,914	167,345	38,038	21,230	184,791	8,438	1,333	9,232	65	11,572	46,015
2000	488,536	561,956	442,605	130,880	58,161	516,025	209,082	83,340	12,320	280,101	33,604	4,357	1,438	36,523	169,426	41,081	21,417	188,792	8,495	2,036	11,950	29	10,036	45,930
2001	467,989	550,183	422,116	133,085	51,578	504,281	199,680	85,153	10,176	274,657	30,819	4,973	1,093	34,698	163,680	40,851	21,433	183,786	9,049	2,078	11,411	51	7,466	45,902
2002	464,329	553,199	421,287	138,089	49,219	510,158	204,352	89,323	10,156	283,519	30,222	6,310	972	35,560	161,391	39,975	21,758	179,607	8,989	2,431	11,000	122	5,351	43,042
2003	456,733	556,660	413,833	143,405	43,478	513,759	203,225	90,417	9,828	283,815	29,785	6,794	991	35,589	157,361	43,819	18,204	182,977	9,005	2,253	11,075	65	4,381	42,900
2004[r]	476,742	594,025	433,134	162,654	45,372	550,416	217,219	104,893	9,847	312,266	30,630	10,029	1,212	39,447	161,168	45,534	19,201	187,501	9,005	2,054	10,357	143	4,755	43,608
2005[p]	481,825	599,523	437,933	164,302	46,604	555,632	223,403	105,816	11,015	318,204	30,233	10,560	1,058	39,735	160,815	44,460	20,053	185,222	9,005	3,217	9,771	250	4,706	43,891

[a] U.S. Department of Agriculture, Forest Service (21); U.S. Geological Survey (79); Data may not add to totals because of rounding; Data have been revised.

[b] Includes pulpwood and the pulpwood equivalent of wood pulp and paper and board.

[c] Includes cooperage logs, poles and piling, fenceposts, hewn ties, round mine timbers, box bolts, excelsior bolts, chemical wood, shingle bolts, and miscellaneous items.

[d] Prior to 1989, pulpwood chips are not included in total production.

[e] Prior to 2000, pulpwood logs are not included in logs.

z Not available.

[r] Revised.

[p] Preliminary.

Table 6a—Production, imports, exports, and consumption of softwood timber products, by major product, 1965–2005 (million cubic feet, roundwood equivalent)[a]

	All products		Industrial roundwood use — Total				Lumber				Plywood and veneer				Pulpwood-based products				Other industrial products, production and consumption[c]	Logs[e]		Pulpwood chip[d] production and		Fuelwood[d] production and consumption
Year	Production	Consumption	Production	Imports	Exports	Consumption	Production	Imports	Exports	Consumption	Production	Imports	Exports	Consumption	Production	Imports[b]	Exports[b]	Consumption[b]		Imports	Exports	Imports	Exports	
1965	8,506	9,337	8,319	1,297	465	9,150	4,583	771	130	5,223	945	14	2	957	2,313	510	155	2,668	300	2	178	z	z	187
1966	8,663	9,456	8,476	1,322	529	9,269	4,514	753	147	5,120	990	17	4	1,003	2,451	546	168	2,829	310	7	210	z	z	187
1967	8,624	9,267	8,432	1,296	653	9,075	4,408	756	163	5,002	981	16	6	991	2,458	518	184	2,791	285	5	300	z	z	192
1968	9,170	9,864	8,972	1,464	770	9,666	4,583	915	163	5,334	1,111	25	5	1,131	2,602	518	206	2,914	281	5	396	z	z	198
1969	9,181	9,933	8,983	1,535	783	9,735	4,437	923	164	5,195	1,035	29	15	1,049	2,812	577	233	3,155	330	7	371	z	z	198
1970	10,303	11,005	10,075	1,652	950	10,777	4,838	1,021	201	5,658	1,082	27	9	1,099	3,376	587	313	3,650	353	17	427	z	z	228
1971	9,621	10,573	9,405	1,710	759	10,357	4,702	1,138	149	5,691	1,253	33	7	1,278	2,760	530	245	3,045	334	9	357	z	z	216
1972	9,855	10,875	9,632	1,945	926	10,652	4,849	1,413	197	6,066	1,379	42	17	1,404	2,623	489	225	2,887	294	2	487	z	z	222
1973	9,942	10,845	9,731	1,957	1,053	10,635	4,947	1,421	293	6,075	1,374	34	31	1,377	2,603	501	210	2,894	287	1	520	z	z	211
1974	9,532	10,281	9,301	1,744	994	10,051	4,630	1,149	279	5,500	1,190	22	41	1,171	2,823	565	270	3,118	255	7	404	z	z	230
1975	9,064	9,552	8,844	1,438	950	9,331	4,602	992	250	5,344	1,198	25	59	1,164	2,393	409	225	2,577	235	11	416	z	z	220
1976	9,596	10,306	9,381	1,754	1,045	10,090	4,624	1,248	261	5,612	1,382	32	54	1,360	2,630	463	225	2,868	240	11	505	z	z	216
1977	9,899	11,094	9,709	2,417	946	10,904	4,966	1,632	233	6,365	1,460	31	22	1,469	2,566	456	214	2,808	240	22	477	z	z	190
1978	10,185	11,606	9,900	2,417	997	11,321	5,009	1,862	235	6,637	1,495	37	22	1,509	2,629	505	212	2,922	240	13	528	z	z	285
1979	10,506	11,672	10,096	2,348	1,182	11,262	4,877	1,742	296	6,322	1,452	29	30	1,451	2,920	558	253	3,225	245	19	603	z	z	410
1980	9,556	10,403	8,981	2,057	1,210	9,828	4,011	1,473	320	5,164	1,187	18	27	1,178	3,041	547	365	3,223	245	18	497	z	z	575
1981	9,191	10,131	8,601	1,996	1,056	9,541	3,839	1,446	310	4,976	1,200	21	49	1,172	2,937	514	317	3,134	245	14	380	z	z	590
1982	9,000	9,861	8,380	1,958	1,097	9,241	3,726	1,442	268	4,899	1,125	25	32	1,118	2,782	476	298	2,960	248	16	498	z	z	620
1983	10,110	11,343	9,515	2,405	1,172	10,748	4,577	1,856	298	6,135	1,379	39	41	1,377	2,767	488	291	2,964	249	23	542	z	z	595
1984	10,351	11,890	9,716	2,633	1,094	11,255	4,715	2,022	258	6,480	1,390	36	26	1,401	2,821	555	271	3,105	250	19	539	z	z	635
1985	10,334	12,032	9,729	2,830	1,132	11,427	4,713	2,212	246	6,678	1,392	46	22	1,415	2,772	561	267	3,066	256	11	597	z	z	605
1986	11,209	12,763	10,591	2,782	1,228	12,144	5,259	2,135	303	7,092	1,501	47	42	1,507	3,011	591	321	3,281	257	8	562	z	z	619
1987	11,748	13,219	11,235	2,879	1,408	12,706	5,629	2,174	381	7,422	1,537	62	53	1,546	3,158	632	341	3,449	277	11	633	z	z	513
1988	11,796	12,825	11,288	2,683	1,654	12,317	5,603	1,992	495	7,100	1,497	51	66	1,482	3,182	631	358	3,456	270	9	735	z	z	508
1989	11,711	12,686	11,169	2,828	1,853	12,144	5,423	2,164	504	7,083	1,357	30	90	1,296	3,223	628	386	3,465	294	3	719	3	154	542
1990	11,520	12,287	10,968	2,537	1,769	11,736	5,154	1,865	439	6,580	1,328	26	101	1,253	3,376	644	417	3,603	298	2	639	0	174	551
1991	11,386	12,030	10,694	2,405	1,761	11,338	5,078	1,773	482	6,370	1,178	23	83	1,118	3,433	608	483	3,558	292	1	556	0	157	691
1992	11,039	11,982	10,498	2,545	1,602	11,440	4,979	1,910	389	6,500	1,209	29	91	1,147	3,436	599	509	3,526	260	6	489	1	125	542
1993	10,457	11,868	9,992	2,840	1,430	11,403	4,752	2,183	350	6,585	1,205	29	88	1,146	3,261	611	443	3,430	225	14	422	4	127	465
1994	10,627	12,265	10,209	3,018	1,380	11,847	4,916	2,344	321	6,940	1,219	27	75	1,172	3,336	622	460	3,498	213	15	387	14	138	418
1995	10,518	12,307	10,166	3,224	1,435	11,955	4,645	2,483	278	6,850	1,195	31	77	1,149	3,580	686	539	3,727	205	9	408	7	132	352
1996	10,473	12,359	10,158	3,262	1,376	12,044	4,791	2,599	264	7,126	1,176	30	75	1,130	3,507	613	534	3,587	181	13	381	1	122	315
1997	10,619	12,563	10,340	3,307	1,362	12,285	4,994	2,596	244	7,346	1,105	35	92	1,048	3,589	661	548	3,701	175	13	332	1	146	278
1998	10,738	13,086	10,428	3,468	1,120	12,775	4,995	2,695	170	7,520	1,089	43	46	1,085	3,771	702	493	3,980	162	24	263	5	149	310
1999	10,738	13,186	10,429	3,541	1,093	12,877	5,272	2,766	204	7,834	1,092	53	46	1,099	3,494	680	430	3,744	158	41	266	1	146	309
2000	10,738	13,241	10,430	3,673	1,170	12,933	5,180	2,805	209	7,776	1,063	58	43	1,078	3,568	746	459	3,856	159	62	330	1	129	308
2001	10,359	13,080	10,051	3,763	1,042	12,772	4,981	2,895	147	7,729	939	73	31	982	3,430	731	437	3,724	272	64	307	1	121	308
2002[f]	10,404	13,288	10,115	3,895	1,011	12,999	5,161	3,026	146	8,040	947	95	27	1,016	3,347	699	447	3,599	269	75	279	0	112	289
2003	10,622	13,731	10,334	4,042	934	13,443	5,273	3,055	145	8,183	933	117	26	1,024	3,587	801	390	3,998	169	69	262	1	111	288
2004	11,105	14,750	10,812	4,590	944	14,457	5,628	3,531	125	9,033	957	176	31	1,102	3,683	819	412	4,090	169	62	256	2	120	293
2005	11,297	14,947	11,002	4,624	974	14,652	5,861	3,550	136	9,275	943	197	26	1,113	3,644	778	426	3,996	169	98	257	1	128	295

[a] U.S. Department of Agriculture, Forest Service (21); U.S. Geological Survey (79). Data may not add to totals because of rounding; Data have been revised.
[b] Includes pulpwood and the pulpwood equivalent of wood pulp and paper and board.
[c] Includes cooperage logs, poles and piling, fence posts, hewn ties, round mine timbers, box bolts, excelsior bolts, chemical wood, shingle bolts, and miscellaneous items.
[d] Prior to 1989, pulpwood chips are not included in total production.
[e] Prior to 2000, Pulpwood Logs are not included in Logs.
z Not Available
[f] Revised

Table 6b—Production, imports, exports, and consumption of softwood timber products, by major product, 1965–2005 (thousand cubic meters, roundwood equivalent)[a]

	All products		Total				Lumber				Plywood and veneer				Pulpwood-based products				Other industrial products, production and consumption[c]	Logs[e]		Pulpwood chip[d]		Fuelwood production and consumption
Year	Production	Consumption	Production	Imports	Exports	Consumption	Production	Imports	Exports	Consumption	Production	Imports	Exports	Consumption	Production	Imports[b]	Exports[b]	Consumption		Imports	Exports	Imports	Exports	
1965	240,852	264,401	235,561	36,729	13,180	259,110	129,769	21,824	3,692	147,901	26,765	396	65	27,097	65,488	14,448	4,380	75,557	8,495	61	5,044	z	z	5,291
1966	245,310	267,766	240,009	37,435	14,980	262,465	127,815	21,326	4,162	144,978	28,048	469	103	28,413	69,409	15,448	4,755	80,103	8,778	193	5,959	z	z	5,301
1967	244,210	262,402	238,777	36,694	18,502	256,969	124,829	21,410	4,605	141,634	27,784	465	181	28,068	69,601	14,665	5,223	79,043	8,070	154	8,493	z	z	5,433
1968	259,656	279,306	254,059	41,446	21,795	273,710	129,772	25,902	4,624	151,050	31,448	716	139	32,025	73,669	14,677	5,830	82,516	7,968	150	11,202	z	z	5,597
1969	259,988	281,283	254,381	43,462	22,167	275,676	125,632	26,133	4,657	147,109	29,304	808	422	29,691	79,618	16,331	6,597	89,353	9,335	189	10,492	z	z	5,607
1970	291,754	311,619	285,307	46,778	26,914	305,171	136,985	28,922	5,684	160,224	30,627	759	259	31,127	95,599	16,615	8,867	103,347	9,992	482	12,103	z	z	6,448
1971	272,441	299,393	266,327	48,436	21,484	293,278	133,148	32,237	4,222	161,163	35,470	943	212	36,201	78,161	15,003	6,951	86,213	9,448	252	10,100	z	z	6,115
1972	279,058	307,935	272,760	55,090	26,213	301,636	137,318	40,022	5,578	171,762	39,039	1,176	471	39,743	74,285	13,841	6,360	81,765	8,314	51	13,804	z	z	6,298
1973	281,514	307,104	275,553	55,420	29,830	301,143	140,075	40,231	8,286	172,020	38,917	950	873	38,994	73,697	14,200	5,940	81,957	8,133	39	14,731	z	z	5,961
1974	269,909	291,131	263,383	49,371	28,149	284,604	131,105	32,548	7,907	155,746	33,696	614	1,158	33,153	79,940	16,001	7,653	88,288	7,210	207	11,431	z	z	6,527
1975	256,670	270,483	250,426	40,714	26,900	264,240	130,302	28,102	7,082	151,321	33,926	722	1,678	32,970	67,764	11,580	6,360	72,984	6,654	310	11,779	z	z	6,244
1976	271,742	291,825	265,632	49,664	29,582	285,715	130,945	35,345	7,377	158,913	39,137	894	1,533	38,497	74,461	13,120	6,377	81,204	6,796	305	14,294	z	z	6,110
1977	280,305	314,155	274,925	60,630	26,781	308,774	140,612	46,219	6,594	180,237	41,356	869	632	41,593	72,662	12,911	6,057	79,516	6,796	632	13,498	z	z	5,380
1978	288,417	328,642	280,347	68,453	28,229	320,571	141,832	52,739	6,643	187,928	42,320	1,051	636	42,735	74,458	14,305	6,010	82,754	6,796	358	14,940	z	z	8,070
1979	297,507	330,524	285,897	66,493	33,476	318,914	138,091	49,332	8,393	179,030	41,110	819	843	41,086	82,690	15,807	7,172	91,325	6,938	536	17,068	z	z	11,610
1980	270,602	294,585	254,320	58,244	34,261	278,303	113,592	41,716	9,070	146,237	33,606	517	773	33,350	86,102	15,495	10,335	91,262	6,938	517	14,083	z	z	16,282
1981	260,264	286,877	243,557	56,519	29,906	270,170	108,722	40,950	8,775	140,897	33,971	607	1,394	33,183	83,160	14,565	8,970	88,755	6,938	397	10,767	z	z	16,707
1982	254,839	279,226	237,282	55,443	31,056	261,670	105,496	40,822	7,585	138,733	31,864	707	910	31,661	78,792	13,466	8,451	83,807	7,021	448	14,109	z	z	17,557
1983	286,296	321,208	269,447	68,107	33,195	304,359	129,618	52,561	8,446	173,733	39,062	1,092	1,150	39,004	78,352	13,810	8,241	83,921	7,057	645	15,358	z	z	16,849
1984	293,099	336,685	275,118	74,555	30,969	318,704	133,526	57,270	7,310	183,485	39,371	1,030	730	39,670	79,874	15,726	7,666	87,934	7,086	529	15,262	z	z	17,981
1985	292,616	340,706	275,485	80,141	32,052	323,574	133,445	62,631	6,965	189,111	39,408	1,290	628	40,070	78,485	15,899	7,555	86,830	7,242	321	16,904	z	z	17,132
1986	317,419	361,415	299,897	78,776	34,780	343,893	148,923	60,469	8,576	200,816	42,513	1,330	1,176	42,667	85,272	16,742	9,103	92,911	7,263	236	15,926	z	z	17,522
1987	332,674	374,328	318,148	81,512	34,859	359,801	159,408	61,550	10,781	210,178	43,534	1,747	1,496	43,785	89,420	17,903	9,645	97,677	7,849	311	17,936	z	z	14,527
1988	334,029	363,166	319,644	81,512	46,845	348,781	158,666	56,404	14,026	201,044	38,426	1,445	2,556	41,975	90,115	17,879	10,139	97,854	8,329	253	20,350	75	4,347	14,385
1989	331,625	359,230	316,282	80,075	52,470	343,887	153,563	61,281	14,276	200,568	37,600	842	2,851	36,712	91,266	17,781	10,940	98,108	8,435	95	18,089	3	4,927	15,343
1990	326,206	347,942	310,594	71,840	50,104	332,330	145,955	52,802	12,421	186,336	33,366	732	2,360	31,650	95,589	18,243	11,816	102,016	8,269	58	15,752	2	4,453	15,612
1991	322,410	340,641	302,835	68,099	49,868	321,067	143,794	50,213	13,639	180,368	34,237	645	2,582	32,477	97,201	17,205	13,663	100,742	7,354	34	13,837	33	3,548	19,574
1992	312,601	339,283	297,258	72,054	45,372	323,940	140,986	54,084	11,004	184,067	34,108	822	2,480	32,441	97,296	16,948	14,402	99,842	6,378	167	11,955	119	3,598	15,343
1993	296,109	336,056	282,952	80,432	40,485	322,899	134,563	61,814	9,920	186,457	34,528	813	2,116	33,186	92,350	17,298	12,532	97,116	6,018	388	10,960	257	3,901	13,157
1994	300,929	347,311	289,080	85,465	39,083	335,462	139,219	66,381	9,081	196,518	33,845	774	2,189	32,547	94,454	17,626	13,024	99,055	5,808	427	11,560	404	3,735	11,849
1995	297,838	348,497	287,872	91,296	40,637	338,531	131,539	70,317	7,878	193,978	33,293	891	2,134	32,002	101,385	19,437	15,275	105,547	5,133	247	10,791	186	3,441	9,966
1996	296,563	349,975	287,644	92,363	38,951	341,057	135,677	73,584	7,469	201,792	31,281	843	2,597	29,679	99,310	17,371	15,115	101,566	4,953	379	9,412	36	4,132	8,919
1997	300,692	355,753	292,811	93,637	38,576	347,872	141,404	73,518	6,910	208,012	30,825	994	1,301	31,116	101,630	18,708	15,525	104,812	4,577	381	7,457	128	4,214	7,880
1998	304,082	370,549	295,296	98,194	31,726	361,763	141,448	76,314	4,806	212,956	30,923	1,206	1,315	30,522	106,775	19,881	13,949	112,707	4,472	666	7,542	37	4,140	8,786
1999	304,059	373,384	295,311	100,263	30,938	364,636	149,298	78,317	5,770	221,845	30,104	1,508	1,219	27,798	98,935	19,250	12,170	106,014	4,502	1,152	9,357	39	3,646	8,748
2000	304,075	374,947	295,343	104,000	33,548	366,215	146,687	79,419	5,907	220,199	29,679	1,637	867	28,653	101,035	21,136	12,987	109,184	7,630	1,768	8,701	23	3,430	8,732
2001	293,328	370,385	284,601	106,556	29,926	361,659	141,054	81,968	4,150	218,872	26,603	2,063	757	28,992	97,128	20,695	12,367	105,456	4,773	1,807	7,904	23	3,185	8,727
2002	297,025	378,826	288,842	110,864	29,064	370,643	146,141	85,679	4,141	227,680	26,816	2,594	729	30,522	94,764	20,457	13,078	102,143	4,773	2,111	7,414	16	3,150	8,183
2003	300,796	388,810	292,640	114,460	26,446	380,654	149,306	86,503	4,102	231,706	26,416	3,305	881	30,992	101,582	22,685	11,051	113,216	4,773	1,951	7,236	43	3,412	8,156
2004	314,457	417,677	306,166	129,964	26,745	409,386	159,358	99,987	3,548	255,797	27,103	4,985	881	31,207	104,284	23,188	11,667	115,806	4,773	1,761	7,236	43	3,412	8,291
2005[P]	319,893	423,249	311,548	130,925	27,568	414,904	165,976	100,512	3,858	262,630	26,702	5,572	748	31,527	103,188	22,019	12,053	113,154	4,773	2,789	7,278	32	3,631	8,344

[a] U.S. Department of Agriculture, Forest Service (21); U.S. Geological Survey (79); Data may not add to totals because of rounding; Data have been revised.

[b] Includes pulpwood and the pulpwood equivalent of wood pulp and paper and board.

[c] Includes cooperage logs, poles and piling, fence posts, hewn ties, round mine timbers, box bolts, excelsior bolts, chemical wood, shingle bolts, and miscellaneous items.

[d] Prior to 1989, pulpwood chips are not included in total production.

[e] Prior to 2000, Pulpwood Logs are not included in Logs.

z Not Available.

P Preliminary

Table 7a—Production, imports, exports, and consumption of hardwood timber products, by major product, 1965–2005 (million cubic feet, roundwood equivalent)[a]

Year	All products Production	All products Consumption	Total Production	Total Imports	Total Exports	Total Consumption	Lumber Production	Lumber Imports	Lumber Exports	Lumber Consumption	Plywood and veneer Production	Plywood and veneer Imports	Plywood and veneer Exports	Plywood and veneer Consumption	Pulpwood-based products Production	Pulpwood-based products Imports[b]	Pulpwood-based products Exports[b]	Pulpwood-based products Consumption	Other industrial products, production and consumption[c]	Logs[e] Imports	Logs[e] Exports	Pulpwood chip[d] Imports	Pulpwood chip[d] Exports	Fuelwood production and consumption
1965	3,763	3,987	2,912	312	89	3,136	1,650	58	17	1,691	125	55	0	180	864	191	58	997	260	9	13	z	z	851
1966	3,897	4,142	3,045	357	112	3,290	1,709	73	35	1,747	128	65	0	193	941	210	65	1,086	255	8	12	z	z	853
1967	3,774	3,979	2,900	323	119	3,105	1,628	60	35	1,653	119	65	1	184	907	191	68	1,030	230	7	16	z	z	874
1968	3,742	3,987	2,842	353	108	3,087	1,529	60	17	1,572	127	98	1	224	937	187	74	1,050	234	7	15	z	z	900
1969	3,881	4,173	2,979	410	118	3,271	1,529	78	17	1,589	118	110	1	227	1,049	216	87	1,178	270	6	13	z	z	902
1970	4,249	4,482	3,211	367	134	3,445	1,674	67	20	1,721	115	107	3	219	1,112	187	100	1,199	299	6	11	z	z	1,037
1971	3,912	4,172	2,895	394	135	3,154	1,480	62	35	1,507	125	132	1	257	1,012	195	90	1,117	268	5	9	z	z	1,017
1972	3,983	4,287	2,935	448	144	3,240	1,489	78	35	1,533	133	164	2	296	1,074	201	92	1,183	223	4	15	z	z	1,048
1973	4,055	4,363	3,064	459	151	3,372	1,543	96	35	1,604	122	132	3	251	1,173	227	95	1,305	208	4	18	z	z	991
1974	4,137	4,381	3,051	426	181	3,295	1,484	78	35	1,528	97	86	4	178	1,277	257	123	1,411	173	5	19	z	z	1,086
1975	3,512	3,682	2,473	310	140	2,643	1,282	44	35	1,291	79	100	5	174	952	163	90	1,025	150	3	11	z	z	1,039
1976	3,738	3,957	2,722	367	148	2,941	1,402	50	35	1,417	84	123	5	202	1,086	192	93	1,184	135	2	15	z	z	1,016
1977	4,059	4,288	2,821	372	143	3,050	1,495	60	35	1,520	91	117	4	205	1,075	192	90	1,177	145	2	14	z	z	1,238
1978	4,602	4,842	3,030	426	186	3,270	1,578	63	70	1,571	92	130	2	220	1,188	230	96	1,321	155	3	18	z	z	1,572
1979	4,944	5,156	3,125	410	198	3,336	1,640	66	70	1,636	89	108	2	195	1,216	234	106	1,344	160	2	21	z	z	1,820
1980	5,163	5,238	3,093	333	259	3,168	1,611	51	87	1,575	78	62	3	138	1,209	218	145	1,282	170	2	24	z	z	2,070
1981	5,084	5,183	2,856	349	250	2,956	1,319	51	87	1,282	75	77	3	149	1,258	219	135	1,342	180	2	25	z	z	2,227
1982	5,860	6,007	2,940	359	212	3,087	1,407	37	64	1,380	95	97	3	189	1,236	222	130	1,328	187	3	15	z	z	2,920
1983	6,166	6,373	3,364	467	260	3,571	1,543	45	86	1,502	104	140	3	241	1,503	278	153	1,628	196	4	18	z	z	2,802
1984	6,643	6,899	3,652	511	256	3,909	1,775	57	92	1,741	103	125	2	226	1,549	325	141	1,732	205	5	20	z	z	2,991
1985	6,521	6,851	3,671	573	244	4,001	1,691	63	71	1,684	93	149	3	239	1,660	357	153	1,864	209	5	18	z	z	2,849
1986	6,967	7,254	4,053	597	310	4,340	1,846	60	91	1,816	96	152	4	244	1,869	381	193	2,057	219	4	22	z	z	2,914
1987	6,566	6,868	4,149	649	347	4,452	1,982	89	130	1,941	102	179	4	277	1,824	380	190	2,014	218	2	24	z	z	2,416
1988	6,722	6,866	4,330	595	451	4,474	2,064	53	208	1,909	101	150	6	245	1,892	390	205	2,078	240	2	33	z	z	2,393
1989	6,861	6,880	4,553	548	529	4,571	2,118	61	150	2,029	97	85	7	174	1,926	395	221	2,100	261	3	34	5	117	2,308
1990	6,957	6,928	4,609	507	537	4,579	2,163	40	151	2,053	95	71	9	157	1,937	394	228	2,103	264	2	35	1	114	2,349
1991	7,438	7,239	4,493	459	658	4,295	1,961	37	164	1,833	89	60	11	138	1,964	361	263	2,063	259	1	45	0	174	2,945
1992	7,025	6,796	4,717	512	741	4,488	2,003	45	172	1,876	85	71	15	142	2,080	393	292	2,182	287	1	36	1	226	2,308
1993	6,901	6,770	4,921	582	713	4,791	2,142	55	182	2,014	89	71	13	148	2,162	454	281	2,335	292	1	38	1	199	1,979
1994	6,738	6,597	4,956	618	760	4,814	2,168	64	193	2,039	101	67	11	156	2,240	480	297	2,423	188	3	42	5	216	1,783
1995	7,086	6,942	5,288	705	849	5,144	2,212	62	184	2,089	107	76	12	172	2,499	559	365	2,692	182	4	43	5	245	1,798
1996	6,795	6,575	5,186	674	893	4,966	2,183	66	190	2,059	105	67	11	161	2,401	530	357	2,574	161	5	41	5	295	1,609
1997	6,743	6,564	5,322	756	935	5,143	2,217	79	213	2,082	109	79	12	176	2,512	589	381	2,721	155	7	51	2	278	1,422
1998[f]	6,580	6,559	5,259	816	837	5,238	2,226	96	185	2,137	112	88	9	191	2,459	624	326	2,757	143	6	53	2	265	1,322
1999	6,571	6,614	5,255	886	842	5,298	2,261	118	206	2,173	116	98	9	205	2,416	663	305	2,774	140	6	60	0	262	1,316
2000	6,514	6,595	5,201	949	869	5,281	2,203	138	226	2,115	124	96	8	212	2,415	704	317	2,802	141	9	92	1	226	1,314
2001	6,169	6,341	4,857	937	765	5,028	2,070	112	213	1,970	149	103	8	244	2,350	712	305	2,757	48	10	96	0	144	1,313
2002[f]	5,993	6,248	4,762	981	727	5,016	2,056	129	202	1,972	120	127	8	240	2,353	712	321	2,744	48	11	109	2	76	1,231
2003	5,507	5,928	4,280	1,022	601	4,701	1,904	138	202	1,840	119	123	9	233	1,970	746	253	2,464	149	11	94	4	43	1,227
2004	5,731	6,228	4,484	1,154	658	4,980	2,043	173	222	1,994	125	178	12	291	2,009	789	266	2,532	149	10	110	4	47	1,247
2005	5,719	6,225	4,463	1,179	672	4,970	2,028	187	253	1,963	125	176	11	290	2,035	792	283	2,545	149	15	88	8	38	1,255

[a] U.S. Department of Agriculture, Forest Service (21); U.S. Geological Survey (79); Data may not add to totals because of rounding; Data have been revised.
[b] Includes pulpwood and the pulpwood equivalent of wood pulp and paper and board.
[c] Includes cooperage logs, poles and piling, fence posts, hewn ties, round mine timbers, box bolts, excelsior bolts, chemical wood, shingle bolts, and miscellaneous items.
[d] Prior to 1989, pulpwood chips are not included in total production.
[e] Prior to 2000, Pulpwood Logs are not included in Logs.
z Not Available.
[f] Revised.

Table 7b—Production, imports, exports, and consumption of hardwood timber products, by major product, 1965–2005 (thousand cubic meters, roundwood equivalent)a

Year	All products Production	All products Consumption	Total Production	Total Imports	Total Exports	Total Consumption	Lumber Production	Lumber Imports	Lumber Exports	Lumber Consumption	Plywood and veneer Production	Plywood and veneer Imports	Plywood and veneer Exports	Plywood and veneer Consumption	Pulpwood-based Production	Pulpwood-based Imports b	Pulpwood-based Exports b	Pulpwood-based Consumption	Other industrial products, production and consumption c	Logs e Imports	Logs e Exports	Pulpwood chip c Imports	Pulpwood chip c Exports	Fuelwood production and consumption
1965	106,552	112,912	82,449	8,848	2,510	88,810	46,720	1,649	493	47,876	3,540	1,544	10	5,097	24,458	5,407	1,638	28,227	7,362	0	369	z	z	24,102
1966	110,360	117,301	86,212	10,106	3,171	93,152	48,383	2,076	987	49,472	3,625	1,849	14	5,465	26,642	5,941	1,828	30,754	7,221	241	342	z	z	24,149
1967	106,874	112,665	82,121	9,142	3,372	87,913	46,113	1,691	987	46,817	3,370	1,835	15	5,210	25,687	5,421	1,930	29,178	6,513	195	439	z	z	24,752
1968	105,974	112,904	80,478	9,991	3,049	87,408	43,292	1,702	493	44,501	3,596	2,782	23	6,343	26,545	5,299	2,103	29,741	6,615	208	430	z	z	25,495
1969	109,904	118,162	84,362	11,603	3,355	92,620	43,286	2,203	493	44,996	3,341	3,108	32	6,428	29,716	6,110	2,467	33,359	7,655	182	363	z	z	25,542
1970	120,307	126,918	90,934	10,382	3,787	97,545	47,395	1,907	566	48,735	3,256	3,019	90	6,201	31,499	5,284	2,819	33,965	8,471	172	312	z	z	29,373
1971	110,785	118,125	81,985	11,159	3,834	89,325	41,909	1,765	987	42,687	3,540	3,749	26	7,277	28,671	5,517	2,554	31,633	7,599	128	267	z	z	28,800
1972	112,774	121,397	83,110	12,690	4,076	91,733	42,172	2,214	987	43,399	3,766	4,655	48	8,382	30,420	5,695	2,616	33,499	6,326	127	425	z	z	29,664
1973	114,839	123,552	86,763	12,986	4,274	95,477	43,696	2,707	987	45,416	3,455	3,727	76	7,108	33,213	6,438	2,695	36,956	5,884	113	516	z	z	28,076
1974	117,135	124,049	86,396	12,054	5,132	93,310	42,035	2,218	987	43,267	2,747	2,425	123	5,040	36,168	7,271	3,485	39,953	4,909	140	538	z	z	30,739
1975	99,447	104,244	70,039	8,766	3,963	74,837	36,307	1,243	987	36,563	2,237	2,829	134	4,927	26,948	4,617	2,543	29,022	4,248	77	300	z	z	29,407
1976	105,842	112,047	77,066	10,401	4,210	83,271	39,694	1,422	987	40,129	2,379	3,475	147	5,720	30,743	5,439	2,648	33,534	3,823	64	427	z	z	28,777
1977	114,931	121,419	79,871	10,532	4,062	86,360	42,341	1,696	987	43,050	2,577	3,325	116	5,805	30,441	5,443	2,553	33,331	4,106	68	406	z	z	35,060
1978	130,318	137,110	85,798	12,054	5,266	92,590	44,672	1,783	1,973	44,482	2,605	3,678	58	6,230	33,630	6,512	2,733	37,409	4,389	81	502	z	z	44,520
1979	140,012	145,999	88,485	11,597	5,617	94,473	46,431	1,866	1,973	46,313	2,520	3,054	60	5,522	34,420	6,621	3,000	38,041	4,531	66	583	z	z	51,527
1980	146,207	148,317	87,579	9,435	7,329	89,690	45,622	1,446	2,467	44,601	2,209	1,768	74	3,908	34,247	6,160	4,101	36,306	4,814	61	688	z	z	58,628
1981	143,952	146,754	80,887	9,891	7,096	83,688	37,336	1,436	2,467	36,306	2,124	2,187	98	4,219	35,618	6,207	3,820	38,005	5,097	61	712	z	z	63,066
1982	165,942	170,097	83,255	10,175	6,004	87,410	39,845	1,041	1,820	39,066	2,690	2,757	79	5,352	35,001	6,294	3,683	37,613	5,297	83	422	z	z	82,687
1983	174,614	180,467	95,261	13,232	7,366	101,114	43,696	1,285	2,442	42,539	2,945	3,975	83	6,824	42,570	7,869	4,335	46,104	5,544	102	505	z	z	79,353
1984	188,108	195,367	103,420	14,479	7,241	110,679	50,273	1,617	2,595	49,294	2,917	3,530	67	6,400	43,865	9,191	4,010	49,051	5,798	136	569	z	z	84,688
1985	184,649	193,982	103,963	16,236	6,903	113,295	47,892	1,794	2,003	47,682	2,631	4,210	73	6,768	47,011	10,103	4,324	52,791	5,925	129	504	z	z	80,687
1986	197,288	205,405	114,765	16,902	8,785	122,883	52,281	1,711	2,580	51,412	2,729	4,296	107	6,918	52,936	10,775	5,465	58,246	6,187	120	633	z	z	82,522
1987	185,916	194,469	117,499	18,389	9,836	126,052	56,124	2,521	3,670	54,975	2,889	5,055	109	7,835	51,642	10,750	5,381	57,012	6,167			z	z	68,417
1988	190,357	194,419	122,607	16,858	12,795	126,669	58,448	1,504	5,895	54,057	2,863	4,257	173	6,948	53,585	11,041	5,805	58,822	6,788			z	z	67,750
1989	194,291	194,786	128,930	15,511	15,016	129,426	59,976	1,724	4,257	57,443	2,738	2,400	199	4,939	54,539	11,171	6,268	59,442	7,386	63	676	133	3,325	65,360
1990	197,007	196,143	130,500	14,358	15,223	129,636	61,249	1,143	4,267	58,125	2,692	2,000	242	4,451	54,847	11,148	6,481	59,514	7,480	83	923	21	3,238	66,507
1991	210,610	204,967	127,224	13,004	18,648	121,581	55,528	1,037	4,647	51,918	2,519	1,699	320	3,898	55,626	10,232	7,463	58,396	7,333	83	966	9	4,934	83,386
1992	198,932	192,407	133,572	14,486	21,012	127,046	56,714	1,282	4,884	53,112	2,416	2,010	419	4,008	58,908	11,133	8,293	61,748	8,118	46	994	31	6,401	65,360
1993	195,408	191,696	139,359	16,492	20,204	135,646	60,648	1,546	5,165	57,030	2,520	2,014	357	4,177	61,210	12,863	7,967	66,106	8,265	27	1,283	31	5,642	65,360
1994	190,805	186,772	140,328	17,500	21,533	136,295	61,399	1,822	5,471	57,749	2,850	1,883	320	4,413	63,433	13,589	8,433	68,590	5,337	30	1,015	134	6,114	56,049
1995	200,644	196,546	149,729	19,963	24,061	145,631	62,629	1,748	5,216	59,161	3,038	2,145	326	4,856	70,751	15,824	10,359	76,217	5,151	37	1,074	129	6,946	50,915
1996	192,403	186,177	146,839	19,077	25,302	140,614	61,828	1,859	5,376	58,311	2,982	1,909	324	4,568	67,982	15,012	10,107	72,887	4,552	73	1,195	155	8,348	45,563
1997	190,949	185,872	150,691	21,405	26,482	145,614	62,765	2,226	6,040	58,951	3,075	2,239	334	4,981	71,146	16,677	10,796	77,027	4,392	117	1,213	66	7,862	40,259
1998 r	186,339	185,832	148,911	23,204	23,711	148,405	63,045	2,707	5,230	60,522	3,174	2,495	252	5,417	69,634	17,670	9,230	78,174	4,059	142	1,147	58	7,497	37,427
1999	186,060	187,286	148,793	25,082	23,856	150,019	64,019	3,336	5,831	61,524	3,276	2,774	247	5,798	68,409	18,788	8,656	78,542	3,966	197	1,449	8	7,432	37,267
2000	184,460	186,725	147,262	26,879	24,614	149,527	62,395	3,920	6,413	59,902	3,500	2,720	219	6,001	68,391	19,945	8,998	79,338	3,993	181	1,502	26	6,389	37,198
2001	174,661	179,537	137,486	26,529	21,653	142,362	58,626	3,185	6,026	55,785	4,216	2,910	226	6,900	66,553	20,156	8,655	78,054	1,346	268	2,593	6	4,035	37,175
2002 r	169,709	176,597	134,850	27,791	20,590	142,052	58,211	3,643	6,015	55,839	3,394	3,610	215	6,789	66,627	20,175	8,546	77,686	1,359	271	2,710	43	2,166	34,859
2003	155,937	167,850	121,192	28,945	17,032	133,105	53,919	3,915	5,726	52,108	3,369	3,489	334	6,597	66,627	21,134	7,153	69,761	4,232	320	3,096	105	1,230	34,744
2004	162,285	176,348	126,968	32,690	18,627	141,031	57,861	4,907	6,298	56,469	3,527	5,043	331	8,240	56,884	22,346	7,534	71,695	4,232	293	3,120	100	1,343	35,318
2005 p	161,932	176,274	126,385	33,378	19,035	140,727	57,427	5,304	7,157	55,574	3,531	4,988	311	8,208	57,627	22,441	8,000	72,068	4,232	428	2,493	217	1,075	35,547

a U.S. Department of Agriculture, Forest Service (21); U.S. Geological Survey (79); Data may not add to totals because of rounding; Data have been revised.

b Includes pulpwood and the pulpwood equivalent of wood pulp and paper and board.

c Includes cooperage logs, poles and piling, fence posts, hewn ties, round mine timbers, box bolts, excelsior bolts, chemical wood, shingle bolts, and miscellaneous items.

d Prior to 1989, pulpwood chips are not included in total production.

e Prior to 2000, Pulpwood Logs are not included in Logs.

z Not Available.

r Revised

p Preliminary

Table 8a—Production, imports, exports, and consumption of timber products (excludes additives and fillers) in tons,[a] by major product, 1965–2005 (million tons,[a] air-dry weight of wood)[b]

The weight of wood in products

Year	All products Production	All products Consumption	Total Production	Total Imports	Total Exports	Total Consumption	Lumber[c] Production	Lumber Imports	Lumber Exports	Lumber Consumption	Plywood and veneer[d] Production	Plywood Imports[j]	Plywood Exports[k]	Plywood Consumption[h]	Panel products[e] Production[i]	Panel Imports[j]	Panel Exports[k]	Panel Consumption	Wood pulp[g] Production	Wood pulp Imports[l]	Wood pulp Exports[k]	Wood pulp Consumption	Other industrial products, production and consumption[f]	Logs[g] Imports	Logs Exports	Pulpwood chip Imports	Pulpwood chip Exports	Fuelwood production and consumption
1965	122.6	131.7	104.4	16.1	7.0	113.5	46.5	5.3	0.9	50.8	6.8	0.7	0.0	7.5	2.9	0.2	0.0	3.2	36.6	9.7	2.9	43.3	8.5	0.2	3.0	z	0.1	18.2
1966	126.8	135.7	108.6	17.2	8.3	117.5	46.6	5.4	1.2	50.7	7.1	0.8	0.0	7.9	3.2	0.2	0.0	3.3	39.4	10.5	3.2	46.7	8.6	0.2	3.4	z	0.3	18.2
1967	126.5	132.4	107.8	16.4	10.5	113.7	45.1	5.2	1.1	49.0	7.0	0.8	0.1	7.8	3.4	0.2	0.0	3.5	39.0	10.0	3.6	45.4	7.8	0.2	4.9	z	0.7	18.7
1968	135.4	143.8	116.2	18.1	13.1	121.2	45.2	6.2	1.1	50.3	7.8	1.2	0.0	9.0	4.0	0.3	0.0	4.3	43.4	10.2	4.0	49.5	7.8	0.2	6.4	z	1.5	19.2
1969	138.3	143.3	119.1	19.4	13.9	124.6	44.2	6.5	1.1	49.5	7.3	1.4	0.1	8.6	4.6	0.3	0.0	4.9	45.6	11.1	4.5	52.2	9.1	0.4	5.9	z	2.2	19.3
1970	141.3	151.0	119.2	18.5	16.5	121.1	42.7	6.2	1.2	47.7	7.6	1.3	0.1	8.8	4.6	0.2	0.1	4.8	44.8	10.4	5.5	49.6	9.9	0.2	6.8	z	2.8	22.1
1971	144.8	151.0	123.2	20.3	14.1	129.4	45.5	7.6	1.2	51.9	8.7	1.7	0.1	10.3	5.9	0.3	0.1	6.1	46.1	10.4	4.8	51.7	9.2	0.2	5.7	z	2.3	21.6
1972	152.9	158.6	130.7	23.1	17.4	136.4	46.5	9.5	1.5	54.5	9.5	2.1	0.1	11.4	7.0	0.5	0.1	7.4	49.1	11.0	5.0	55.1	7.9	0.1	7.8	z	2.9	22.2
1973	156.4	160.4	135.4	23.8	19.7	139.4	47.7	9.7	2.1	55.3	9.4	1.7	0.2	10.8	7.6	0.5	0.1	8.0	50.9	11.9	5.0	57.8	7.5	0.1	8.3	z	4.0	21.0
1974	149.0	151.0	126.0	21.2	19.2	128.0	43.1	7.4	1.9	48.6	8.0	1.1	0.3	8.8	6.8	0.3	0.1	7.0	50.5	12.3	5.9	56.9	6.5	0.2	6.6	z	4.4	23.0
1975	136.4	135.5	114.4	16.6	17.5	113.5	40.1	6.0	1.7	44.4	7.9	1.6	0.5	8.7	6.0	0.1	0.1	6.0	44.2	9.0	5.0	48.3	5.9	0.2	6.6	z	3.7	22.0
1976	150.3	150.9	128.7	20.8	20.2	129.3	44.3	8.2	1.9	50.6	9.0	1.5	0.2	10.1	7.4	0.2	0.1	7.5	49.7	10.6	5.2	55.1	5.7	0.2	8.1	z	4.5	21.6
1977	159.6	163.9	134.6	23.9	19.6	138.9	47.3	10.7	1.7	56.3	9.5	1.7	0.2	10.8	8.4	0.3	0.1	8.6	51.2	11.1	5.2	57.1	5.9	0.4	7.6	z	4.8	25.0
1978	170.3	177.1	137.8	26.8	20.1	144.6	48.4	12.2	2.0	58.5	9.8	1.7	0.2	11.2	8.7	0.4	0.1	9.1	52.3	12.3	5.2	59.5	6.0	0.2	8.5	z	4.2	32.5
1979	179.5	182.5	140.4	26.4	23.4	143.5	48.4	11.5	2.4	57.5	9.6	1.4	0.2	10.7	8.2	0.4	0.1	8.5	53.3	12.8	5.8	60.3	6.2	0.3	9.7	z	5.2	39.0
1980	177.5	176.5	131.2	23.3	24.4	130.2	42.9	9.8	2.8	49.9	8.0	1.0	0.2	8.6	7.0	0.3	0.1	7.2	53.8	12.1	8.0	57.8	6.3	0.3	8.1	z	5.2	46.3
1981	173.1	175.1	123.8	22.9	20.9	125.8	38.3	9.5	2.7	45.1	8.2	0.8	0.2	8.8	6.7	0.3	0.1	6.9	53.8	11.9	7.3	58.3	6.5	0.3	6.3	z	4.1	49.3
1982	184.0	185.6	122.1	22.2	20.7	123.7	38.3	9.3	2.2	45.4	8.0	1.2	0.3	9.0	5.7	0.4	0.0	6.1	52.2	11.0	6.9	56.3	6.6	0.3	8.0	z	3.3	62.0
1983	195.5	200.9	136.1	27.4	22.0	141.5	45.7	12.1	2.6	55.2	9.7	1.8	0.3	11.2	7.4	0.6	0.1	7.9	54.9	12.5	7.4	60.0	6.8	0.4	8.7	z	2.9	59.5
1984	207.8	217.5	144.3	31.0	21.7	154.1	49.5	13.5	2.4	60.6	9.9	1.2	0.2	11.4	7.6	0.8	0.1	8.3	59.0	14.6	7.1	66.5	6.9	0.4	8.7	z	2.7	63.4
1985	201.2	212.4	140.8	32.9	21.7	151.9	48.8	14.9	2.2	61.5	9.9	2.0	0.1	11.8	7.7	0.8	0.1	8.4	55.1	14.9	7.1	62.9	7.1	0.2	9.5	z	2.7	60.5
1986	211.5	221.9	149.7	33.9	23.5	160.1	54.4	14.5	2.7	66.1	10.9	2.1	0.1	12.6	7.9	0.9	0.1	8.7	57.4	15.5	8.4	64.5	7.2	0.2	9.1	0.8	2.8	61.8
1987	209.9	219.6	158.7	36.1	26.4	168.4	58.8	15.2	3.6	70.3	11.3	2.6	0.1	13.4	8.1	0.9	0.1	8.8	59.8	16.7	9.0	67.5	7.5	0.2	10.2	0.6	2.9	51.3
1988	214.4	217.8	163.7	35.0	31.7	167.0	59.5	15.1	5.2	68.0	11.2	2.2	0.2	12.7	8.3	0.8	0.2	8.9	61.0	17.2	9.8	68.5	7.8	0.2	11.9	1.0	4.0	50.8
1989	215.0	216.9	165.2	34.8	33.0	167.0	59.5	15.1	4.7	69.8	10.6	1.3	0.2	11.0	8.4	0.5	0.2	8.7	61.6	17.0	10.5	68.1	8.4	0.1	11.7	0.8	5.0	49.9
1990	214.2	214.1	163.4	32.4	32.4	163.4	58.2	12.9	4.3	66.8	10.4	1.1	0.3	10.5	8.2	0.5	0.3	8.4	62.3	17.1	11.1	68.3	8.6	0.1	10.4	0.7	5.3	50.8
1991	220.9	214.6	157.3	29.7	34.0	153.0	53.4	11.6	4.6	60.5	9.3	1.8	0.4	9.4	8.1	0.5	0.3	8.2	62.5	16.1	12.8	65.8	8.4	0.5	9.3	0.7	6.1	63.6
1992	209.7	207.4	159.8	32.2	34.5	157.5	55.3	13.3	4.2	64.4	9.3	1.5	0.4	9.8	8.7	0.4	0.4	8.7	63.3	16.8	14.2	65.8	8.3	0.0	8.1	0.5	6.5	49.9
1993	201.1	205.5	158.3	36.3	31.9	162.7	55.1	15.2	4.0	66.3	9.7	1.9	0.4	9.9	9.1	0.5	0.4	9.2	63.5	18.4	13.3	68.5	7.9	0.2	7.1	0.8	6.0	42.8
1994	199.0	204.5	160.5	38.2	32.8	166.0	56.6	16.4	4.0	69.0	10.0	1.1	0.5	10.3	9.6	0.8	0.5	9.8	65.1	19.3	14.3	70.1	6.1	0.3	6.7	0.4	6.5	38.5
1995	196.5	202.2	158.9	40.6	32.8	164.6	55.1	17.3	3.6	68.8	9.9	0.9	0.6	10.3	8.9	0.8	0.6	9.1	65.1	20.2	15.9	69.5	5.9	0.3	7.0	0.9	7.0	37.6
1996	192.7	197.1	159.0	40.0	35.5	163.5	55.9	18.2	3.6	70.5	9.7	1.2	0.6	10.1	9.5	0.8	0.6	9.7	64.4	18.7	16.3	66.9	5.2	0.3	6.5	0.9	7.7	33.7
1997	191.3	197.5	161.6	42.6	36.3	167.8	57.6	18.3	3.7	72.3	9.2	1.4	0.5	9.6	9.6	0.9	0.5	9.9	66.4	20.9	17.4	69.9	5.0	0.3	5.9	0.8	7.8	29.8
1998	187.7	200.7	159.1	44.5	31.5	172.1	57.7	19.1	2.9	74.0	9.2	1.8	0.4	10.2	9.6	1.3	0.4	10.5	65.4	21.6	15.1	71.8	4.6	0.5	4.9	0.7	7.7	28.6
1999	188.7	204.6	160.3	47.5	31.7	176.2	60.0	19.8	3.5	76.5	9.3	1.6	0.6	10.5	9.9	1.5	0.4	11.0	63.9	23.3	14.8	72.5	4.5	0.7	8.1	0.5	7.6	28.4
2000	187.8	204.9	159.4	49.8	32.7	176.5	58.8	20.3	3.5	75.5	9.2	1.9	0.5	10.6	9.8	1.6	0.4	11.1	63.8	24.6	15.1	73.3	4.6	1.1	6.5	0.3	6.5	28.4
2001	176.8	197.6	148.5	49.9	29.1	169.2	56.1	20.6	3.0	73.7	8.1	2.0	0.4	9.7	8.7	2.1	0.4	10.4	59.6	23.8	14.2	69.2	4.9	1.1	6.2	0.2	4.9	28.4
2002[p]	174.8	198.3	148.2	51.9	28.4	171.7	57.2	21.7	3.0	75.9	8.1	2.6	0.4	10.4	9.3	2.3	0.3	11.3	59.3	23.8	15.2	67.9	4.8	1.3	6.0	0.4	6.0	26.6
2003	171.8	202.1	145.3	54.2	24.0	175.5	56.4	22.0	2.9	75.5	7.9	2.8	0.3	10.3	9.1	3.0	0.3	11.8	58.7	24.8	12.1	71.5	4.8	1.2	5.5	0.4	3.5	26.5
2004	178.1	215.1	151.1	62.7	25.6	188.2	60.4	25.5	3.3	83.0	7.8	4.1	0.4	11.5	9.5	5.2	0.4	14.3	59.8	25.8	13.0	72.6	4.8	1.1	5.7	1.0	2.9	27.0
2005	180.3	216.8	153.2	62.7	26.1	189.7	61.9	25.8	3.3	84.3	7.7	4.3	0.4	11.6	9.5	5.2	0.5	14.3	60.8	24.7	13.5	72.0	4.8	1.8	5.3	0.9	3.1	27.1

[a] U.S. Department of Agriculture, Forest Service (49).
[b] Pine Chemicals Association, Inc. (31); Data may not add to totals because of rounding; Data for wood pulp have been revised; Air-dry weight contains 15% moisture content.
[c] Includes hardwood and softwood pallets. Pallets equate 20% of lumber.
[d] Includes hardwood and softwood plywood and laminated veneer lumber. LVL begins in 1980.
[e] Includes hardboard, particleboard, insulating board, OSB and MDF.
[f] Excludes wood pulp used in hardboard and insulating board. Includes wood pulp and other. Wood pulp/1000 added to other/100 (Table 42).
[g] Prior to 2000, Pulpwood Logs are not included in logs.
[h] Excludes veneer produced and consumed in industries other than the plywood industry.
[i] Doesn't include OSB until 1980.
[j] Doesn't include OSB.
[k] Doesn't include OSB, MDF, and Paperboard until 1967.
[l] Includes both wood pulp and the wood pulp equivalent of paper and board except hardboard and insulating board.
[m] Includes pulpwood (except chips), wood pulp, and the wood pulp equivalent of paper and board except hardboard and insulating board.
[n] Includes cooperage logs, poles and piling, fence posts, hewn ties, round mine timbers, box bolts, excelsior bolts, chemical wood, shingle bolts, and miscellaneous items.
[z] Not Available.
[p] Preliminary
[r] Revised

Table 8b—Production, imports, exports, and consumption of timber products (excludes additives and fillers) in tons, by major product, 1965–2005 (thousand metric tons,[a] air-dry weight of wood)[b]

	All products		The weight of wood in products: Total				Lumber[c]				Plywood and veneer[d]				Panel products[e]				Wood pulp[f]				Other industrial products, production and consumption[n]	Logs[g]		Pulpwood chip		Fuelwood production and consumption
Year	Production	Consumption	Production	Imports	Exports	Consumption	Production	Imports	Exports	Consumption	Production	Imports	Exports	Consumption[h]	Production[i]	Imports[j]	Exports[k]	Consumption	Production	Imports[l]	Exports[m]	Consumption		Imports	Exports	Imports	Exports	
1965	111,188	119,465	94,712	14,613	6,336	102,989	42,142	4,836	859	46,120	6,198	626	18	6,806	2,663	224	22	2,865	33,203	8,773	2,660	39,316	7,729	153	2,687	z	91	16,476
1966	115,016	123,083	98,509	15,564	7,497	106,576	42,257	4,863	1,100	46,021	6,463	749	28	7,184	2,860	181	27	3,013	35,730	9,556	2,941	42,345	7,798	215	3,128	z	272	16,507
1967	114,715	120,073	97,795	14,913	9,555	103,153	40,898	4,761	1,188	44,471	6,340	743	47	7,036	3,044	180	26	3,199	35,335	9,056	3,225	41,166	7,108	173	4,435	z	635	16,920
1968	122,832	127,365	105,404	16,439	11,907	109,936	41,008	5,658	1,036	45,630	7,105	1,129	40	8,194	3,672	246	30	3,888	39,376	9,228	3,665	44,939	7,108	178	5,775	z	1,361	17,428
1969	125,455	130,455	107,995	17,633	12,633	112,996	40,124	5,852	1,036	44,940	6,619	1,263	108	7,775	4,202	275	42	4,435	41,385	10,059	4,063	47,381	8,281	184	5,389	z	1,995	17,460
1970	128,161	129,948	108,082	16,748	14,961	109,869	38,739	5,617	1,124	43,232	6,848	1,221	91	7,978	4,183	191	46	4,328	40,626	9,395	5,014	45,007	8,999	325	6,164	z	2,523	20,079
1971	131,357	136,915	111,786	18,372	12,814	117,344	41,244	6,934	1,100	47,078	7,861	1,516	58	9,320	5,331	258	55	5,534	41,829	9,475	4,390	46,915	8,309	189	5,147	z	2,064	19,571
1972	138,714	143,839	118,556	20,955	15,830	123,680	42,185	8,621	1,365	49,441	8,613	1,884	125	10,372	6,360	409	69	6,700	44,565	9,952	4,574	49,943	7,136	88	7,064	z	2,634	20,158
1973	141,844	145,413	122,765	21,482	17,913	126,334	43,225	8,804	1,895	50,135	8,490	1,510	226	9,774	6,888	412	92	7,208	46,129	10,755	4,499	52,385	6,832	0	7,570	z	3,631	19,079
1974	135,125	136,943	114,237	19,258	17,440	116,055	39,089	6,711	1,718	44,082	7,278	982	308	7,952	6,177	281	124	6,333	45,811	11,112	5,315	51,608	5,907	172	5,942	z	4,033	20,888
1975	123,706	122,908	103,723	15,091	15,889	102,925	36,377	5,440	1,542	40,276	7,168	1,146	431	7,884	5,442	107	102	5,447	40,110	8,198	4,503	43,805	5,314	199	5,997	z	3,315	19,983
1976	136,278	136,843	116,723	18,896	18,331	117,288	40,175	7,470	1,718	45,927	8,171	1,410	400	9,180	6,723	198	111	6,810	45,053	9,619	4,676	49,996	5,176	199	7,308	z	4,117	19,555
1977	144,783	148,678	122,115	21,702	17,807	126,010	42,898	9,684	1,542	51,041	8,611	1,352	183	9,780	7,596	292	104	7,784	46,422	10,026	4,704	51,744	5,314	347	6,903	z	4,371	22,668
1978	154,456	160,578	124,978	24,352	18,230	131,100	43,929	11,022	1,846	53,105	8,853	1,516	165	10,203	7,869	408	78	8,199	47,435	11,188	4,700	53,923	5,452	218	7,667	z	3,774	29,478
1979	162,773	165,522	127,383	23,954	21,205	130,132	43,906	10,426	2,200	52,133	8,706	1,247	216	9,737	7,393	390	73	7,710	48,331	11,592	5,260	54,663	5,590	299	8,763	z	4,693	35,390
1980	161,015	160,042	119,026	21,145	22,118	118,053	38,873	8,904	2,529	45,248	7,278	732	208	7,802	6,341	280	78	6,543	48,801	10,942	7,299	52,445	5,728	287	7,333	z	4,672	41,989
1981	157,004	158,828	112,289	20,784	18,960	114,113	34,744	8,599	2,440	40,903	7,419	898	367	7,950	6,073	297	126	6,244	48,788	10,763	6,628	52,923	5,866	227	5,699	z	3,699	44,715
1982	166,933	168,329	110,743	20,140	18,743	112,140	34,748	8,404	2,000	41,153	7,257	1,118	248	8,128	5,211	398	49	5,559	47,325	9,956	6,248	51,033	6,004	263	7,214	z	2,984	56,189
1983	177,339	182,218	123,415	24,866	19,986	128,295	41,467	10,992	2,381	50,078	8,806	1,635	308	10,133	6,677	576	61	7,192	49,826	11,292	6,739	54,379	6,142	371	7,875	z	2,623	53,924
1984	188,447	197,289	130,898	28,083	19,240	139,740	44,917	12,253	2,212	54,957	9,003	1,501	205	10,299	6,893	722	66	7,549	53,520	13,277	6,472	60,325	6,280	330	7,859	z	2,426	57,549
1985	182,531	192,606	127,701	29,810	19,735	137,776	44,266	13,480	1,955	55,791	9,018	1,849	184	10,683	6,952	734	108	7,578	49,986	13,524	6,426	57,083	6,418	223	8,642	z	2,418	54,830
1986	191,835	201,266	135,757	30,768	21,338	145,188	49,323	13,107	2,474	59,956	9,848	1,921	340	11,429	7,185	773	124	7,833	52,093	14,062	7,646	58,509	6,556	177	8,221	729	2,533	56,078
1987	190,402	199,165	143,909	32,723	23,960	152,672	53,315	13,748	3,307	63,755	10,239	2,330	428	12,141	7,362	784	165	7,982	54,264	15,151	8,163	61,252	6,832	186	9,241	524	2,657	46,492
1988	194,498	197,490	148,458	31,771	28,778	151,451	53,981	12,367	4,696	61,651	10,130	1,991	557	11,564	7,497	753	221	8,028	55,368	15,620	8,859	62,129	7,039	153	10,790	887	3,655	46,039
1989	195,038	196,633	149,801	31,606	30,011	151,397	53,943	13,703	4,300	63,346	9,623	1,177	783	10,018	7,618	474	294	7,798	55,828	15,447	9,504	61,771	7,660	88	10,583	716	4,546	45,237
1990	194,250	194,100	148,220	29,351	29,501	148,070	52,745	11,727	3,916	60,556	9,429	1,001	887	9,543	7,466	429	346	7,549	56,510	15,498	10,039	61,969	7,757	52	9,474	643	4,838	46,030
1991	200,346	196,371	142,633	26,924	30,898	138,659	48,475	10,493	4,134	54,833	8,472	866	790	8,548	7,391	340	369	7,362	56,670	14,587	11,585	59,673	7,605	31	8,458	607	5,562	57,712
1992	190,199	188,005	144,963	29,174	31,368	142,768	50,143	12,048	3,817	58,374	8,715	1,053	901	8,867	7,862	406	463	7,805	57,433	15,201	12,919	59,716	7,541	0	7,373	464	5,896	45,237
1993	182,407	186,294	143,615	32,915	29,028	147,502	49,955	13,805	3,667	60,093	8,754	1,060	855	8,959	8,268	465	469	8,264	57,558	16,692	12,094	62,156	7,137	211	6,468	682	5,475	38,792
1994	180,521	185,422	145,585	34,690	29,789	150,486	51,292	14,895	3,594	62,592	9,037	1,004	743	9,298	8,706	690	545	8,852	59,047	17,506	12,937	63,616	5,535	248	6,035	346	5,935	34,935
1995	178,214	183,332	144,088	36,848	31,730	149,206	49,973	15,736	3,265	62,445	8,946	1,157	774	9,329	8,074	719	615	8,178	59,082	18,328	14,405	63,005	5,341	181	6,342	727	6,330	34,126
1996	174,750	178,774	144,211	36,304	32,280	148,235	50,679	16,494	3,241	63,932	8,840	1,052	765	9,126	8,621	723	588	8,755	58,439	16,974	14,773	60,641	4,720	259	5,927	802	6,986	30,539
1997	173,543	179,128	146,560	38,603	33,018	152,145	52,269	16,589	3,320	65,538	8,383	1,247	915	8,714	8,670	804	540	8,934	60,184	18,966	15,743	63,407	4,555	287	5,393	710	7,107	26,983
1998	170,222	181,996	144,318	40,386	28,612	156,092	52,368	17,344	2,613	67,098	8,352	1,429	499	9,282	8,711	1,186	392	9,504	59,291	19,551	13,721	65,121	4,210	417	4,448	460	6,939	25,904
1999	171,167	185,536	145,374	43,119	28,750	159,743	54,465	17,973	3,008	69,429	8,396	1,653	506	9,543	9,008	1,378	408	9,978	57,951	21,167	13,387	65,731	4,113	662	4,583	286	6,857	25,793
2000	170,324	185,801	144,579	45,173	29,696	160,056	53,348	18,392	3,218	68,522	8,385	1,688	470	9,602	8,929	1,487	424	9,992	57,894	22,297	13,705	66,486	4,141	1,011	5,933	298	5,947	25,745
2001	160,371	179,151	134,663	45,217	26,437	153,422	50,850	18,718	2,717	66,851	7,330	1,851	350	8,830	7,866	1,875	378	9,363	54,100	21,584	12,902	62,782	4,410	1,032	5,665	157	4,424	25,729
2002[r]	159,126	180,656	134,444	47,062	24,938	156,529	51,870	19,664	2,712	68,822	7,358	2,359	324	9,393	8,407	2,100	343	9,464	53,807	21,599	13,813	61,593	4,381	1,207	5,461	132	3,171	24,126
2003	155,866	183,263	131,820	49,188	21,792	159,216	51,199	19,927	2,614	68,511	7,129	2,541	339	9,331	8,229	2,732	280	10,681	53,276	22,493	10,961	64,808	4,389	1,119	5,002	377	2,596	24,047
2004	161,522	195,140	137,079	56,828	23,210	170,696	54,755	23,158	2,671	75,242	7,099	3,743	416	10,426	8,657	4,672	403	12,927	54,219	23,366	11,761	65,824	4,389	1,020	5,142	870	2,818	24,444
2005	163,516	196,647	138,914	56,848	23,716	172,045	56,114	23,393	3,003	76,505	6,948	3,902	367	10,483	8,650	4,715	428	12,938	55,173	22,421	12,279	65,315	4,389	1,597	4,851	819	2,789	24,602

[a]U.S. Department of Agriculture, Forest Service (49).
[b]Pine Chemicals Association, Inc. (31); Data may not add to totals because of rounding; Data for wood pulp have been revised; Air-dry weight contains 15% moisture content.
[c]Includes hardwood and softwood pallets. Pallets equate 20% of lumber.
[d]Includes hardwood and softwood plywood and laminated veneer lumber. LVL begins in 1980.
[e]Includes hardboard, particleboard, insulating board, OSB and MDF.
[f]Excludes wood pulp used in hardboard and insulating board. Includes wood pulp and other. Wood pulp/1000 added to other/100 (Table 42).
[g]Prior to 2000, Pulpwood Logs are not included in logs.
[r]Revised.
[h]Excludes veneer produced and consumed in industries other than the plywood industry.
[i]Doesn't include OSB until 1980.
[j]Doesn't include OSB.
[k]Doesn't include OSB, MDF, and Paperboard until 1967.
[l]Includes both wood pulp and the wood pulp equivalent of paper and board except hardboard and insulating board.
[m]Includes pulpwood (except chips), wood pulp, and the wood pulp equivalent of paper and board except hardboard and insulating board.
[n]Includes cooperage logs, poles and piling, fence posts, hewn ties, round mine timbers, box bolts, excelsior bolts, chemical wood, shingle bolts, and miscellaneous items.
[z]Not available.

Table 9—U.S. annual industrial wood product production in thousands of short tons, product weight, 1965 -2005[a]

Year	Total	Softwood plywood[b]	Oriented strandboard[b]	Laminated veneer lumber[b]	Hardwood plywood and veneer[c]	Softwood lumber[d]	Hardwood lumber[d]	Lumber made at pallet plants[e]	Particleboard production[f]	Hardboard production[g]	Medium-density fiberboard production[f]	Pulp paper and board[h]	Other industrial products, production and consumption[i]	Insulating board[j]
1965	108,868	6,807	z	z	1,345	28,599	15,929	171	1,059	913	105	43,465	9,240	1,234
1966	113,194	7,140	z	z	1,362	28,162	16,488	203	1,333	964	117	46,971	9,323	1,131
1967	110,997	7,086	z	z	1,257	27,503	15,712	204	1,510	949	130	46,969	8,498	1,178
1968	116,505	8,036	z	z	1,318	28,589	14,740	225	1,956	1,160	145	50,561	8,498	1,276
1969	119,987	7,489	z	z	1,227	27,669	14,727	262	2,365	1,327	161	53,530	9,900	1,330
1970	119,523	7,842	z	z	1,179	26,876	14,057	247	2,434	1,370	179	53,408	10,758	1,173
1971	124,453	9,097	z	z	1,263	29,326	14,254	270	3,317	1,633	198	53,753	9,933	1,410
1972	130,569	10,021	z	z	1,332	30,239	14,334	303	4,330	1,812	220	58,009	8,531	1,439
1973	134,386	10,011	z	z	1,186	30,836	14,837	363	4,866	1,891	245	60,548	8,168	1,437
1974	126,340	8,683	z	z	919	27,046	14,257	402	4,324	1,767	272	60,403	7,062	1,205
1975	113,646	8,777	z	z	690	26,112	12,325	312	3,520	1,775	302	52,393	6,353	1,087
1976	128,233	10,084	z	z	711	29,873	13,462	383	4,485	2,120	394	59,283	6,188	1,251
1977	134,926	10,596	z	z	779	31,923	14,343	462	5,019	2,411	620	61,149	6,353	1,271
1978	139,305	10,918	z	z	778	32,704	15,120	529	5,231	2,445	714	63,085	6,518	1,262
1979	141,932	10,748	z	z	755	32,509	15,706	580	4,748	2,402	713	65,873	6,683	1,215
1980	134,084	8,932	84	53	681	27,530	15,452	505	4,148	1,919	693	66,217	6,848	1,021
1981	129,344	9,161	169	70	641	24,797	12,622	494	4,035	1,908	726	66,931	7,013	780
1982	124,212	8,666	348	70	909	23,222	13,494	447	3,365	1,746	627	63,483	7,178	657
1983	141,762	10,653	838	88	971	29,020	14,794	505	4,231	2,282	849	69,352	7,343	836
1984	150,006	10,897	1,276	88	988	30,434	17,027	591	4,494	2,137	892	72,742	7,508	934
1985	148,775	11,030	1,668	123	881	30,577	16,196	650	4,684	1,969	963	71,459	7,673	904
1986	160,772	12,096	2,196	140	912	34,435	17,680	721	5,067	1,819	1,098	75,964	7,838	806
1987	170,449	12,523	2,548	158	1,000	37,415	19,006	797	5,212	1,705	1,264	79,830	8,168	823
1988	174,787	12,359	2,878	193	1,019	37,224	19,813	876	5,385	1,599	1,320	82,847	8,415	859
1989	175,777	11,695	3,191	210	1,011	36,653	20,345	943	5,425	1,624	1,364	83,257	9,158	901
1990	176,550	11,440	3,386	280	1,009	34,941	20,792	996	5,352	1,570	1,336	85,307	9,273	868
1991	171,867	10,200	3,508	280	982	32,373	18,847	1,005	5,304	1,530	1,347	86,546	9,092	853
1992	179,502	10,572	4,158	298	934	33,706	19,276	1,046	5,597	1,648	1,499	90,885	9,016	868
1993	180,831	10,563	4,376	368	992	32,165	20,620	960	5,964	1,640	1,633	92,154	8,532	866
1994	185,905	10,740	4,679	403	1,182	33,297	20,900	863	6,387	1,627	1,759	96,595	6,617	857
1995	185,630	10,591	4,939	490	1,209	31,467	21,337	768	5,906	1,541	1,557	98,582	6,386	857
1996	186,758	10,490	5,821	560	1,171	32,476	21,074	660	6,270	1,650	1,752	98,334	5,643	857
1997	193,114	9,824	6,584	665	1,229	33,844	21,386	733	6,372	1,407	1,948	102,822	5,445	857
1998	191,746	9,721	7,017	718	1,288	33,853	21,480	744	6,459	1,344	1,970	101,262	5,033	857
1999	196,307	9,743	7,258	838	1,323	35,736	21,814	735	6,773	1,371	1,987	102,955	4,917	857
2000	193,159	9,557	7,441	833	1,487	35,110	21,259	735	6,756	1,182	2,093	100,900	4,950	857
2001	182,836	8,269	7,833	935	1,381	33,760	19,970	735	5,760	1,038	1,946	95,080	5,273	857
2002[r]	185,987	8,313	8,391	982	1,376	34,979	19,828	735	6,207	912	2,280	95,890	5,238	857
2003	183,454	8,042	8,509	1,181	1,343	35,738	18,360	735	5,603	1,345	2,261	94,232	5,247	857
2004	192,318	8,020	8,919	1,510	1,327	38,147	19,708	735	6,053	1,212	2,457	98,124	5,247	857
2005	193,212	7,837	9,366	1,586	1,311	39,731	19,560	735	5,781	1,358	2,588	97,256	5,247	857

[a]Sources for recent production data (some earlier data are Forest Service estimates or from Dept. of Commerce):
[b]APA--The Engineered Wood Association (11).
[c]Dept. of Commerce (to 1988); 1989-1990 data from Hardwood Plywood & Veneer Association;
  later estimates based on trends in value of shipments (Dept. of Commerce); hardwood veneer based on Census of Manufactures data and trend in value of shipments.
[d]1965-1976 based on Commerce Department data and Forest Service estimates; 1976-1998 American Forest & Paper Association (AF&PA)
  American Forest & Paper Association (4) (1996 hardwood estimated by Forest Service; 1997-1998 hardwood estimate from Miller Freeman).
  [Note that Commerce Dept. reported hardwood lumber production is understood to underestimate actual production as reflected in Forest Service estimates since 1900.]
[e]Forest Service estimate of lumber cut from roundwood at pallet plants.
  Other lumber (e.g., purchased lumber) used by pallet makers is accounted for under hardwood and softwood lumber production.
[f]Composite Panel Association (based on production data 1959-1977, and 1995-1997; otherwise based on shipments; 1998 data are estimated) (15).
[g]Composite Panel Association (1965-1997) and as reported by Miller Freeman (1998); 1998 figure is estimated (15).
[h]AF&PA, formerly API (Statistics of Paper, Paperboard & Woodpulp) (5). Paper and paperboard production includes "Total Paper", "Total Paperboard", and "Building Paper" production.
  Total production of pulp, paper and paperboard includes market pulp produced for export.
[i]Data through 1988 was obtained from U.S. Timber Production, Trade, Consumption, and Price Statistics reports (USDA Forest Service).
  Miscellaneous wood product production for 1996 based on timber product output tables in (draft) 1997 RPA Inventory Data Tables; intervening and subsequent data are extrapolated.
[j]Derived using earlier data from Commerce Department MA26A reports (in square feet of product output) to convert tonnage reported in AF&PA and earlier API reports.
zNot available.
rRevised.

Table 10—Industrial wood productivity, 1965-2005[a]

| | Industrial wood productivity (industrial wood product output per unit of roundwood input) | | Total industrial wood product production (from table 9) | Roundwood equivalents of production | | | | | Recovered paper utilization rate (percent)[e] | U.S. population | Per capita industrial wood product production |
| | | | | Hardwoods[b] | Softwoods[c] | Totals | | | | | |
Year	Lbs/ft^3	Tons/ton	Thousand tons	Million ft^3	Million ft^3	Million ft^3	Thousand short tons[d]	Thousand metric tons		Millions	Lb/capita
1965	19 28	0.6929	108,261	2,912	8,319	11,230	156,247	141,744	23.5%	194.3	1,114
1966	19 52	0.7007	112,432	3,045	8,476	11,520	160,461	145,567	22.6%	196.6	1,144
1967	19.44	0.6991	110,134	2,900	8,432	11,332	157,547	142,924	21.2%	198.7	1,109
1968	19 54	0.7052	115,421	2,842	8,972	11,814	163,678	148,485	20.4%	200.7	1,150
1969	19 85	0.7149	118,703	2,979	8,983	11,963	166,052	150,639	22.1%	202.7	1,171
1970	17.79	0.6420	118,211	3,211	10,075	13,287	184,128	167,038	22.8%	205.1	1,153
1971	19 94	0.7206	122,665	2,895	9,405	12,300	170,218	154,419	22.8%	207.7	1,181
1972	20.40	0.7376	128,216	2,935	9,632	12,567	173,840	157,704	22.5%	209.9	1,222
1973	20 59	0.7433	131,730	3,064	9,731	12,795	177,225	160,775	23.5%	211.9	1,243
1974	20 08	0.7235	123,996	3,051	9,301	12,352	171,383	155,475	23.7%	213.9	1,159
1975	19.76	0.7165	111,787	2,473	8,844	11,317	156,016	141,534	23.0%	216.0	1,035
1976	20 80	0.7533	125,859	2,722	9,381	12,102	167,078	151,570	23.4%	218.0	1,155
1977	21.12	0.7647	132,289	2,821	9,709	12,529	172,986	156,929	23.4%	220.2	1,202
1978	21.12	0.7633	136,542	3,030	9,900	12,930	178,891	162,286	23.8%	222.6	1,227
1979	21 09	0.7620	139,443	3,125	10,096	13,221	182,998	166,012	23.9%	225.1	1,239
1980	21 85	0.7857	131,899	3,093	8,981	12,074	167,867	152,286	23.5%	227.7	1,159
1981	22 22	0.8002	127,276	2,856	8,601	11,458	159,052	144,289	23.4%	230.0	1,107
1982	21.66	0.7782	122,574	2,940	8,380	11,320	157,505	142,886	23.7%	232.2	1,056
1983	21.72	0.7803	139,888	3,364	9,515	12,879	179,269	162,629	23.4%	234.3	1,194
1984	22.16	0.7938	148,099	3,652	9,716	13,368	186,568	169,251	23.8%	236.3	1,253
1985	21 92	0.7852	146,873	3,671	9,729	13,400	187,048	169,686	23.8%	238.5	1,232
1986	21.69	0.7764	158,793	4,053	10,591	14,644	204,535	185,550	24.7%	240.7	1,319
1987	21 90	0.7853	168,479	4,149	11,235	15,385	214,546	194,632	24.6%	242.8	1,388
1988	22.13	0.7921	172,817	4,330	11,288	15,618	218,165	197,915	25.1%	245.0	1,411
1989	22.12	0.7897	173,912	4,553	11,169	15,722	220,233	199,791	25.7%	247.3	1,406
1990	22.44	0.8000	174,796	4,609	10,968	15,577	218,500	198,219	27.0%	249.9	1,399
1991	22.41	0.7989	170,201	4,493	10,694	15,187	213,032	193,259	29.1%	252.7	1,347
1992	23 39	0.8311	177,932	4,717	10,498	15,215	214,088	194,217	30.9%	255.4	1,393
1993	24 02	0.8498	179,125	4,921	9,992	14,914	210,784	191,219	32.3%	258.1	1,388
1994	24 28	0.8594	184,058	4,956	10,209	15,164	214,175	194,295	33.7%	260.7	1,412
1995	23 83	0.8409	184,152	5,288	10,166	15,454	219,002	198,674	34.4%	263.0	1,400
1996	24.17	0.8536	185,428	5,186	10,158	15,344	217,241	197,077	36.9%	265.5	1,397
1997	24 51	0.8653	191,964	5,322	10,340	15,662	221,839	201,248	36.4%	267.9	1,433
1998	24 31	0.8591	190,698	5,259	10,428	15,687	221,969	201,366	37.1%	270.3	1,411
1999	25.18	0.8858	197,420	5,255	10,429	15,683	221,908	201,310	37.1%	273.2	1,445
2000	24 85	0.8786	194,210	5,201	10,430	15,631	221,050	200,532	39.1%	282.1	1,377
2001	24 80	0.8781	184,844	4,857	10,051	14,907	210,499	190,960	39.1%	284.8	1,298
2002	25 33	0.8983	188,404	4,762	10,115	14,878	209,813	190,338	40.0%	287.5	1,311
2003	25.11	0.8955	183,454	4,280	10,334	14,614	204,859	185,844	37.5%	291.1	1,261
2004	25.15	0.8969	192,318	4,484	10,812	15,296	214,427	194,524	37.2%	294.0	1,309
2005	24 99	0.8921	193,212	4,463	11,002	15,465	216,584	196,480	37.8%	296.7	1,303

[a] U.S. Department of Agriculture, Forest Products Laboratory (20).
[b] The average specific gravity for hardwood is 0.52.
[c] The average specific gravity for softwood is 0.42.
[d] The weight density of a cubic foot of water in pounds is 62.4. Example: ((0.52*62.4/2000)+(0.42*62.4/2000))*1000.
[e] Utiliza ion rate is the ratio of recovered paper consumption to total production of paper and board.

Table 11a—Per capita consumption of timber products, by major product, 1965–2005[a]

Year	All products	Total roundwood	Industrial roundwood used for							Fuelwood	
			Lumber		Plywood and veneer		Pulp products		Other industrial products[b]		
	Cubic feet	Cubic feet	Cubic feet	Board feet (lumber tally)	Cubic feet	Board feet (local log rule)	Cubic feet	Cords	Cubic feet	Cubic feet	Cords
1965	68.5	63.2	35.6	194	5.9	27	18.9	0.2	2.9	5.3	0.067
1966	69.1	63.8	34.9	190	6.1	28	19.9	0.2	2.9	5.3	0.066
1967	66.6	61.2	33.5	182	5.9	27	19.2	0.2	2.6	5.4	0.067
1968	68.9	63.5	34.4	187	6.8	31	19.8	0.2	2.6	5.5	0.068
1969	69.5	64.1	33.5	182	6.3	29	21.4	0.3	3.0	5.4	0.068
1970	75.4	69.2	36.0	196	6.4	30	23.6	0.3	3.2	6.2	0.077
1971	70.9	65.0	34.7	189	7.4	34	20.0	0.3	2.9	5.9	0.074
1972	72.2	66.2	36.2	197	8.1	37	19.4	0.2	2.5	6.1	0.076
1973	71.7	66.1	36.2	197	7.7	35	19.8	0.2	2.3	5.7	0.071
1974	68.5	62.3	32.9	179	6.3	29	21.2	0.3	2.0	6.2	0.077
1975	61.2	55.4	30.7	167	6.2	29	16.7	0.2	1.8	5.8	0.073
1976	65.4	59.7	32.2	175	7.2	33	18.6	0.2	1.7	5.7	0.071
1977	69.7	63.3	35.8	195	7.6	35	18.1	0.2	1.7	6.5	0.081
1978	73.8	65.5	36.9	201	7.8	36	19.1	0.2	1.8	8.3	0.104
1979	74.7	64.8	35.4	192	7.3	34	20.3	0.3	1.8	9.9	0.124
1980	68.6	57.0	29.6	161	5.8	27	19.8	0.2	1.8	11.6	0.145
1981	66.5	54.3	27.2	148	5.7	26	19.5	0.2	1.8	12.2	0.153
1982	68.3	53.0	27.0	147	5.6	26	18.5	0.2	1.9	15.2	0.191
1983	75.5	61.0	32.6	177	6.9	32	19.6	0.2	1.9	14.5	0.181
1984	79.4	64.1	34.8	189	6.9	32	20.5	0.3	1.9	15.3	0.192
1985	79.1	64.6	35.1	191	6.9	32	20.7	0.3	1.9	14.5	0.181
1986	83.1	68.4	37.0	201	7.3	34	22.2	0.3	2.0	14.7	0.183
1987	82.7	70.6	38.6	210	7.5	35	22.5	0.3	2.0	12.1	0.151
1988	80.3	68.5	36.8	200	7.1	33	22.6	0.3	2.1	11.8	0.148
1989	79.1	67.5	36.8	200	5.9	27	22.5	0.3	2.2	11.5	0.144
1990	76.9	65.3	34.5	188	5.6	26	22.8	0.3	2.2	11.6	0.145
1991	76.2	61.9	32.5	177	5.0	23	22.2	0.3	2.2	14.4	0.180
1992	73.5	62.3	32.8	178	5.0	23	22.3	0.3	2.1	11.2	0.139
1993	72.1	62.7	33.3	181	5.0	23	22.3	0.3	2.0	9.5	0.118
1994	72.2	63.8	34.4	187	5.1	23	22.7	0.3	1.5	8.4	0.106
1995	73.1	64.9	34.0	185	5.0	23	24.4	0.3	1.5	8.2	0.102
1996	71.2	64.0	34.6	188	4.9	22	23.2	0.3	1.3	7.2	0.091
1997	71.3	65.0	35.2	191	4.6	21	24.0	0.3	1.2	6.3	0.079
1998	72.5	66.5	35.7	194	4.7	22	24.9	0.3	1.1	6.0	0.075
1999	72.3	66.3	36.6	199	4.8	22	23.9	0.3	1.1	5.9	0.074
2000	70.0	64.3	35.1	191	4.6	21	23.6	0.3	1.1	5.7	0.072
2001	67.9	62.2	34.1	185	4.3	20	22.8	0.3	1.1	5.7	0.071
2002[r]	67.7	62.4	34.8	189	4.4	20	22.1	0.3	1.1	5.3	0.066
2003	67.2	62.0	34.4	187	4.3	20	22.2	0.3	1.1	5.2	0.065
2004	71.1	65.9	37.5	204	4.7	22	22.5	0.3	1.1	5.2	0.065
2005	71.0	65.7	37.9	206	4.7	22	22.0	0.3	1.1	5.2	0.065

[a]U.S. Department of Agriculture, Forest Service (21,32); U.S. Council of Economic Advisors (40);
 Data may not add to totals because of rounding.

[b]Includes cooperage logs, poles and piling, fence posts, hewn ties, round mine timbers, box bolts,
 excelsior bolts, chemical wood, shingle bolts, and miscellaneous items.

[r]Revised.

Table 11b—Per capita consumption of timber products, by major product, 1965–2005 (cubic meters)[a]

		Industrial roundwood used for					
Year	All products	Total roundwood	Lumber	Plywood and veneer	Pulp products	Other industrial products[b]	Fuelwood
1965	1.940	1.789	1.008	0.166	0.534	0.082	0.151
1966	1.956	1.807	0.989	0.172	0.564	0.081	0.150
1967	1.886	1.734	0.948	0.167	0.545	0.073	0.152
1968	1.952	1.798	0.974	0.191	0.559	0.073	0.155
1969	1.969	1.815	0.948	0.178	0.605	0.084	0.154
1970	2.135	1.960	1.019	0.182	0.669	0.090	0.175
1971	2.008	1.840	0.981	0.209	0.567	0.082	0.168
1972	2.045	1.873	1.025	0.229	0.549	0.070	0.171
1973	2.032	1.871	1.026	0.218	0.561	0.066	0.161
1974	1.939	1.765	0.930	0.179	0.600	0.057	0.174
1975	1.733	1.568	0.870	0.175	0.472	0.050	0.165
1976	1.851	1.691	0.913	0.203	0.526	0.049	0.160
1977	1.975	1.791	1.014	0.215	0.512	0.050	0.184
1978	2.090	1.854	1.044	0.220	0.540	0.050	0.236
1979	2.114	1.834	1.001	0.207	0.575	0.051	0.280
1980	1.943	1.614	0.838	0.164	0.560	0.052	0.329
1981	1.883	1.537	0.770	0.163	0.551	0.052	0.347
1982	1.933	1.501	0.766	0.159	0.523	0.053	0.432
1983	2.138	1.727	0.923	0.196	0.555	0.054	0.411
1984	2.249	1.814	0.985	0.195	0.580	0.055	0.434
1985	2.240	1.830	0.993	0.196	0.585	0.055	0.410
1986	2.353	1.938	1.048	0.206	0.628	0.056	0.416
1987	2.341	2.000	1.092	0.213	0.637	0.058	0.342
1988	2.275	1.939	1.041	0.200	0.640	0.059	0.335
1989	2.239	1.912	1.043	0.168	0.637	0.064	0.326
1990	2.177	1.848	0.978	0.160	0.646	0.064	0.329
1991	2.159	1.751	0.919	0.141	0.630	0.062	0.407
1992	2.081	1.765	0.929	0.143	0.633	0.061	0.316
1993	2.043	1.774	0.943	0.142	0.632	0.057	0.268
1994	2.045	1.806	0.975	0.144	0.643	0.044	0.239
1995	2.069	1.838	0.963	0.142	0.691	0.042	0.231
1996	2.016	1.811	0.980	0.138	0.657	0.036	0.205
1997	2.019	1.840	0.997	0.129	0.679	0.035	0.180
1998	2.054	1.883	1.012	0.134	0.706	0.032	0.171
1999	2.047	1.879	1.037	0.135	0.676	0.031	0.168
2000	1.983	1.821	0.993	0.129	0.668	0.030	0.163
2001	1.923	1.762	0.964	0.122	0.644	0.032	0.161
2002[r]	1.916	1.766	0.986	0.124	0.625	0.031	0.150
2003	1.904	1.757	0.975	0.122	0.629	0.031	0.147
2004	2.013	1.865	1.062	0.134	0.638	0.031	0.148
2005	2.009	1.861	1.073	0.134	0.624	0.030	0.148

[a] U.S. Department of Agriculture, Forest Service (21,32); U.S. Council of Economic Advisors (40); Data may not add to totals because of rounding.

[b] Includes cooperage logs, poles and piling, fence posts, hewn ties, round mine timbers, box bolts, excelsior bolts, chemical wood, shingle bolts, and miscellaneous items.

[r] Revised.

Table 12—Consumption of selected timber products and other materials used in construction, manufacturing, and shipping, 1965–2005[a]

Year	Lumber						Plywood					
	Total		Softwoods		Hardwoods		Total		Softwoods		Hardwoods	
	Consumption	Index 1996=100	Consumption	Index 1996=100	Consumption	Index 1996=100	Consumption	Index 1996=100	Consumption	Index 1996=100	Consumption	Index 1996=100
	Billion board feet		*Billion board feet*		*Billion board feet*		*Billion square feet (3/8-in. basis)*		*Billion square feet (3/8-in. basis)*		*Billion square feet (3/8-in. basis)*	
1965	43.1	70.3	33.4	67 5	9.7	82.2	15.5	73 0	12.4	68.9	3.1	95.7
1966	42.7	69.7	32.7	66.1	10.0	84.9	16.3	76 9	13.0	72.2	3.3	102.9
1967	41.4	67.6	32.0	64.6	9 5	80.3	16.0	75.4	12.9	71.5	3.2	97.6
1968	43.1	70.3	34.1	68 9	9 0	76.3	18.5	87 2	14.6	81.3	3.9	120 2
1969	42 3	69.0	33.2	67.1	9.1	77.1	17.5	82 2	13.5	75.0	4.0	122.7
1970	40 8	66.5	32.2	65.1	8.6	72.8	18.0	84 8	14.2	79.0	3.8	117 3
1971	45 0	73.4	36.4	73 5	8.6	73.1	21.0	98 8	16.5	91.8	4.5	137 9
1972	47 5	77.5	38.8	78 3	8.7	74.2	23.3	109.5	18.1	100.5	5.2	159 9
1973	47 9	78.3	38.8	78.4	9.1	77.6	22.2	104.5	17.9	99.4	4.3	133 0
1974	41.6	67.9	32.9	66 5	8.7	73.9	18.3	86 2	15.3	85.1	3.0	92.2
1975	38.4	62.7	31.1	62 8	7.4	62.5	18.2	85 5	15.3	84.7	2.9	89.9
1976	44.1	72.0	36.1	72 8	8.1	68.5	21.1	99 3	17.7	98.4	3.4	104.1
1977	49.4	80.5	40.7	82 2	8.6	73.4	22.5	105.8	19.1	106.0	3.4	104.4
1978	51.4	83.9	42.5	85 9	8 9	75.8	23.4	110.0	19.7	109.5	3.6	113 0
1979	50.1	81.7	40.8	82.4	9 3	78.8	22.5	105.8	19.3	107.0	3.2	98.8
1980	42 8	69.8	33.8	68 3	9 0	76.0	18.2	85.6	16.0	88.8	2.2	68.0
1981	39 3	64.1	32.0	64.7	7 3	61.7	18.5	87.1	16.1	89.3	2.4	74.7
1982	39.1	63.9	31.3	63 3	7 8	66.6	18.6	87.6	15.4	85.5	3.2	99.5
1983	48.4	79.0	39.9	80.6	8 5	72.5	23.1	108.7	18.9	105.0	4.2	129.1
1984	52 8	86.1	42.9	86.6	9 9	84.0	23.6	110.8	19.6	108.8	3.9	122 3
1985	54 0	88.1	44.4	89 8	9.6	81.1	24.3	114.2	19.9	110.5	4.4	134 9
1986	57 9	94.5	47.6	96 2	10.3	87.5	26.1	122.7	21.6	119.7	4.5	139.4
1987	61 5	100.3	50.5	101.9	11.0	93.7	27.5	129.4	22.2	123.4	5.3	163.2
1988	59 2	96.6	48.3	97.7	10.9	92.2	26.4	124.3	21.7	120.4	4.7	145.9
1989	60.6	98.9	49.1	99.1	11.5	98.0	23.3	109.9	20.0	111.0	3.4	104.0
1990	57.4	93.7	45.7	92.4	11.7	99.3	22.4	105.3	19.3	107.4	3.0	94.0
1991	52.1	85.0	41.6	84.1	10.4	88.6	20.1	94.4	17.4	96.3	2.7	83.5
1992	55 8	91.1	45.1	91.1	10.7	90.8	20.8	97 8	17.9	99.5	2.8	87.8
1993	57 2	93.3	45.7	92 3	11.5	97.5	20.9	98 5	17.9	99.6	3.0	92.6
1994	59 8	97.6	48.2	97 3	11.6	98.9	21.7	102.0	18.5	102.5	3.2	99.2
1995	59 5	97.1	47.6	96.1	11.9	101.4	21.6	101.9	18.2	100.8	3.5	107 9
1996	61 3	100.0	49.5	100.0	11.8	100 0	21.2	100.0	18.0	100.0	3.2	100.0
1997	62 9	102.7	51.0	103.1	11.9	101.1	20.1	94 8	16.5	91.7	3.6	112.3
1998	64 5	105.2	52.2	105.5	12.2	103 8	21.2	99 8	17.2	95.4	4.0	124.1
1999	66 8	109.1	54.4	109.9	12.4	105 5	21.7	102.0	17.3	96.3	4.3	134.2
2000	66.1	107.9	54.0	109.1	12.1	102.7	21.7	102.3	17.1	95.2	4.6	141.9
2001	64 9	106.0	53.7	108.5	11.3	95.6	19.8	93 0	15.3	84.8	4.5	139.3
2002r	67.1	109.5	55.8	112.8	11.3	95.7	20.8	97 9	15.7	87.0	5.1	158.7
2003	67.4	109.9	56.8	114.8	10.5	89.3	20.6	97 0	15.6	86.6	5.0	154.9
2004	74.1	121.0	62.8	126.8	11.4	96.8	22.5	106.1	16.2	89.9	6.3	196.3
2005	75.6	123.5	64.4	130.2	11.2	95.2	22.6	106.4	16.3	90.7	6.3	194.1

Table 12—Consumption of selected timber products and other materials used in construction, manufacturing, and shipping, 1965–2005a—Con.

Year	Particleboard[b] Consumption Million square feet (3/4-in. basis)	Index 1996=100	Insulating board Consumption Million square feet (1/2-in. basis)	Index 1996=100	Hardboard Shipments Million square feet (1/8-in. basis)	Index 1996=100	Portland cement[c] Shipments Thousand tons	Index 1996=100	Steel products[d] Shipments Thousand tons	Index 1996=100	Brick[e] Shipments Million bricks	Index 1996=100
1965	832	13.1	3,395	137.4	2,921	55 3	70,328	71.2	11,836	149.0	8,089	108.6
1966	1,032	16.2	3,098	125.4	3,083	58.4	71,570	72.5	11,862	149.3	7,552	101.4
1967	1,166	18.3	3,233	130.9	3,038	57 5	70,315	71.2	11,375	143.2	7,117	95.6
1968	1,489	23.4	3,525	142.7	3,710	70 3	74,740	75.7	12,195	153.5	7,557	101.5
1969	1,794	28.2	3,656	148.0	4,247	80.4	77,047	78.0	11,402	143.5	7,290	97 9
1970	1,851	29.1	3,246	131.4	4,384	83 0	73,407	74.4	10,565	133.0	6,496	87 2
1971	2,488	39.1	3,889	157.4	5,225	99 0	79,005	80.0	8,666	109.1	7,570	101.6
1972	3,205	50.3	3,973	160.9	5,798	109.8	82,808	83.9	8,589	108.1	8,402	112.8
1973	3,574	56.2	3,975	160.9	6,050	114.6	88,459	89.6	10,731	135.1	8,674	116.5
1974	3,163	49.7	3,252	131.7	5,654	107.1	81,125	82.2	11,360	143.0	6,673	89.6
1975	2,650	41.6	2,919	118.2	5,681	107.6	69,078	70.0	8,119	102.2	6,262	84.1
1976	3,449	54.2	3,375	136.6	6,785	128.5	72,833	73.8	7,508	94.5	7,218	96 9
1977	4,105	64.5	3,485	141.1	7,714	146.1	78,730	79.7	7,553	95.1	8,663	116.3
1978	4,360	68.5	3,470	140.5	7,825	148.2	84,838	85.9	9,612	121.0	8,586	115.3
1979	4,020	63.2	3,399	137.6	7,688	145.6	84,860	86.0	9,978	125.6	7,708	103.5
1980	3,601	56.6	2,818	114.1	6,140	116.3	76,059	77.0	8,742	110.1	6,090	81 8
1981	3,522	55.3	2,118	85.7	6,105	115.6	71,901	72.8	8,446	106.3	5,059	67 9
1982	3,564	56.0	1,841	74.5	5,587	105.8	64,602	65.4	6,260	78.8	5,119	68.7
1983	4,560	71.6	2,398	97.1	7,303	138.3	70,849	71.8	6,276	79.0	6,218	83 5
1984	5,107	80.2	2,742	111.0	6,837	129.5	81,928	83.0	6,052	76.2	6,991	93 9
1985	5,292	83.1	2,724	110.3	6,300	119.3	84,779	85.9	6,407	80.7	6,605	88.7
1986	5,693	89.4	2,415	97.8	5,822	110.3	88,946	90.1	5,141	64.7	7,184	96 5
1987	6,042	94.9	2,388	96.7	5,458	103.4	90,458	91.6	5,619	70.7	7,601	102.1
1988	6,239	98.0	2,457	99.5	5,118	96 9	90,299	91.5	6,014	75.7	6,930	93 0
1989	4,920	77.3	2,621	106.1	5,196	98.4	89,081	90.2	7,041	88.6	7,494	100.6
1990	4,746	74.6	2,480	100.4	5,025	95 2	87,675	88.8	7,206	90.7	6,873	92 3
1991	4,654	73.1	2,332	94.4	4,895	92.7	78,058	79.1	7,112	89.5	5,975	80 2
1992	5,057	79.5	2,458	99.5	5,273	99 9	82,845	83.9	6,848	86.2	6,231	83.7
1993	5,656	88.9	2,435	98.6	5,248	99.4	86,388	87.5	6,755	85.0	6,655	89.4
1994	6,271	98.5	2,470	100.0	5,206	98.6	92,698	93.9	7,319	92.1	7,238	97 2
1995	5,828	91.6	2,470	100.0	4,930	93.4	93,392	94.6	6,988	88.0	6,665	89 5
1996	6,365	100 0	2,470	100.0	5,280	100.0	98,728	100.0	7,943	100.0	7,448	100.0
1997	6,691	105.1	2,470	100.0	4,501	85 2	99,812	101.1	7,546	95.0	7,576	101.7
1998	8,320	130.7	2,470	100.0	4,300	81.4	114,329	115.8	8,400	105.8	8,241	110.6
1999	8,619	135.4	2,470	100.0	4,386	83.1	120,024	121.6	8,800	110.8	8,932	119.9
2000	9,098	142 9	2,470	100.0	3,781	71.6	121,332	122.9	8,767	110.4	8,617	115.7
2001	9,030	141 9	2,470	100.0	3,322	62 9	124,736	126.3	9,188	115.7	7,955	106.8
2002r	9,927	156 0	2,470	100.0	2,919	55 3	121,279	122.8	8,869	111.7	8,110	108.9
2003	11,383	178 8	2,470	100.0	4,304	81 5	124,506	126.1	9,953	125.3	8,520	114.4
2004	17,786	279.4	2,470	100.0	3,880	73 5	133,110	134.8	10,011	126.0	9,389	126.1
2005	17,061	268.1	2,470	100.0	4,347	82 3	136,714	138.5	9,208	115.9	9,374	125.9

[a]APA–The Engineered Wood Association (12,13); Composite Panel Association (15); U.S. Department of Commerce, Bureau of Industrial Economics (71); Wood Technology (86); U.S. International Trade Commission (80).
[b]Includes medium-density fiberboard.
[c]U.S. Geological Survey (79).
[d]American Iron and Steel Institute (8). Construction, including maintenance; Net shipments.
[e]U.S. Department of Commerce, Bureau of the Census (52)
[p]Preliminary
[r]Revised

Table 13—Volume and value of imports and exports of timber products by product, 2005

Product	Standard unit of measure	Imports[a] Volume	Value[b] Million dollars	Exports Volume	Value[c] Million dollars	Trade Balance[d] Volume	Value[c] Million dollars
Logs:[e,f,j]	Thousand cubic meters						
Softwoods		2,789.0	233.6	7,279.0	847.9	4,490.0	614.3
Hardwoods		428.0	47.2	2,493.0	591.4	2,065.0	544.2
Total		3,217.0	280.8	9,772.0	1,439.3	6,555.0	1,158.5
Lumber:[f]	Thousand cubic meters						
Softwoods		41,864.5	8,401.8	1,524.6	516.3	(40,339.9)	(7,885.5)
Hardwoods		2,537.3	1,118.0	3,485.7	1,624.0	948.4	506.0
Railroad ties[e]		86.0	16.8	728.0	62.4	642.0	45.6
Total		44,487.8	9,536.6	5,738.3	2,202.7	(38,749.5)	(7,333.9)
Veneer:	Thousand square meters						
Softwoods[e]		326,309.0	237.3	54,838.0	69.1	(271,471.0)	(168.2)
Hardwoods[e,f]		207,351.0	337.7	327,774.0	441.1	120,423.0	103.4
Total		533,660.0	575.0	382,612.0	510.2	(151,048.0)	(64.9)
Plywood:[e]	Thousand cubic meters						
Softwoods	3/8" thickness	2,371.0	639.1	341.0	113.1	(2,030.0)	(526.0)
Hardwoods	3/8" thickness	3,227.0	1,225.0	162.0	52.7	(3,065.0)	(1,172.4)
Total		5,598.0	1,864.2	503.0	165.8	(5,095.0)	(1,698.4)
Particleboard[e]	Thousand cubic meters 3/4" thickness	1,285.0	241.6	100.0	24.8	(1,185.0)	(216.8)
Med. Dens. Fiberboard[e]	Thousand cubic meters 3/4" thickness	1,509.9	420.4	252.0	76.9	(1,257.9)	(343.6)
OSB/Waferboard[e]	Thousand cubic meters 3/8" thickness	9,342.0	2,703.7	150.0	36.4	(9,192.0)	(2,667.3)
Hardboard[e]	Thousand cubic meters 1/8" thickness	1,412.0	851.6	317.0	96.3	(1,095.0)	(755.4)
Pulpwood:	Thousand cubic meters						
Round[e,f]		50.5	9.0	143.2	70.8	92.8	61.8
Chips[f]		119.5	35.5	353.2	191.8	233.7	156.3
Total		170.0	44.5	496.4	262.6	326.4	218.2
Wood pulp[f]	Thousand metric tons	6,134.5	2,970.0	5,817.8	3,197.9	(316.7)	227.9
Paper and board:[f,g]	Thousand metric tons						
Newsprint		5,375.3	3,074.0	654.2	382.5	(4,721.2)	(2,691.4)
Printing & Writing Paper		8,193.7	6,366.4	1,663.2	1,798.7	(6,530.5)	(4,567.6)
Paperboard		1,780.8	1,128.7	6,107.0	3,615.2	4,326.3	2,486.5
Other paper & board[h]		1,383.3	1,913.2	1,185.2	1,501.9	(198.0)	(411.3)
Converted products		1,803.8	4,562.7	2,575.2	4,473.9	771.4	(88.8)
Total		18,536.8	17,044.9	12,184.9	11,772.2	(6,351.9)	(5,272.7)
Recovered Paper[f]	Thousand metric tons	494.9	67.7	14,523.7	1,715.2	14,028.9	1,647.4
Other wood products[i]			7,313.2		1,227.6		(6,085.6)
Total all products[j,e,k]			43,914.3		22,727.7		(21,186.6)

[a]Imports for consumption.

[b]Customs value, which is generally defined as the price actually paid or payable for merchandise when sold for exportation to the U.S., excluding U.S. import duties, freight, insurance, and other charges.

[c]Value (free alongside ship) at U.S. ports of export, based on the transaction price, including inland freight, insurance, and other charges.

[d]Negative amounts, given in parentheses, indicate imports exceed exports.

[e]U.S. International Trade Commission (80).

[f]American Forest & Paper Association (3,4,5).

[g]Includes wet machine board and converted paper and paperboard products.

[h]Includes tissue, packaging and industrial papers, wet machine board and construction paper & board

[i]Includes poles and piling, fuelwood, wood charcoal, cork, wood containers wood doors, and other miscellaneous products. Does not include wood furniture nor printed material.

[j]Includes Pulpwood Logs.

[k]Data may not add to totals because of rounding.

Table 14—Value of imports and exports of all commodities[a] and timber products,[b] 1965–2005

Year	Imports[c] All commodities		Timber products Total		Proportion[e]	Exports[d] All commodities		Timber products Total		Proportion[e]
	Million current dollars	Million 1997 dollars[f]	Million current dollars	Million 1997 dollars	Percent	Million current dollars	Million 1997 dollars	Million current dollars	Million 1997 dollars	Percent
1965	21,285	84,086	1,977	7,810	9.3	27,135	107,196	917	3,623	3.4
1966	25,360	97,175	2,165	8,296	8.5	29,884	114,510	1,024	3,924	3.4
1967	26,733	102,130	2,087	7,973	7.8	31,142	118,974	1,150	4,393	3.7
1968	32,970	123,011	2,446	9,126	7.4	33,953	126,678	1,362	5,082	4.0
1969	35,863	128,543	2,734	9,799	7.6	37,462	134,274	1,509	5,409	4.0
1970	39,756	137,476	2,546	8,804	6.4	42,590	147,276	1,816	6,280	4.3
1971	45,516	152,437	2,937	9,836	6.5	43,492	145,658	1,692	5,667	3.9
1972	55,290	177,261	3,632	11,644	6.6	48,887	156,733	2,038	6,534	4.2
1973	69,024	195,721	4,468	12,669	6.5	70,246	199,186	3,006	8,524	4.3
1974	100,140	238,839	4,778	11,396	4.8	97,144	231,693	4,165	9,934	4.3
1975	96,477	210,796	4,141	9,048	4.3	106,102	231,826	4,088	8,932	3.9
1976	121,121	252,947	5,590	11,674	4.6	113,319	236,653	4,695	9,805	4.1
1977	147,976	290,936	6,720	13,212	4.5	117,926	231,855	4,664	9,170	4.0
1978	172,912	315,645	8,028	14,655	4.6	141,126	257,621	4,963	9,060	3.5
1979	205,850	333,754	9,181	14,886	4.5	178,591	289,558	6,854	11,113	3.8
1980	239,943	340,944	8,648	12,288	3.6	216,592	307,763	8,516	12,101	3.9
1981	259,012	337,244	9,042	11,773	3.5	228,961	298,117	7,925	10,319	3.5
1982	242,340	309,226	8,382	10,695	3.5	207,158	264,334	7,151	9,125	3.5
1983	256,680	323,321	10,067	12,681	3.9	195,969	246,847	7,044	8,873	3.6
1984	322,949	397,380	12,235	15,055	3.8	212,056	260,929	7,210	8,872	3.4
1985	343,067	424,180	12,539	15,504	3.7	206,926	255,850	6,699	8,283	3.2
1986	368,251	468,950	13,271	16,900	3.6	206,628	263,131	7,692	9,795	3.7
1987	402,084	499,085	15,268	18,951	3.8	244,417	303,381	9,940	12,338	4.1
1988	437,475	522,187	16,749	19,992	3.8	310,333	370,426	12,782	15,257	4.1
1989	477,400	542,925	19,106	21,728	4.0	362,100	411,800	17,224	19,588	4.8
1990	498,300	546,716	18,806	20,633	3.8	389,300	427,125	18,542	20,344	4.8
1991	491,000	537,782	17,100	18,729	3.5	416,900	456,622	19,500	21,358	4.7
1992	536,500	584,108	18,700	20,359	3.5	440,400	479,480	20,700	22,537	4.7
1993	589,400	632,527	18,874	20,255	3.2	456,800	490,224	16,889	18,125	3.7
1994	668,600	708,583	17,117	18,141	2.6	502,400	532,444	15,320	16,236	3.0
1995	749,600	767,033	19,023	19,465	2.5	575,800	589,191	17,582	17,991	3.1
1996	803,300	802,671	21,264	21,247	2.6	612,000	611,521	18,315	18,301	3.0
1997	877,300	877,300	27,375	27,375	3.1	679,300	679,300	21,386	21,386	3.1
1998	918,800	942,435	28,684	29,422	3.1	670,600	687,850	19,261	19,757	2.9
1999	1,030,400	1,047,642	32,263	32,803	3.1	683,200	694,632	19,483	19,809	2.9
2000	1,224,400	1,177,343	34,300	32,982	2.8	772,000	742,330	21,760	20,924	2.8
2001	1,145,900	1,089,544	32,250	30,664	2.8	718,800	683,449	18,931	18,000	2.6
2002	1,166,900	1,135,747	32,348	31,484	2.8	682,600	664,377	18,739	18,238	2.7
2003	1,260,700	1,164,847	33,644	31,086	2.7	713,400	659,159	19,230	17,768	2.7
2004	1,472,900	1,281,132	42,042	36,568	2.9	807,500	702,365	21,136	18,384	2.6
2005	1,674,300	1,357,311	43,914	35,600	2.6	892,600	723,607	22,728	18,425	2.5

[a] U.S. Council of Economic Advisors (39).

[b] U.S. International Trade Commission (80).

[c] Imports for consumption. Customs value, which is generally defined as the price actually paid or payable for merchandise. when sold for exportation to the United States, excluding U.S. import duties, freight, insurance, and other charges.

[d] Value (free alongside ship) at U.S. ports of export, based on the transaction price, including inland freight, insurance, and other charges.

[e] Timber products as a percentage of all commodities.

[f] Converted to 1997 dollars by dividing current dollars by the implicit deflators for gross domestic product for imports and exports.

Table 15—Foreign exchange rates by selected country and year, 1975–2005[a]

Country	Currency	Foreign currency units per U.S. dollar																	
		2005	2004	2003	2002	2001	2000	1999	1998	1997	1996	1995	1994	1993	1990	1985	1980	1975
North America																		
Canada	Dollar	1.2115	1.3017	1.4008	1.5704	1.5487	1.4855	1.4858	1.4836	1.3849	1.3638	1.3725	1.3664	1.2902	1.1668	1.3658	1.1693	1.0173
Asia																		
China, PR	Yuan	8.1936	8.2768	8.277	8.277	8.277	8.2784	8.2781	8.3008	8.3193	8.3389	8.37	8.6404	5.7795	4.7921	2.9434	z	z
Hong Kong	Dollar	7.7775	7.7891	7.7875	7.7997	7.7997	7.7924	7.7594	7.7467	7.7431	7.7345	7.7357	7.729	7.7357	7.7899	7.7911	z	z
India	Rupee	44	45.26	46.59	48.63	47.22	45.00	43.13	41.36	36.365	35.506	32.418	31.394	31.291	17.492	12.332	7.8866	8.3854
Japan	Yen	110.11	108.15	115.94	125.22	121.57	107.8	113.73	130.99	121.06	108.78	93.96	102.18	111.08	145	238.47	226.63	296.69
Malaysia	Ringgit	3.7869	3.8	3.8000	3.8000	3.8000	3.8000	3.8000	3.9254	2.8173	2.5154	2.5073	2.6237	2.5738	2.7057	2.4806	2.1767	2.395
Singapore	Dollar	1.6639	1.6902	1.743	1.791	1.793	1.7250	1.6951	1.6722	1.4857	1.41	1.4171	1.5275	1.6158	1.8134	2.2008	z	z
South Korea	Won	1023.75	1145.24	1192.08	1250.31	1292.01	1,130.90	1,189.84	950.77	950.77	805	772.69	806.93	805.75	710.64	861.89	z	z
Sri Lanka	Rupee	100.383	101.268	96.541	95.773	89.602	76.964	70.868	59.026	59.026	55.289	51.047	49.17	48.211	40.078	27.187	16.167	6.95
Taiwan	Dollar	32.131	33.372	34.405	34.536	33.824	31.260	32.322	33.547	28.775	27.468	26.495	26.465	26.416	26.918	39.889	z	z
Thailand	Baht	40.252	40.271	41.556	43.019	44.532	40.210	37.887	41.262	31.072	25.359	24.921	25.161	25.333	25.609	27.193	z	z
Africa																		
South Africa	Rand	6.3606	6.4402	7.5550	10.5176	8.6093	6.9468	6.1191	5.5417	4.6072	4.3011	3.6284	3.5526	3.2729	2.5885	2.2343	0.778	0.7328
Europe																		
Austria	Schilling	17.130	17.115	15.578	13.009	12.318	12.704	14.659	12.379	12.206	10.589	10.076	11.409	11.639	11.331	20.676	12.945	17.401
Belgium	Franc	50.219	50.175	45.669	38.137	36.112	37.242	42.974	36.31	35.807	30.968	29.472	33.426	34.581	33.424	59.336	29.237	36.694
Denmark	Krone	5.9953	5.9891	6.5774	7.8862	8.3323	8.0953	6.9900	6.703	6.6092	5.8003	5.5999	6.3561	6.4863	6.1899	10.598	5.6345	5.7351
European Union	Euro	1.2449	1.2438	1.1321	0.9454	0.8952	0.9232	1.0653	z	z	z	z	z	z	z	z	z	z
Finland	Markka	7.4018	7.3953	6.7312	5.6211	5.3226	5.4891	6.3340	5.3473	5.1956	4.5948	4.3763	5.234	5.7251	3.83	6.1971	3.7206	3.6651
France	Franc	8.1660	8.1588	7.4261	6.2014	5.8721	6.0558	6.9879	5.8995	5.8393	5.1158	4.9864	5.5459	5.6669	5.4467	8.9799	4.225	4.2819
Germany	Deutsche mark	2.4348	2.4327	2.2142	1.8490	1.7509	1.8056	2.0835	1.7597	1.7348	1.5049	1.4321	1.6216	1.6545	1.6166	2.9419	1.8175	2.4553
Greece	Drachma	z	z	z	z	z	365.92	306.30	295.7	273.28	240.82	231.68	242.5	229.64	158.59	138.4	z	z
Ireland	Pound[b]	0.9804	0.9796	0.8916	0.7446	0.7050	0.7271	0.8390	142.48	151.63	159.95	160.35	149.69	146.47	165.76	106.62	205.77	222.16
Italy	Lira	2,410.46	2,408.33	2,192.05	1,830.55	1,733.35	1,787.56	2,062.71	1736.85	1703.81	1542.76	1629.5	1,611.49	1,573.41	1,198.27	######	856.2	652.4
Netherlands	Guilder	2.7434	2.7410	2.4948	2.0834	1.9728	2.0345	2.3476	1.9837	1.9525	1.6863	1.6044	1.819	1.8585	1.8215	3.3184	1.9875	2.5232
Norway	Krone	6.4412	6.7399	7.0803	7.9839	8.9964	8.8131	7.8017	7.5521	7.0857	6.4594	6.3355	7.0553	7.1009	6.2541	8.5933	4.9381	5.2137
Portugal	Escudo	249.58	249.36	226.97	189.54	179.47	185.08	213.57	180.25	175.44	154.28	149.88	165.93	161.08	142.7	172.07	50.082	25.454
Spain	Peseta	207.13	206.95	188.37	157.30	148.95	153.61	177.25	149.41	146.53	124.64	126.68	133.88	127.48	101.96	169.98	71.758	57.393
Sweden	Krona	7.471	7.348	8.0787	9.7233	10.3425	9.1735	8.2740	7.9522	7.6446	6.7082	7.1406	7.7161	7.7956	5.9231	8.6031	4.2309	4.1424
Switzerland	Franc	1.2459	1.2428	1.3450	1.5567	1.6891	1.6904	1.5045	1.4506	1.4514	1.2361	1.1812	1.3667	1.4781	1.3901	2.4551	1.6772	2.5811
United Kingdom	Pound[b]	182.04	183.3	163.47	150.25	143.96	151.56	161.72	165.73	163.76	156.07	157.85	153.19	150.16	178.41	129.74	232.58	222.16
Other																		
Australia	Dollar[b]	76.27	73.65	65.24	54.37	51.69	58.15	64.54	62.91	74.368	78.283	74.073	73.161	67.993	78.069	70.026	114	130.77
New Zealand	Dollar[b]	70.49	66.43	58.22	46.45	42.02	45.68	52.94	53.61	66.247	68.765	65.625	59.358	54.127	59.619	49.752	97.34	121.16
Index																		
United States	Dollar[c,d]	83.78	85.37	93	103.09	104.32	98.32	94.07	98.85	96.38	87.34	84.25	91.32	93.18	89.09	143.01	87.39	98.5

[a] U.S. Federal Reserve System, Board of Governors (77).

[b] Value in U.S. cents.

[c] Index of weighted-average exchange value of U.S. dollar against the currencies of ten industrial countries. The weight for each of the ten countries is the 1972–1976 average world trade of that country divided by the average world trade of all ten countries combined. Series revised as of August 1978.

[d] Data prior to 1999 was reported using the G-10 index. Data for 1999 and later is reported using the major currency scale.

z Not available.

Table 16—Log imports by major species, 1965–2005 (cubic meters)[a,b]

			Hardwoods				
Year	Total	Softwoods[c]	Total	Mahogany	Philippine mahogany or lauan	Birch and maple	Other
1965	308,493	61,155	247,338	57,984	49,830	28,086	111,438
1966	433,068	192,525	240,543	72,933	12,684	28,539	126,387
1967	348,810	153,567	195,243	47,565	20,838	29,898	96,942
1968	357,870	149,943	207,927	38,505	8,607	29,445	131,370
1969	371,007	188,901	182,106	29,445	14,043	34,428	104,190
1970	654,132	482,445	171,687	30,804	3,171	37,146	100,566
1971	380,520	252,321	128,199	14,949	906	39,411	72,933
1972	178,029	51,189	126,840	16,308	3,171	35,787	71,574
1973	151,755	38,505	113,250	9,513	14,496	41,676	47,565
1974	346,998	206,568	140,430	15,402	4,077	55,719	65,232
1975	387,315	310,305	77,010	7,248	1,359	32,616	35,787
1976	369,648	305,322	64,326	5,436	2,718	39,411	16,761
1977	699,885	631,935	67,950	10,872	2,265	40,317	14,496
1978	438,957	358,323	80,634	6,795	[d]	41,223	32,616
1979	602,490	536,352	66,138	4,983	1,359	38,052	21,744
1980	577,575	516,873	60,702	4,530	[d]	33,522	22,650
1981	457,983	396,828	61,155	2,718	[d]	39,411	19,026
1982	530,463	447,564	82,899	3,624	[d]	46,206	33,069
1983	747,450	645,344	102,106	1,359	1,359	23,103	76,285
1984	665,548	529,195	136,353	2,265	1,359	19,932	112,797
1985	449,557	320,905	128,652	1,359	1,359	13,137	112,797
1986	355,832	236,194	119,637	5,889	7,248	13,590	92,910
1987	373,725	311,030	62,695	1,359	1,359	17,214	42,763
1988	308,538	253,272	55,266	7,701	[d]	17,214	30,351
1989	178,210	94,858	83,352	3,624	453	30,351	48,924
1990	104,688	58,301	46,387	4,983	[d]	16,761	24,643
1991	61,653	34,473	27,180	4,077	[d]	11,778	11,325
1992	196,647	166,749	29,898	3,171	453	19,932	6,342
1993	425,276	388,130	37,146	4,983	[d]	17,667	14,496
1994	499,931	427,360	72,571	5,889	[d]	28,539	38,143
1995	364,111	246,963	117,148	7,248	1,359	29,746	78,795
1996	521,009	378,574	142,435	7,701	1,359	53,303	80,072
1997	577,912	381,000	196,912	10,419	1,359	36,572	148,562
1998	839,334	665,599	173,735	10,419	1,359	39,516	122,441
1999	1,333,038	1,151,979	181,059	10,419	1,359	45,628	123,653
2000	2,036,683	1,768,635	268,048	10,419	1,359	42,671	213,599
2001	2,078,600	1,807,473	271,127	10,419	1,359	34,598	224,751
2002	2,431,352	2,110,926	320,426	10,419	1,359	57,202	251,446
2003	2,253,254	1,951,567	301,687	10,419	1,359	24,081	265,828
2004	2,054,482	1,760,982	293,500	10,419	1,359	32,851	248,871
2005	3,217,000	2,789,000	428,000	10,419	1,359	52,000	364,222

[a]U.S. Department of Commerce, Bureau of the Census (67);
U.S. International Trade Commission (80);
American Forest & Paper Association (4).
Data may not add to totals because of rounding.
[b]Prior to 2000, pulpwood logs are not included in logs.
[c]Western Wood Products Association 1965-1999(82); U.S. International Trade
Commission 2000-present(80).
[d]Fewer than 50,000 board feet.

Table 17—Log imports by major region of origin, 1965–2005 (million board feet, log scale)[a,b]

Year	Total	Canada[c]	Mexico and Central America[d]	South America	Africa	Asia	Other[e]
1965	68.1	20.3	3.4	18.0	14.1	11.7	0.6
1966	95.6	49.4	3.7	21.3	17.4	3.6	0.2
1967	77.0	40.6	3.0	18.3	9.7	4.9	0.5
1968	79.0	39.9	3.1	26.8	6.8	2.1	0.3
1969	81.9	49.5	2.1	18.3	8.3	3.5	0.2
1970	144.4	114.9	2.3	17.6	8.3	1.0	0.3
1971	84.0	64.6	2.2	13.1	3.2	0.9	f
1972	39.3	17.3	2.6	13.9	3.8	1.4	0.3
1973	33.5	17.8	3.0	2.9	4.8	4.8	0.2
1974	76.6	57.0	z	1.3	4.0	9.1	5.2
1975	85.5	80.3	0.3	z	1.4	0.1	3.4
1976	81.6	78.0	z	z	1.3	0.7	1.6
1977	154.5	150.5	z	z	2.5	0.6	0.9
1978	96.9	85.9	0.4	5.5	4.1	0.5	0.5
1979	133.0	111.2	0.2	17.4	1.5	1.1	1.6
1980	127.5	121.4	0.2	f	1.3	0.2	4.4
1981	101.1	94.4	0.4	f	0.7	0.6	5.0
1982	117.1	115.4	0.2	0.1	0.9	0.4	0.1
1983	165.0	161.5	1.0	0.1	0.3	1.7	0.4
1984	146.9	143.1	0.2	0.1	0.7	1.8	1.0
1985	99.2	81.1	0.1	0.5	3.2	13.9	0.4
1986	78.6	61.1	0.1	0.2	1.2	5.4	10.6
1987	82.5	75.6	0.2	0.2	0.3	2.1	4.1
1988	68.1	62.6	0.4	0.2	1.4	2.6	0.9
1989	39.3	20.0	2.3	0.7	2.1	8.1	6.1
1990	23.1	19.3	0.6	0.5	0.5	1.6	0.6
1991	13.6	9.0	0.4	0.2	0.3	1.1	2.6
1992	43.4	40.7	0.8	0.2	0.6	0.6	0.5
1993	93.9	89.3	f	0.2	0.4	0.6	3.4
1994	110.4	85.0	1.2	0.6	0.6	0.7	22.3
1995	80.4	56.3	1.5	0.6	0.6	0.1	21.3
1996	115.0	94.6	2.1	0.8	0.1	0.1	17.3
1997	127.6	105.7	1.7	1.2	0.1	0.1	18.8
1998	185.3	168.4	0.5	1.2	0.1	0.2	14.9
1999[r]	294.3	280.3	0.6	1.8	0.3	1.3	9.9
2000	449.6	426.2	0.5	4.6	2.6	0.3	15.4
2001	458.9	445.0	0.7	3.9	0.2	0.8	8.2
2002	536.7	521.4	4.2	3.1	0.2	0.2	7.5
2003	497.4	486.7	0.9	3.8	0.1	0.8	5.2
2004	453.5	446.8	0.5	2.0	0.3	0.5	3.4
2005	710.2	605.0	0.9	3.5	0.2	1.5	99.0

[a]U.S. Department of Agriculture, Forest Service (41); U.S. International Trade Commission (80); Western Wood Products Association (82). Data may not add to totals because of rounding.
[b]Prior to 2000, pulpwood logs are not included in logs.
[c]American Forest & Paper Association 1965-1999 (2); U.S. International Trade Commission (80)
[d]Includes the West Indies.
[e]For the years 1974–1977, all imports with a value of less than $500 are included in Other.
[f]Fewer than 50,000 board feet.
[z]Not Available.
[r]Revised

44

Table 18—Log exports by major species, 1965–2005 (cubic meters, Scribner log scale)[d]

Year	Total	Softwoods Total[a]	Douglas-fir[b]	Port-Orford-cedar[b]	Western hemlock[b]	Other	Hardwoods Total[a]	Walnut[b]	Other
1965	5,413,350	5,044,608	504,189	177,123	[c]	4,363,296	368,742	106,908	261,834
1966	6,302,136	5,960,121	591,165	186,636	[c]	5,182,320	342,015	56,625	285,390
1967	8,933,613	8,494,203	1,220,835	156,738	[c]	7,116,630	439,410	72,933	366,477
1968	11,633,493	11,203,596	1,796,145	173,952	[c]	9,233,499	429,897	98,754	331,143
1969	10,856,145	10,492,839	1,724,118	184,371	[c]	8,584,350	363,306	93,318	269,988
1970	12,416,277	12,104,160	2,206,110	245,073	6,508,251	3,144,726	312,117	78,822	233,295
1971	10,368,264	10,100,994	2,013,585	182,106	5,503,044	2,402,259	267,270	58,437	208,833
1972	14,230,542	13,805,175	3,472,245	208,833	6,571,671	3,552,426	425,367	70,215	355,152
1973	15,248,433	14,732,466	4,407,690	134,541	6,654,570	3,535,665	515,967	71,121	444,846
1974	11,970,072	11,432,361	3,409,731	161,268	5,638,038	2,223,324	537,711	35,334	502,377
1975	12,081,057	11,780,718	3,716,412	175,311	5,297,835	2,591,160	300,339	38,505	261,834
1976	14,722,500	14,295,321	4,631,472	173,952	6,186,621	3,303,276	427,179	33,522	393,657
1977	13,905,741	13,499,400	4,562,616	93,771	5,919,804	2,923,209	406,341	34,428	371,913
1978	15,443,807	14,941,942	5,400,748	132,240	6,539,657	2,869,297	501,865	40,023	461,842
1979	17,653,505	17,070,163	6,120,229	111,320	7,219,284	3,619,330	583,342	30,845	552,497
1980	14,771,936	14,084,259	5,764,040	63,384	5,359,583	2,897,252	687,677	42,790	644,887
1981	11,480,034	10,768,258	4,651,907	76,562	3,929,671	2,110,118	711,776	34,681	677,095
1982	14,532,915	14,110,896	6,552,432	56,009	5,096,001	2,406,454	422,019	21,477	400,542
1983	15,864,631	15,359,500	7,322,097	42,876	5,198,143	2,796,384	505,131	21,055	484,076
1984	15,832,011	15,263,251	7,196,064	58,768	5,073,441	2,934,978	568,760	25,101	543,659
1985	17,409,547	16,905,829	8,088,510	67,216	5,910,092	2,840,011	503,718	25,078	478,640
1986	16,560,027	15,927,331	7,364,856	60,634	5,645,612	2,856,229	632,696	25,522	607,174
1987	18,614,694	17,938,374	8,447,612	57,603	6,275,463	3,157,696	676,320	28,294	648,026
1988	21,735,380	20,812,537	10,469,727	89,649	6,502,774	3,750,387	922,843	36,272	886,571
1989	21,318,404	20,351,989	9,350,773	62,613	7,301,367	3,637,236	966,415	62,105	904,310
1990	19,085,282	18,091,013	8,569,609	50,016	5,407,488	4,063,900	994,269	61,419	932,850
1991	17,037,272	15,753,913	7,287,197	42,000	4,751,809	3,672,907	1,283,359	52,699	1,230,660
1992	14,853,177	13,838,454	6,355,299	46,603	4,033,243	3,403,309	1,014,723	56,088	958,635
1993	13,029,867	11,955,773	5,375,330	18,958	3,051,000	3,510,485	1,074,094	42,653	1,031,441
1994	12,156,559	10,961,351	5,322,522	18,616	2,424,749	3,195,464	1,195,208	50,842	1,144,366
1995	12,774,600	11,561,013	5,110,746	10,419	2,992,971	3,446,877	1,213,587	34,428	1,179,159
1996	11,939,721	10,792,272	5,503,044	10,419	2,202,486	3,076,323	1,147,449	27,633	1,119,816
1997	10,862,940	9,413,340	3,661,599	13,137	1,900,335	3,838,269	1,449,600	28,992	1,420,608
1998	8,959,268	7,457,408	3,316,460	3,344	793,227	3,344,377	1,501,860	33,119	1,468,741
1999	9,233,046	7,542,903	3,047,148	4,829	1,006,688	3,484,238	1,690,143	36,184	1,653,959
2000	11,951,675	9,358,160	3,053,550	3,851	843,212	5,457,547	2,593,515	51,491	2,542,024
2001	11,411,898	8,702,102	2,515,403	1,673	703,513	5,481,513	2,709,796	59,203	2,650,593
2002	11,001,033	7,904,525	2,423,384	3,068	550,953	4,927,120	3,096,508	80,585	3,015,923
2003	10,076,496	7,414,695	2,245,153	3,961	560,022	4,605,559	2,661,801	86,987	2,574,814
2004	10,357,741	7,237,211	2,461,102	1,024	414,435	4,360,650	3,120,530	101,806	3,018,724
2005	9,772,000	7,279,000	2,157,000	2,000	348,000	4,772,000	2,493,000	112,000	2,381,000

[a]Prior to 2000, pulpwood logs are not included in logs.
[b]American Forest & Paper Association 1965-1999 (4); U.S. International Trade Commission 2000-present (80).
[c]U.S. International Trade Commission (80).
[d]Western hemlock is included in Other.
Data may not add to totals because of rounding.

Table 19—Log exports by major region of destination, 1965–2005 (million board feet, Scribner log scale)[a,b]

Year	Total	Canada	European Union[c]	Japan	South Korea	China	Other
1965	1,195.0	355.1	29.4	804.4	2.8	[d]	3.3
1966	1,391.2	266.1	17.2	1,081.4	25.2	[d]	1.3
1967	1,972.1	335.5	20.5	1,585.5	29.9	[d]	0.7
1968	2,568.1	341.8	28.7	2,119.2	75.1	[d]	3.3
1969	2,396.5	324.6	29.6	2,007.3	32.2	[d]	2.8
1970	2,740.9	291.8	23.1	2,366.1	48.2	[d]	11.7
1971	2,288.8	339.9	20.5	1,847.1	73.9	[d]	7.4
1972	3,141.4	519.1	31.9	2,528.0	53.8	[d]	8.6
1973	3,366.1	417.8	41.5	2,779.5	113.7	[d]	13.6
1974	2,642.4	332.3	39.1	2,114.2	149.2	[d]	7.6
1975	2,666.9	277.6	35.3	2,256.4	86.4	[d]	11.2
1976	3,250.0	362.5	48.6	2,675.1	150.5	[d]	13.3
1977	3,069.7	350.0	46.0	2,460.1	203.3	[d]	10.3
1978	3,409.2	368.5	57.5	2,646.1	321.8	[d]	15.3
1979	3,897.0	407.6	65.4	3,149.1	258.9	[d]	16.0
1980	3,260.9	317.8	90.4	2,544.2	201.7	87.8	19.0
1981	2,534.2	247.4	56.1	1,774.2	151.6	222.4	82.5
1982	3,208.1	302.5	47.8	1,978.7	277.7	547.0	54.4
1983	3,502.1	347.1	57.4	2,028.0	320.9	723.2	25.6
1984	3,494.9	421.2	52.6	1,759.8	289.1	866.6	105.7
1985	3,843.2	445.4	39.1	1,899.1	327.5	1069.0	63.1
1986	3,655.6	450.0	76.7	2,089.4	364.5	615.4	59.6
1987	4,109.2	421.4	62.6	2,397.2	492.5	579.3	156.3
1988	4,798.1	378.9	78.8	2,415.6	612.0	1121.4	191.4
1989	4,706.0	272.7	93.6	2,992.7	761.5	454.3	131.2
1990	4,213.1	395.8	69.2	2,626.2	619.2	361.9	140.8
1991	3,761.0	423.6	53.4	2,126.8	624.7	371.8	160.8
1992	3,278.8	415.0	44.2	2,043.0	416.6	236.9	123.1
1993	2,876.4	389.9	41.1	1,881.9	303.1	131.3	129.1
1994	2,683.6	435.1	56.8	1,821.6	206.1	75.0	89.0
1995	2,820.0	715.7	47.5	1,728.3	235.2	20.2	73.1
1996	2,635.7	518.0	32.1	1,807.5	200.3	15.9	61.9
1997	2,398.0	711.0	42.1	1,347.7	205.6	18.2	73.4
1998	1,977.8	778.5	47.1	1,004.0	61.9	17.8	68.5
1999	2,038.2	787.8	48.2	998.3	130.1	7.8	66.1
2000	2,638.3	1,349.6	117.7	934.1	137.3	21.5	78.2
2001	2,519.2	1,453.9	78.0	745.7	129.6	29.5	82.5
2002	2,428.5	1,362.2	58.1	676.0	136.8	45.0	150.4
2003	2,224.4	1,194.6	75.5	649.7	168.7	40.0	95.8
2004	2,286.5	1,110.3	72.6	642.2	157.2	74.4	229.8
2005	2,157.2	1,168.0	54.3	573.5	174.6	93.8	92.9

[a]U.S. International Trade Commission (80). Data may not add to totals because of rounding
[b]Prior to 2000, pulpwood logs are not included in logs.
[c]European Union includes Austria, Belguim–Luxembourg, Denmark, Finland, France, Germany, Greece, Ireland, Italy, the Netherlands, Portugal, Spain, Sweden, and UK.
[d]Fewer than 50,000 board feet.

Table 20—Average stumpage prices for sawtimber sold from national forests, by selected species, 1965–2005 (dollars per thousand board feet)[a]

Year	Softwoods								Hardwoods					
	Douglas-fir[b]		Southern pine[c]		Ponderosa pine[d]		Western hemlock[e]		All eastern hardwoods[f]		Oak white, red, and black		Sugar maple[g]	
	Current dollars	1997 dollars	Current dollars	1997 dollars	Current dollars	1997 dollars	Current dollars	1997 dollars	Current dollars	1997 dollars	Current dollars	1997 dollars	Current dollars	1997 dollars
1965	42.6	168.3	31.7	125.2	19.8	78.2	19.1	75.5	25.0	98.8	21.3	84.1	z	z
1966	50.0	191.6	38.6	147.9	19.8	75.9	20.5	78.6	29.3	112.3	23.2	88.9	z	z
1967	41.7	159.3	38.3	146.3	22.2	84.8	21.8	83.3	27.0	103.1	16.8	64.2	z	z
1968	61.2	228.3	42.2	157.4	30.2	112.7	35.6	132.8	23.6	88.1	17.3	64.5	z	z
1969	82.2	294.6	51.7	185.3	71.0	254.5	45.1	161.7	30.2	108.2	28.2	101.1	z	z
1970	41.9	144.9	44.1	152.5	32.1	111.0	20.5	70.9	26.9	93.0	26.6	92.0	z	z
1971	49.0	164.1	52.2	174.8	37.6	125.9	20.6	69.0	24.6	82.4	21.2	71.0	z	z
1972	71.7	229.9	65.6	210.3	65.8	211.0	49.0	157.1	34.3	110.0	26.6	85.3	z	z
1973	138.1	391.6	93.4	264.8	92.3	261.7	99.2	281.3	46.0	130.4	43.6	123.6	93.6	265.4
1974	202.4	482.7	76.2	181.7	100.6	239.9	110.8	264.3	45.9	109.5	54.7	130.5	75.9	181.0
1975	169.5	370.3	57.0	124.5	71.2	155.6	68.8	150.3	33.9	74.1	29.7	64.9	42.1	92.0
1976	176.2	368.0	87.0	181.7	101.8	212.6	79.7	166.4	34.9	72.9	43.4	90.6	27.7	57.8
1977	225.9	444.1	100.3	197.2	131.4	258.3	89.3	175.6	37.9	74.5	60.0	118.0	47.4	93.2
1978	250.3	456.9	134.5	245.5	164.7	300.7	113.6	207.4	41.1	75.0	59.2	108.1	60.5	110.4
1979	394.4	639.5	155.2	251.6	239.0	387.5	200.8	325.6	46.8	75.9	68.8	111.5	68.9	111.7
1980	432.2	614.1	155.4	220.8	206.1	292.9	212.7	302.2	52.4	74.5	65.6	93.2	70.1	99.6
1981	350.2	456.0	172.0	224.0	195.2	254.2	163.4	212.8	50.9	66.3	63.2	82.3	67.8	88.3
1982	118.2	150.8	127.2	162.3	66.9	85.4	44.5	56.8	56.4	72.0	70.8	90.3	71.1	90.7
1983	161.6	203.6	140.6	177.1	104.0	131.0	62.2	78.3	60.1	75.7	87.9	110.7	55.1	69.4
1984	132.9	163.5	139.4	171.5	122.7	151.0	61.8	76.0	90.1	110.9	145.0	178.4	80.5	99.1
1985	126.2	156.0	90.7	112.1	101.4	125.4	50.5	62.4	65.4	80.9	94.5	116.8	70.0	86.6
1986	160.7	204.6	103.6	131.9	156.6	199.4	74.7	95.1	69.9	89.0	108.1	137.7	66.2	84.3
1987	190.2	236.1	135.7	168.4	209.3	259.8	105.4	130.8	88.1	109.4	146.8	182.2	80.5	99.9
1988	256.0	305.6	141.9	169.4	182.1	217.4	162.9	194.4	151.3	180.6	146.3	174.6	108.4	129.4
1989	389.8	443.3	313.4	356.4	292.0	332.1	223.3	253.9	135.8	154.4	178.9	203.5	128.6	146.3
1990	466.4	511.7	126.7	139.0	252.2	276.7	203.0	222.7	146.1	160.3	188.3	206.6	135.3	148.4
1991	395.0	432.6	166.1	181.9	237.6	260.2	164.1	179.7	160.1	175.4	163.6	179.2	120.7	132.2
1992	477.2	519.5	198.4	216.0	292.3	318.2	164.6	179.2	166.6	181.4	211.2	229.9	144.6	157.4
1993	317.8	341.1	217.2	233.1	535.2	574.4	363.7	390.3	264.1	283.4	194.6	208.8	219.5	235.6
1994	652.4	691.4	265.9	281.8	291.4	308.8	334.8	354.8	352.1	373.2	317.4	336.4	313.4	332.1
1995	453.5	464.1	248.5	254.3	149.9	153.4	297.1	304.0	313.9	321.2	296.6	303.5	285.6	292.2
1996	453.0	452.7	251.1	250.9	270.0	269.8	289.3	289.1	312.6	312.3	264.4	264.2	213.2	213.0
1997	331.4	331.4	307.3	307.3	270.2	270.2	211.3	211.3	286.9	286.9	264.5	264.5	357.1	357.1
1998	254.2	260.8	287.8	295.2	204.9	210.2	161.4	165.6	240.9	247.1	270.2	277.1	394.8	405.0
1999	314.7	319.9	268.5	273.0	181.0	184.1	95.7	97.3	195.1	198.4	317.4	322.7	448.1	455.6
2000	433.4	416.7	258.1	248.2	154.6	148.7	46.1	44.3	368.6	354.4	265.6	255.4	445.8	428.7
2001	255.4	242.8	153.5	145.9	115.5	109.8	34.0	32.3	530.5	504.4	326.4	310.3	587.2	558.3
2002	184.8	179.9	166.4	162.0	117.8	114.6	73.2	71.2	382.0	371.8	273.8	266.4	485.0	472.0
2003	193.2	178.5	163.6	151.2	111.2	102.7	86.0	79.5	284.8	263.2	303.7	280.6	560.2	517.6
2004	93.1	81.0	183.0	159.2	65.4	56.9	63.2	55.0	427.2	371.6	291.2	253.3	618.0	537.5
2005	320.5	259.8	192.8	156.3	103.3	83.8	70.1	56.8	415.1	336.5	329.2	266.9	648.0	525.3

[a] U.S. Department of Agriculture, Forest Service (42,47). Forest Service National Forest prices in this table are for timber sold on a Scribner Decimal C log rule basis, except in the Northeastern states where International 1/4-in. log rule is used. Prices include KV payments and exclude timber sold by land exchanges and from land utilization project lands. Data for the years 1965 to 1983 are statistical high bid prices. Data from 1984 to April 1999 are high bid prices that include specified road costs. After April 1999, it no longer included specific road costs. 1997 dollars derived by dividing the price in current dollars by the Bureau of Labor Statistics producer price index for all commodities (1997 = 100).

[b] Western Washington and western Oregon.

[c] Southern Region.

[d] Pacific Southwest Region (prior to January 1979 called the California Region); Includes Jeffrey pine.

[e] Pacific Northwest Region.

[f] Eastern and Southern Regions.

[g] Eastern Region.

[z] Not Available.

Table 21—Volume and value of sawtimber stumpage sold from national forests, by selected species and region, 2005[a]

Species and region[b]	Volume[c]	Value[d]	Average price per thousand board feet	Species and region	Volume	Value	Average price per thousand board feet
	Thousand board feet	Thousand dollars	Dollars		Thousand board feet	Thousand dollars	Dollars
SOFTWOODS, WESTERN				SOFTWOODS, WESTERN—Con.			
Cedar				Fir—Con.			
Alaska cedar:				True fir:			
Pacific Northwest[6]	2	0 5	217.46	Rocky Mountain[2]	3,308	243.2	73.52
Alaska[10]	5,520	193.6	35.08	Southwestern[3]	1,667	26.0	15.62
Total	5,522	194.1	35.15	Pacific Southwest[5]	71,724	7,835.5	109.24
Incense cedar:				Pacific Northwest[6]	136	16.6	121.90
Pacific Southwest[5]	19,750	3,663 0	185.47	Total	76,836	8,121.4	105.70
Pacific Northwest[6]	0	0 0	0.00	Hemlock			
Total	19,750	3,663 0	185.47	Mountain hemlock:			
Port-Orford-cedar:				Pacific Southwest[5]	0	0.0	0.00
Pacific Southwest[5]	6	0.1	22.34	Pacific Northwest[6]	346	1.7	4.81
Pacific Northwest[6]	0	0 0	0.00	Total	346	2	4.81
Total	6	0.1	22.34	Western hemlock:			
Western redcedar:				Northern[1]	84	8.7	102.96
Northern[1]	1,825	244 9	134.17	Pacific Northwest[6]	21,359	1,497.1	70.09
Pacific Northwest[6]	4,143	1,054.7	254.60	Alaska[10]	20,146	46.9	2.33
Alaska[10]	3,712	92.1	24.80	Total	41,590	1,552.7	37.33
Total	9,680	1,391.7	143.77	Western larch			
Douglas-fir				Northern[1]	18,862	1,727.2	91.57
East side:				Intermountain[4]	0	0.0	0.00
Northern[1]	85,878	13,038.7	151.83	Pacific Northwest[6]	68	19.4	284.29
Rocky Mountain[2]	1,452	65 2	44.92	Total	18,930	1,746.6	92.26
Southwestern[3]	4,388	64 3	14.66	Pine			
Intermountain[4]	18,766	2,189.6	116.68	Lodgepole pine:			
Pacific Northwest[6]	220,476	34,553 9	156.72	Northern[1]	26,739	4,354.6	162.86
Total	330,960	49,911 8	150.81	Rocky Mountain[2]	33,530	2,132.4	63.60
West side:				Intermountain[4]	3,511	442.7	126.08
Pacific Southwest[5]	24,679	4,749 9	192.47	Pacific Southwest[5]	481	39.9	82.90
Pacific Northwest[6]	4,235	1,357 3	320.51	Pacific Northwest[6]	11,903	1,248.4	104.88
Total	28,914	6,107 2	211.22	Total	76,164	8,217.9	107.90
Fir				Ponderosa pine[e]:			
Grand fir:				Northern[1]	8,297	1,405.4	169.38
Northern[1]	15,834	2,430 5	153.50	Rocky Mountain[2]	69,463	6,750.1	97.18
Intermountain[4]	10,847	1,027 0	94.68	Southwestern[3]	44,679	1,085.6	24.30
Pacific Northwest[6]	8,302	1,419.6	170.99	Intermountain[4]	6,181	721.7	116.76
Total	34,983	4,877.1	139.41	Pacific Southwest[5]	0	0.0	0.00
Noble fir:				Pacific Northwest[6]	82,535	6,192.1	75.02
Pacific Northwest[6]	0	0 0	0.00	Total	211,156	16,154.9	76.51
Shasta fir:				Sugar pine:			
Pacific Northwest[6]	0	0 0	0.00	Pacific Southwest[5]	17,673	2,098.5	118.74
Subalpine fir:				Pacific Northwest[6]	1,027	35.5	34.60
Northern[1]	6,921	509 9	73.68	Total	18,700	2,134.0	114.12
Rocky Mountain[2]	1	0.1	141.58	Western white pine:			
Southwestern[3]	223	0 5	2.10	Northern[1]	3,653	415.2	113.64
Intermountain[4]	2,185	214 5	98.16	Southwestern[3]	120	1.7	13.97
Pacific Northwest[6]	0	0 0	0.00	Pacific Southwest[5]	0	0.0	0.00
Total	9,330	725 0	77.71	Pacific Northwest[6]	24	4.9	206.34
White fir:				Total	3,796	421.7	111.08
Rocky Mountain[2]	0	0 0	0.00	Pine not specified			
Intermountain[4]	0	0 0	0.00	by species:			
Pacific Northwest[6]	48,911	2,736 2	55.94	Northern[1]	0	0.0	0.00
Total	48,911	2,736 2	55.94	Southwestern[3]	0	0.0	0.00
				Total	0	0.0	0.00
				Spruce			
				Black, red, and white spruce			
				Alaska[10]	19	0.1	5.32

Table 21—Volume and value of sawtimber stumpage sold from national forests, by selected species and region, 2005[a]—con.

Species and region[b]	Volume[c] Thousand board feet	Value[d] Thousand dollars	Average price per thousand board feet Dollars	Species and region	Volume Thousand board feet	Value Thousand dollars	Average price per thousand board feet Dollars
SOFTWOODS, WESTERN—Con.				SOFTWOODS, EASTERN—Con.			
Spruce—Con.				Softwoods not specified			
Engelmann spruce:				by species:			
Northern [1]	3,589	930.2	259.20	Southern [8]	13	0.2	19.16
Rocky Mountain [2]	6,213	632.7	101.84	Eastern [9]	884	54.0	61.03
Southwestern [3]	1,505	12.0	8.00	Total	897	54.2	60.42
Intermountain [4]	5,849	887.0	151.66	Total, eastern softwoods	203,507	34,686.3	170.44
Pacific Northwest [6]	11	0.8	69.15	Total, softwoods	1,217,433	145,064.7	119.16
Total	17,166	11.8	0.69	HARDWOODS, WESTERN			
Sitka spruce:				Alder			
Pacific Northwest [6]	294	51.1	173.91	Pacific Northwest [6]	841	102.1	121.45
Alaska [10]	27,258	630.3	23.12	Aspen			
Total	27,552	681.4	24.73	Rocky Mountain [2]	0	0.0	0.00
Softwoods not specified				Southwestern [3]	0	0.0	0.00
by species:				Intermountain [4]	56	0.0	0.30
Northern [1]	2,800	423.6	151.28	Total	56	0.0	0.30
Rocky Mountain [2]	18,921	762.3	40.29	Hardwoods not specified			
Southwestern [3]	1,269	2.5	2.00	by species:			
Intermountain [4]	4,572	388.9	85.05	Rocky Mountain [2]	0	0.0	0.00
Pacific Southwest [5]	265	4.0	14.95	Pacific Southwest [5]	431	0.3	0.62
Pacific Northwest [6]	5,789	147.0	25.40	Pacific Northwest [6]	0	0.0	0.00
Alaska [10]	0	0.0	0.00	Total	431	0.3	0.00
Total	33,616	1,728.2	51	Total, western hardwoods	1,327	102.4	77.14
Total, western softwoods	1,013,926	110,378	108.86				
				HARDWOODS, EASTERN			
SOFTWOODS, EASTERN				Ash			
Cedar				Southern [8]	107	15.4	143 83
Southern [8]	9	0.3	30.62	Eastern [9]	931	184.6	198 26
Eastern [9]	7	0.1	11.67	Total	1,038	200.0	192 66
Total	16	0.4	22.61	Aspen			
Cypress				Eastern [9]	3,466	323.7	93.39
Southern [8]	0	0.0	0.00	Basswood			
Fir				Southern [8]	0	0.0	0.00
True fir:				Eastern [9]	654	16.7	25.61
Eastern [9]	107	8.6	79.92	Total	654	16.7	25.61
Hemlock				Beech			
Eastern hemlock:				Eastern [9]	1,496	92.1	61.58
Southern [8]	62	1.5	23.82	Birch			
Eastern [9]	376	73.6	195.70	Paper birch:			
Total	438	75.1	171.41	Eastern [9]	605	118.9	196 38
Pine				Yellow birch:			
Eastern white pine:				Eastern [9]	1,133	475.9	420.13
Southern [8]	8,871	1,162.3	131.01	Cherry			
Eastern [9]	412	27.2	66.01	Black cherry:			
Total	9,284	1,189.5	128.13	Southern [8]	246	249.3	1,013 97
Jack pine:				Eastern [9]	10,237	24,488.0	2,392.11
Eastern [9]	5,053	396.2	78.41	Total	10,483	24,737.3	2,359.79
Red pine:				Hickory			
Eastern [9]	14,638	2,276.6	155.52	Southern [8]	68	9.5	140 24
Red and white eastern pine:				Maple			
Eastern [9]	3,900	536.8	137.64	Red maple:			
Southern pine:				Southern [8]	183	22.7	123.73
Southern [8]	159,641	29,212.7	182.99	Eastern [9]	5,600	888.2	158.62
Eastern [9]	6,427	565.8	88.04	Total	5,783	910.9	157.52
Total	166,068	29,778.5	179.31	Sugar maple:			
Virginia pine:				Southern [8]	33	17.4	534 00
Southern [8]	3	1.6	545.60	Eastern [9]	4,929	3,194.2	648 04
Pine not specified				Total	4,962	3,211.5	647 29
by species:				Maple not specified			
Eastern [9]	605	36.6	60.58	by species:			
Spruce				Southern [8]	2	0.1	73 99
Black, red, and white spruce:				Eastern [9]	95	48.2	505 53
Eastern [9]	2,498	332.2	132.95	Total	97	48.3	498.42

Table 21—Volume and value of sawtimber stumpage sold from national forests, by selected species and region, 2005[a]—con.

Species and region[b]	Volume[c] Thousand board feet	Value[d] Thousand dollars	Average price per thousand board feet Dollars	Species and region	Volume Thousand board feet	Value Thousand dollars	Average price per thousand board feet Dollars
HARDWOODS, EASTERN—Con.				Poplar			
Oak				Yellow poplar:			
Chestnut oak:				Southern [8]	1,191	105.7	88.75
Southern [8]	1,062	157.2	148.02	Eastern [9]	5,364	531.2	99.03
Eastern [9]	65	18.7	285.19	Total	6,555	636.9	97.17
Total	1,127	175.9	155.98	Yellow poplar, basswood			
Red and black oak:				and cucumber:			
Southern [8]	5,156	1,681.5	326.12	Southern [8]	5,456	695.9	127.54
Eastern [9]	2,160	1,000.3	463.09	Hardwoods not specified			
Total	7,316	2,681.8	366.56	by species:			
Scarlet oak:				Southern [8]	14,463	1,135.5	78.51
Southern [8]	0	0.0	0.00	Eastern [9]	5,315	618.8	116.43
Eastern [9]	2	0.4	196.08	Total	19,778	1,754.3	88.70
Total	2	0.4	196.08	Total, eastern hardwoods	101,995	42,337.3	415.09
White oak:				Total, hardwoods	103,322	42,439.6	410.75
Southern [8]	1,816	331.1	182.33	Total, softwoods and			
Eastern [9]	96	24.9	260.44	hardwoods	1,320,754	187,504.4	141.97
Total	1,911	356.0	186.24				
Oak not specified							
by species:							
Southern [8]	5,406	886.4	163.97				
Eastern [9]	24,659	5,004.9	202.96				
Total	30,065	5,891.3	195.95				

[a]U.S. Department of Agriculture, Forest Service (47); Data may not add to totals because of rounding; The stumpage prices shown in this table do not necessarily indicate values for any specific tract of public or private timber, and prices received for individual tracts may vary widely because of differences in timber quality, degree of competition timber accessibility, variations in special costs, methods of allocating overhead costs by species, or other factors; Excludes pulpwood and miscellaneous products and also excludes timber sold by land exchanges and from land in utilization projects.

[b]Administrative regions of the Forest Service.

[c]Scribner Decimal C log rule except in the Northeastern states timber where international 1/4-in. log rule is used.

[d]High bid prices, which include specified road costs KV payments.

[e]Includes small amounts of Jeffrey pine.

[1-6,8-10]Region area numbers.

Table 22—Average stumpage prices for sawtimber sold from private lands in Louisiana, by selected species, 1965–2005 (dollars per thousand board feet, Doyle log scale)[a]

Year	Southern pine		Ash		Gums		Oaks	
	Current dollars	1997 dollars[b]	Current dollars	1997 dollars	Current dollars	1997 dollars	Current dollars	1997 dollars
1965	28.40	112.19	22.60	89.08	17.50	68.97	16.20	64.00
1966	34.30	131.43	23.00	88.10	19.50	74.69	17.90	68.59
1967	36.80	140.59	23.30	88.93	19.50	74.43	17.70	67.62
1968	40.70	151.85	25.60	95.37	20.00	74.51	19.00	70.89
1969	50.10	179.57	31.80	113.79	22.60	80.87	21.50	77.06
1970	46.40	160.45	28.10	97.04	21.00	72.52	20.40	70.54
1971	56.00	187.55	26.60	89.03	21.90	73.30	20.80	69.66
1972	66.30	212.56	28.50	91.18	23.80	76.15	23.10	74.06
1973	84.20	238.75	41.50	117.56	32.30	91.50	30.20	85.63
1974	90.90	216.80	48.20	114.98	36.80	87.79	35.50	84.67
1975	81.60	178.29	45.70	99.83	35.40	77.33	34.10	74.51
1976	101.10	211.14	45.80	95.63	37.20	77.67	37.30	77.90
1977	119.90	235.74	49.70	97.59	39.70	77.95	40.60	79.82
1978	156.20	285.14	59.40	108.42	46.20	84.32	46.50	84.88
1979	211.50	342.91	74.20	120.11	51.90	84.01	53.40	86.58
1980	189.20	268.84	70.20	99.69	53.10	75.41	55.50	78.86
1981	185.00	240.88	70.20	91.35	52.00	67.66	55.60	72.39
1982	144.60	184.51	71.10	90.67	53.70	68.48	57.50	73.37
1983	160.70	202.42	103.80	130.69	67.30	84.73	71.60	90.19
1984	158.80	195.40	109.00	133.98	68.00	83.58	72.70	89.46
1985	118.20	146.15	88.30	109.03	57.30	70.75	62.50	77.28
1986	112.30	143.01	87.90	111.84	53.70	68.32	64.70	82.39
1987	147.30	182.84	z	z	59.30	73.55	79.00	98.06
1988	161.00	192.18	134.20	160.07	62.10	74.07	101.20	120.80
1989	169.10	192.31	133.80	152.09	65.30	74.23	98.30	111.79
1990	182.60	200.34	141.10	154.73	81.90	89.81	106.50	116.85
1991	194.30	212.81	123.60	135.27	67.60	73.98	89.00	97.48
1992	222.60	242.35	289.30	314.71	78.10	84.96	136.90	149.05
1993	273.30	293.30	z	z	z	z	153.00	164.20
1994	330.50	350.26	z	z	z	z	205.00	217.26
1995	389.56	398.62	z	z	z	z	252.75	258.63
1996	344.57	344.30	z	z	z	z	203.00	202.84
1997	412.39	412.39	z	z	z	z	289.75	289.75
1998	406.76	417.22	z	z	z	z	276.50	283.61
1999	368.70	374.87	z	z	z	z	285.00	289.77
2000	392.35	377.27	z	z	z	z	270.00	259.62
2001	351.12	333.85	z	z	z	z	321.00	305.21
2002	368.41	358.57	z	z	z	z	290.00	282.26
2003	348.46	321.97	z	z	z	z	319.00	294.75
2004	372.40	323.91	z	z	z	z	306.00	266.16
2005	384.37	311.60	z	z	z	z	315.00	255.36

[a]Timber Mart South (36); Louisiana Department of Agriculture (23).

[b]Derived by dividing the price in current dollars by the Bureau of Labor Statistics producer price index for all commodities (1997 = 100).

[z]Not available.

Table 23—Veneer log production, by softwoods and hardwoods, 1965–2005(million board feet, local log rule)[a]

Year	All species[b]	Softwoods	Hardwoods
1965	6,275	5,425	850
1966	6,315	5,610	705
1967	6,305	5,610	695
1968	6,880	6,150	730
1969	6,430	5,750	680
1970	6,642	5,863	779
1971	7,215	6,515	700
1972	7,810	7,070	740
1973	7,750	7,090	660
1974	7,560	6,945	615
1975	8,185	7,545	640
1976	8,417	7,795	623
1977	7,960	7,360	600
1978	8,150	7,560	590
1979	7,690	7,085	605
1980	7,649	7,040	609
1981	7,710	7,095	615
1982	7,504	6,885	619
1983	7,736	7,110	626
1984	7,970	7,335	635
1985	8,460	7,810	650
1986	9,062	8,398	664
1987	9,370	8,700	670
1988	9,261	8,580	681
1989	8,814	8,119	695
1990	8,662	7,942	720
1991	8,037	7,276	761
1992	7,876	7,101	775
1993	7,796	6,995	801
1994	7,735	6,881	854
1995	7,626	6,700	926
1996	7,560	6,583	977
1997	7,581	6,601	980
1998	7,671	6,707	964
1999	7,802	6,812	990
2000	7,870	6,855	1,015
2001	7,984	6,931	1,052
2002	7,518	6,521	997
2003[E]	7,105	6,089	1,016
2004[E]	7,093	6,071	1,022
2005[E]	6,921	5,913	1,008

[a]Data may not add to totals because of rounding.

[b]U.S. Department of Agriculture, Forest Service (49).

[E]Estimated

Table 24—Pulpwood consumption, production, imports, exports, and the equivalent wood volumes of imports and exports of paper, board, and wood pulp, 1965–2005 (thousand cords)[a]

Year	U.S. total consump- tion[pc]	Consumption in U.S. mills						Net imports	Imports	Exports	Paper, board, and wood pulp (pulpwood equivalent)		
		Total	Domestic productions								Net imports	Imports	Exports
			Total	Roundwood[r]			Residue[b]						
				Total	Softwoods	Hardwoods							
1965	63,519	54,034	52,884	39,129	28,201	10,928	13,755	1,150	1,305	155	9,485	13,487	4,001
1966	67,429	57,399	56,294	41,809	29,900	11,910	14,484	1,105	1,385	280	10,030	14,367	4,337
1967	67,377	58,419	57,469	41,441	29,967	11,474	16,028	950	1,590	640	8,958	13,789	4,831
1968	69,214	60,969	60,734	43,535	31,690	11,845	17,199	235	1,425	1,190	8,245	13,643	5,398
1969	73,428	64,577	65,257	47,499	34,239	13,260	17,758	-680	980	1,660	8,851	14,956	6,105
1970	73,308	66,732	67,577	49,467	37,212	12,255	18,110	-845	1,120	1,965	6,576	14,310	7,734
1971	74,286	66,601	66,906	46,295	33,533	12,763	20,610	-305	1,225	1,530	7,685	14,375	6,690
1972	75,685	68,068	69,023	45,311	31,784	13,527	23,712	-955	1,020	1,975	7,616	14,263	6,646
1973	80,294	71,421	72,891	46,269	31,496	14,773	26,622	-1,470	1,200	2,670	8,873	15,483	6,610
1974	84,452	75,787	77,957	50,394	34,268	16,126	27,563	-2,170	965	3,135	8,665	17,057	8,392
1975	69,231	63,941	65,821	41,029	29,035	11,993	24,792	-1,880	765	2,645	5,290	12,172	6,882
1976	78,092	71,094	73,249	45,527	31,856	13,671	27,722	-2,155	1,115	3,270	6,998	14,019	7,021
1977	80,486	72,952	74,972	44,538	31,022	13,516	30,434	-2,020	1,350	3,370	7,534	14,548	7,014
1978	84,346	75,073	76,453	46,722	31,778	14,943	29,731	-1,380	1,675	3,055	9,272	16,205	6,933
1979	87,651	78,680	81,065	50,699	35,389	15,310	30,366	-2,385	1,405	3,790	8,971	16,847	7,876
1980	87,055	81,921	84,031	52,107	36,941	15,166	31,925	-2,110	1,590	3,700	5,134	16,256	11,122
1981	86,814	81,003	82,468	51,390	35,685	15,704	31,079	-1,465	1,490	2,955	5,811	15,579	9,768
1982	82,127	76,912	77,862	49,093	33,829	15,264	28,769	-950	1,405	2,355	5,215	14,302	9,087
1983	91,044	84,504	84,829	51,612	33,413	18,199	33,217	-325	1,715	2,040	6,540	16,312	9,772
1984	95,854	86,282	86,377	52,324	33,945	18,379	34,054	-95	1,825	1,920	9,572	18,697	9,125
1985	95,325	85,380	86,600	52,698	33,097	19,602	33,901	-1,220	650	1,870	9,945	19,198	9,253
1986	100,144	91,187	92,502	57,723	35,630	22,094	34,779	-1,315	630	1,945	8,957	19,974	11,017
1987	102,445	93,005	94,590	58,538	37,172	21,367	36,052	-1,585	430	2,015	9,440	20,882	11,442
1988	101,737	93,000	95,030	59,342	37,359	21,984	35,688	-2,030	735	2,765	8,737	20,779	12,042
1989	100,276	92,615	93,831	59,924	37,755	22,169	33,907	-1,216	988	2,204	7,661	20,341	12,679
1990	99,361	92,561	93,936	61,758	39,559	22,199	32,178	-1,376	917	2,293	6,801	19,847	13,046
1991	95,484	91,925	93,246	62,701	40,213	22,488	30,545	-1,321	1,025	2,346	3,559	18,305	14,746
1992	96,146	93,642	95,238	63,489	39,918	23,571	31,749	-1,596	857	2,453	2,504	18,451	15,947
1993	96,089	90,996	92,759	62,122	37,621	24,501	30,637	-1,764	745	2,509	5,094	19,485	14,392
1994	98,142	93,259	95,327	63,698	38,312	25,387	31,629	-2,068	544	2,612	4,883	19,965	15,082
1995[r]	97,052	93,013	94,999	69,808	41,173	28,635	25,191	-1,986	303	2,290	4,039	20,474	16,435
1996[r]	90,190	88,246	90,439	66,697	39,641	27,056	23,742	-2,193	334	2,527	1,943	17,979	16,036
1997[r]	95,247	92,312	95,038	68,354	39,943	28,411	26,684	-2,726	357	3,083	2,935	20,186	17,251
1998[r]	96,305	90,591	93,371	68,134	40,580	27,554	25,237	-2,780	231	3,011	5,713	20,653	14,939
1999	94,265	86,969	89,908	64,048	37,157	26,890	25,861	-2,940	144	3,084	7,296	21,077	13,780
2000	95,904	87,453	89,888	64,775	37,965	26,810	25,113	-2,435	150	2,585	8,452	22,951	14,499
2001	92,181	83,384	85,240	62,033	36,200	25,833	23,207	-1,856	79	1,935	8,797	22,618	13,821
2002	90,500	82,715	84,030	60,494	34,901	25,593	23,536	-1,315	66	1,381	7,785	22,222	14,437
2003	97,295	85,001	85,375	62,616	37,742	24,874	22,758	-373	189	563	12,294	24,080	11,786
2004	98,954	86,903	87,704	64,014	38,657	25,357	23,690	-801	437	1,238	12,052	24,494	12,443
2005	96,804	86,284	87,088	63,681	37,989	25,692	23,407	-804	411	1,215	10,520	23,522	13,002

[a]American Forest & Paper Association (3); American Pulpwood Association (10).

[b]Chips produced from roundwood and byproducts from primary processing plants, such as slabs, edgings, and veneer cores.

[r]Revised.

[c]American Forest & Paper Association (7) for 2005

Table 25—Pulpwood production, by region[a] and softwoods and hardwoods, 1965–2005 (million cords)[b]

Year[c]	All section			North			South			West		
	Total	Soft-woods	Hard-woods	Total	Soft-woods	Hard-woods	Total	Soft-woods	Hard-woods	Total	Soft-woods	Hard-woods
1965	52.88	40.1	12.8	9.0	4.1	4.9	31.2	23.8	7.4	12.7	12.2	0.5
1966	56.29	42.1	14.2	10.3	4.4	5.9	33.1	25.4	7.7	12.9	12.3	0.6
1967	57.47	43.6	13.9	10.3	4.5	5.8	33.6	25.9	7.7	13.6	13.2	0.4
1968	60.73	46.6	14.1	9.8	4.3	5.5	36.5	28.3	8.2	14.4	14.0	0.4
1969	65.26	48.8	16.5	10.3	4.1	6.2	40.0	30.2	9.8	15.0	14.5	0.5
1970	67.58	50.7	16.9	11.3	4.6	6.7	41.1	31.4	9.7	15.2	14.7	0.5
1971	66.91	50.3	16.6	10.5	4.0	6.5	41.1	31.5	9.6	15.3	14.8	0.5
1972	69.02	51.0	18.0	10.7	4.0	6.7	42.3	31.7	10.6	16.0	15.3	0.7
1973	72.89	52.7	20.2	12.8	4.6	8.2	43.4	32.1	11.3	16.7	16.0	0.7
1974	77.96	55.8	22.2	13.9	5.1	8.8	46.1	33.6	12.5	18.0	17.1	0.9
1975	65.82	50.1	15.7	10.4	4.2	6.2	40.7	31.7	9.0	14.7	14.2	0.5
1976	73.25	54.1	19.1	12.2	4.8	7.4	44.3	33.2	11.1	16.7	16.1	0.6
1977	74.97	55.7	19.3	12.5	4.9	7.6	45.2	34.2	11.0	17.3	16.6	0.7
1978	76.45	55.3	21.2	13.0	5.2	7.8	47.7	35.0	12.7	15.8	15.1	0.7
1979	81.06	58.3	22.8	14.0	5.5	8.5	50.2	36.7	13.5	16.9	16.1	0.8
1980	84.03	60.6	23.4	14.3	5.7	8.6	50.7	36.9	13.8	19.0	18.0	1.0
1981	82.47	59.6	22.9	13.9	5.6	8.3	51.6	37.7	13.9	17.0	16.3	0.7
1982	77.86	56.3	21.6	13.1	5.9	7.2	50.2	36.6	13.6	14.6	13.8	0.8
1983	84.83	59.9	24.9	14.4	5.6	8.8	53.9	38.5	15.4	16.5	15.8	0.7
1984	86.38	61.1	25.3	14.7	6.0	8.7	54.4	38.7	15.7	17.3	16.4	0.9
1985	86.60	60.6	26.0	14.6	5.8	8.8	56.2	39.9	16.3	15.8	14.9	0.9
1986	92.50	64.0	28.5	15.2	5.7	9.5	59.9	42.0	17.9	17.4	16.3	1.1
1987	94.59	65.6	29.0	15.4	5.8	9.6	61.5	43.2	18.3	17.7	16.6	1.1
1988	95.03	65.7	29.3	14.8	5.4	9.4	61.8	42.9	18.9	18.4	17.4	1.0
1989	93.83	64.3	29.5	14.0	5.1	8.9	62.8	43.3	19.5	17.0	15.9	1.1
1990	93.94	63.1	30.8	14.0	5.0	9.0	65.4	44.6	20.8	14.5	13.5	1.0
1991	93.25	62.4	30.8	14.2	5.2	9.0	66.8	45.8	21.0	12.2	11.4	0.8
1992	95.24	59.8	35.4	13.9	5.0	8.9	70.9	45.0	25.9	10.4	9.8	0.6
1993	92.76	55.7	37.1	15.0	5.6	9.4	71.9	44.8	27.1	5.9	5.3	0.6
1994	95.33	56.1	39.2	15.4	5.6	9.8	74.7	45.8	28.9	5.2	4.7	0.5
1995	95.00	61.1	33.9	15.0	6.7	8.3	72.6	48.1	24.5	7.4	6.3	1.1
1996	90.44	58.7	31.8	14.5	6.6	7.9	69.6	46.7	22.9	6.4	5.4	0.9
1997	95.04	61.4	33.6	15.2	6.8	8.4	74.1	50.0	24.1	5.7	4.6	1.1
1998	93.37	60.3	33.1	14.6	6.3	8.3	72.4	48.9	23.5	6.3	5.1	1.2
1999	89.91	57.7	32.2	13.8	6.0	7.8	70.7	47.5	23.2	5.4	4.3	1.2
2000	89.89	57.8	32.1	14.1	6.1	8.1	70.1	47.2	22.9	5.7	4.6	1.1
2001	85.24	54.4	30.9	13.4	5.8	7.7	67.0	44.8	22.2	4.8	3.8	1.0
2002	84.03	53.7	30.3	13.1	5.5	7.6	66.4	44.8	21.7	4.5	3.5	1.1
2003	85.37	55.6	29.7	13.3	5.4	8.0	67.3	46.5	20.9	4.7	3.8	0.9
2004	87.70	57.4	30.3	14.1	5.5	8.6	68.6	48.0	20.6	5.0	3.8	1.1
2005	87.09	57.0	30.1	14.1	5.5	8.6	68.2	47.7	20.4	4.9	3.8	1.1

[a]The West includes: Alaska, Arizona, California, Idaho, Montana, Oregon, and Washington.
The South includes: Alabama, Arkansas, Florida, Georgia, Kentucky, Louisiana, Maryland,
Mississippi, North Carolina, Oklahoma, South Carolina, Tennessee, Texas, and Virginia.
The North includes: Illinois, Indiana, Iowa, Maine, Michigan, Minnesota, Missouri, New York,
Ohio, Pennsylvania, and Wisconsin.
[b]American Pulpwood Association (10); data may not add to totals because of rounding.
All numbers were revised; values include chip production.
[c]Data for the years 1989 to present are domestic receipts at pulp mills.

Table 26—Pulpwood stumpage prices of Louisiana and northern New Hampshire, 1965–2005 (dollars per cord)

Year	Louisiana[a]				Northern New Hampshire[b]			
	Southern pine		Hardwoods		Hemlock and pine[c]		Spruce and fir	
	Current dollars	1992 dollars[d]	Current dollars	1992 dollars	Current dollars	1992 dollars	Current dollars	1992 dollars
1965	1.21	4.80	0.44	1.74	0.48	1.91	1.24	4.90
1966	1.26	4.81	0.47	1.80	0.72	2.75	1.45	5.55
1967	1.27	4.85	0.48	1.84	0.58	2.21	1.45	5.53
1968	1.28	4.79	0.51	1.90	0.55	2.06	1.45	5.40
1969	1.28	4.60	0.52	1.88	0.51	1.83	1.24	4.45
1970	1.30	4.48	0.54	1.86	0.48	1.67	1.24	4.29
1971	1.31	4.39	z	z	0.48	1.62	1.24	4.16
1972	1.31	4.20	0.58	1.86	0.55	1.77	1.24	3.98
1973	1.43	4.07	0.66	1.88	0.55	1.56	1.24	3.52
1974	1.67	3.98	0.74	1.78	0.73	1.74	1.52	3.62
1975	1.77	3.86	0.77	1.69	0.73	1.60	1.66	3.62
1976	1.85	3.86	0.77	1.61	0.73	1.53	1.79	3.74
1977	1.96	3.85	0.81	1.60	0.73	1.44	1.79	3.53
1978	2.15	3.93	0.87	1.59	0.80	1.46	1.93	3.53
1979	2.57	4.16	1.01	1.63	1.03	1.68	2.21	3.58
1980	2.84	4.04	1.13	1.61	1.38	1.96	2.21	3.14
1981	3.49	4.54	1.19	1.54	1.38	1.80	2.21	2.87
1982	3.94	5.03	1.24	1.58	1.38	1.76	2.21	2.82
1983	4.10	5.16	1.32	1.67	1.38	1.74	2.34	2.95
1984	4.87	5.99	1.20	1.48	1.38	1.70	2.34	2.89
1985	4.19	5.18	1.21	1.50	1.10	1.36	2.48	3.07
1986	3.32	4.23	1.19	1.51	1.03	1.32	2.48	3.16
1987	3.82	4.74	1.48	1.83	1.03	1.28	2.48	3.08
1988	4.40	5.25	1.43	1.71	0.97	1.15	2.76	3.29
1989	5.06	5.75	1.53	1.74	1.10	1.25	3.03	3.45
1990	4.93	5.41	1.50	1.65	1.66	1.82	3.45	3.78
1991	5.74	6.28	2.26	2.47	1.66	1.81	3.86	4.23
1992	6.48	7.06	2.16	2.35	1.59	1.73	3.24	3.53
1993	6.92	7.42	2.70	2.89	1.66	1.78	4.55	4.88
1994	6.49	6.87	2.79	2.96	3.17	3.36	3.31	3.32
1995	6.72	6.87	2.87	2.94	z	z	z	z
1996	6.58	6.57	3.48	3.48	z	z	z	z
1997	6.61	6.61	4.15	4.15	z	z	z	z
1998	8.07	8.27	4.71	4.83	z	z	z	z
1999	7.25	7.37	3.79	3.86	0.82	0.83	0.63	0.64
2000	6.44	6.19	2.85	2.74	0.75	0.72	0.69	0.66
2001	5.89	5.60	3.73	3.55	0.75	0.72	0.69	0.66
2002	5.39	5.24	4.12	4.01	0.75	0.73	0.69	0.67
2003	5.27	4.87	4.46	4.12	0.61	0.57	1.00	0.93
2004	5.21	4.53	4.53	3.94	0.73	0.63	1.12	0.97
2005	6.26	5.07	5.43	4.40	0.68	0.55	0.92	0.74

[a] Louisiana Department of Agriculture, Office of Marketing (23);

[b] New Hampshire University, Cooperative Extension Service, and New Hampshire Department of Resources and Economic Development (30).

[c] Includes tamarack.

[d] Derived by dividing the price in current dollars by the Bureau of Labor Statistics producers price index for all commodities (1997 = 100).

[z] Not available.

Table 27—Pulpwood prices of Louisiana and northern New Hampshire, 1965–2005 (dollars per standard cord, including bark)[a]

Year	Louisiana[b]				Northern New Hampshire[c]					
	Southern pine		Hardwoods		Hemlock and pine[d]		Spruce and fir		Hardwoods	
	Current dollars	1997 dollars[e]	Current dollars	1997 dollars	Current dollars	1997 dollars	Current dollars	1997 dollars	Current dollars	1997 dollars
1965	15.70	62.02	13.65	53.92	16.85	66.57	21.00	82.96	16.50	65.18
1966	16.50	63.23	14.80	56.71	17.75	68.02	22.00	84.30	17.50	67.06
1967	16.50	63.04	14.85	56.73	20.25	77.36	22.40	85.58	17.50	66.86
1968	17.00	63.43	16.30	60.82	19.55	72.94	22.15	82.64	z	z
1969	17.75	63.62	17.40	62.37	19.45	69.71	23.20	83.16	18.90	67.74
1970	17.75	61.38	17.45	60.34	19.50	67.43	23.40	80.92	20.00	69.16
1971	z	z	z	z	19.50	65.31	23.40	78.37	20.25	67.82
1972	19.25	61.72	19.00	60.91	19.25	61.72	23.75	76.14	22.00	70.53
1973	22.50	63.80	22.00	62.38	20.40	57.85	25.50	72.31	23.50	66.64
1974	28.30	67.50	24.95	59.51	21.25	50.68	30.00	71.55	26.50	63.20
1975	29.25	63.91	26.20	57.25	25.15	54.95	30.50	66.64	28.50	62.27
1976	30.45	63.59	26.10	54.51	30.40	63.49	31.50	65.78	31.65	66.10
1977	31.65	62.23	27.20	53.48	32.50	63.90	36.50	71.76	33.00	64.88
1978	34.55	63.07	28.30	51.66	34.50	62.98	39.00	71.19	35.00	63.89
1979	38.95	63.15	32.05	51.96	36.65	59.42	44.00	71.34	37.00	59.99
1980	41.45	58.90	33.60	47.74	36.65	52.08	46.00	65.36	41.50	58.97
1981	44.20	57.55	34.20	44.53	41.50	54.03	49.00	63.80	44.00	57.29
1982	46.95	59.91	35.25	44.98	41.50	52.95	49.00	62.52	44.00	56.14
1983	47.60	59.96	35.30	44.46	41.50	52.27	49.00	61.72	46.50	58.57
1984	42.75	52.60	z	z	41.50	51.06	49.00	60.29	47.50	58.45
1985	49.20	60.83	37.50	46.37	41.50	51.31	49.00	60.59	46.50	57.49
1986	48.10	61.25	35.40	45.08	41.50	52.85	49.50	63.04	47.00	59.85
1987	50.65	62.87	45.35	56.29	41.50	51.51	49.50	61.44	47.00	58.34
1988	52.25	62.37	46.85	55.92	41.50	49.54	50.50	60.28	47.50	56.70
1989	55.19	62.77	46.49	52.87	41.50	47.20	50.50	57.43	51.00	58.00
1990	55.64	61.05	47.86	52.51	48.50	53.21	56.75	62.26	50.75	55.68
1991	61.04	66.86	52.37	57.36	50.00	54.76	66.75	73.11	50.75	55.59
1992	64.11	69.80	46.85	51.01	47.00	51.17	66.00	71.86	49.50	53.89
1993	66.15	70.99	51.54	55.31	49.00	52.59	65.00	69.76	49.50	53.12
1994	57.55	60.99	55.23	58.53	65.50	69.42	44.00	46.63	50.50	53.52
1995	67.93	69.51	73.06	74.76	z	z	z	z	z	z
1996	62.55	62.50	57.45	57.41	z	z	z	z	z	z
1997	72.30	72.30	70.19	70.19	z	z	z	z	z	z
1998	74.87	76.80	58.55	60.06	49.77	51.05	27.50	28.21	58.50	60.00
1999	64.61	65.69	53.24	54.13	49.77	50.60	27.50	27.96	58.50	59.48
2000	59.11	56.84	51.53	49.55	49.77	47.86	22.83	21.95	58.50	56.25
2001	59.64	56.70	64.97	61.77	49.77	47.32	27.50	26.15	58.50	55.62
2002	60.66	59.04	65.59	63.84	49.77	48.44	27.50	26.77	58.50	56.94
2003	61.74	57.05	69.16	63.90	64.17	59.29	35.09	32.43	33.21	30.68
2004	62.41	54.28	67.28	58.52	66.13	57.52	34.25	29.79	33.30	28.97
2005	67.58	54.79	75.67	61.34	53.14	43.08	36.50	29.59	31.17	25.27

[a]All numbers reflect the delivered timber price.

[b]Timber Mart-South (36); Louisiana Department of Agriculture, Office of Marketing (23); f.o.b. car.

[c]New Hampshire University, Cooperative Extension Service, and New Hampshire Department of Resources and Economic Development (30).

[d]Includes tamarack.

[e]Derived by dividing price in current dollars by the Bureau of Labor Statistics producer price index for all commodities (1997 = 100).

[z]Not available.

Table 28—Lumber production, imports, exports, and consumption, by softwoods and hardwoods, 1965–2005[a]

Year	Production			Imports			Exports			Consumption			Per capita consumption		
	Total	Soft-woods	Hard-woods	Total	Soft-woods	Hard-woods	Total	Soft-woods[b]	Hard-woods	Total	Soft-woods	Hard-woods	Total	Soft-woods	Hard-woods
	Billion board feet	*Billion board feet*	*Billion board feet*	*Billion board feet*	*Billion board feet*	*Billion board feet*	*Billion board feet*	*Billion board feet*	*Billion board feet*	*Billion board feet*	*Billion board feet*	*Billion board feet*	*Board feet*	*Board feet*	*Board feet*
1965	38.7	29.3	9.4	5.2	4.9	0.3	0.9	0.8	0.1	43.1	33.4	9.7	222	172	50
1966	38.6	28.8	9.8	5.2	4.8	0.4	1.1	0.9	0.2	42.7	32.7	10.0	217	166	51
1967	37.5	28 2	9.3	5.1	4.8	0.3	1.2	1.0	0.2	41.4	32.0	9.5	208	161	48
1968	38.0	29.3	8.7	6.2	5.8	0.3	1.1	1.0	0.1	43.1	34.1	9.0	215	170	45
1969	37.1	28.3	8.7	6.3	5.9	0.4	1.1	1.0	0.1	42.3	33.2	9.1	209	164	45
1970	35.9	27.5	8.3	6.1	5.8	0.3	1.2	1.1	0.1	40.8	32.2	8.6	199	157	42
1971	38.5	30 0	8.4	7.6	7.2	0.4	1.1	0.9	0.2	45.0	36.4	8.6	217	175	41
1972	39.5	31 0	8.5	9.4	9.0	0.4	1.4	1.2	0.2	47.5	38.8	8.7	226	185	42
1973	40.4	31.6	8.8	9.6	9.0	0.5	2.0	1.8	0.2	47.9	38.8	9.1	226	183	43
1974	36.2	27.7	8.4	7.3	6.8	0.4	1.8	1.6	0.2	41.6	32.9	8.7	195	154	41
1975	34.1	26.7	7.3	6.0	5.7	0.3	1.6	1.4	0.2	38.4	31.1	7.4	178	144	34
1976	37.7	29.7	8.0	8.2	8.0	0.3	1.8	1.6	0.2	44.1	36.1	8.1	202	165	37
1977	40.2	31.7	8.5	10.7	10.4	0.3	1.6	1.4	0.2	49.4	40.7	8.6	224	185	39
1978	41.0	32.1	9.0	12.2	11.9	0.4	1.8	1.4	0.4	51.4	42.5	8.9	231	191	40
1979	40.7	31.4	9.3	11.5	11.2	0.4	2.2	1.8	0.4	50.1	40.8	9.3	222	181	41
1980	35.4	26 2	9.2	9.9	9.6	0.3	2.5	2.0	0.5	42.8	33.8	9.0	188	149	39
1981	32.2	24.7	7.5	9.5	9.2	0.3	2.4	1.9	0.5	39.3	32.0	7.3	171	139	32
1982	31.8	23.8	8.0	9.4	9.1	0.2	2.0	1.6	0.4	39.1	31.3	7.8	169	135	34
1983	38.5	29.7	8.8	12.3	12.0	0.3	2.3	1.8	0.5	48.4	39.9	8.5	207	170	36
1984	41.3	31 2	10.1	13.6	13.3	0.3	2.1	1.6	0.5	52.8	42.9	9.9	223	181	42
1985	40.9	31.3	9.6	15.0	14.6	0.4	1.9	1.5	0.4	54.0	44.4	9.6	226	186	40
1986	45.8	35.3	10.5	14.6	14.2	0.3	2.4	1.9	0.5	57.9	47.6	10.3	241	198	43
1987	49.5	38 2	11.3	15.2	14.7	0.5	3.2	2.5	0.7	61.5	50.5	11.0	253	208	45
1988	49.9	38.1	11.7	13.8	13.5	0.3	4.5	3.3	1.2	59.2	48.3	10.9	242	197	44
1989	49.6	37.5	12.1	15.3	14.9	0.3	4.2	3.4	0.9	60.6	49.1	11.5	245	198	47
1990	48.1	35.8	12.3	13.1	12.9	0.2	3.8	2.9	0.9	57.4	45.7	11.7	230	183	47
1991	44.3	33 2	11.2	11.7	11.5	0.2	4.0	3.1	0.9	52.1	41.6	10.4	206	165	41
1992	45.9	34.5	11.4	13.4	13.2	0.3	3.6	2.6	1.0	55.8	45.1	10.7	218	177	42
1993	45.2	32 9	12.2	15.4	15.1	0.3	3.4	2.3	1.0	57.2	45.7	11.5	222	177	45
1994	46.5	34.1	12.4	16.6	16.2	0.4	3.3	2.2	1.1	59.8	48.2	11.6	229	185	45
1995	44.9	32 2	12.6	17.6	17.2	0.4	2.9	1.9	1.1	59.5	47.6	11.9	226	181	45
1996	45.8	33.3	12.5	18.4	18.0	0.4	2.9	1.8	1.1	61.3	49.5	11.8	231	186	44
1997	47.3	34.7	12.7	18.5	18.0	0.5	2.9	1.6	1.2	62.9	51.0	11.9	235	190	44
1998	47.4	34.7	12.7	19.2	18.7	0.5	2.2	1.1	1.1	64.5	52.2	12.2	238	193	45
1999	49.5	36.6	12.9	19.9	19.2	0.7	2.5	1.4	1.2	66.8	54.4	12.4	245	199	45
2000	48.6	36 0	12.6	20.2	19.4	0.8	2.7	1.4	1.3	66.1	54.0	12.1	234	191	43
2001	46.4	34.6	11.8	20.7	20.1	0.6	2.2	1.0	1.2	64.9	53.7	11.3	228	188	40
2002	47.6	35.8	11.8	21.7	21.0	0.7	2.2	1.0	1.2	67.1	55.8	11.3	233	194	39
2003	47.5	36.6	10.9	22.0	21.2	0.8	2.1	1.0	1.2	67.4	56.8	10.5	231	195	36
2004	50.8	39.1	11.7	25.5	24.5	1.0	2.1	0.8	1.3	74.1	62.8	11.4	252	213	39
2005	52.3	40.7	11.6	25.7	24.6	1.1	2.3	0.9	1.5	75.6	64.4	11.2	255	217	38

[a]U.S. Department of Commerce, Bureau of the Census (57); American Forest & Paper Association (4); Luppold and Dempsey (24); U.S. International Trade Commission (80); Western Wood Products Association (83).

Data may not add to totals because of rounding; Data has been revised.

[b]Includes small volumes of mixed species (not classified as softwoods or hardwoods).

Table 29—Lumber production, by region[a] and softwoods and hardwoods, 1965–2006 (billion board feet)[b]

Year	All regions			North			South			West[c]		
	Total	Soft-woods	Hard-woods	Total	Soft-woods	Hard-woods	Total	Soft-woods	Hard-woods	Total	Soft-woods	Hard-woods
1965	38.7	29.3	9.4	4.4	1.1	3.3	12.7	6.8	5.9	21.6	21.4	0.2
1966	38.6	28.8	9.8	4.5	1.1	3.4	12.9	6.7	6.2	21.2	21.0	0.2
1967	37.5	28.2	9.3	5.3	1.7	3.6	12.5	6.7	5.8	19.7	19.6	0.1
1968	38.0	29.3	8.7	4.5	1.1	3.4	12.2	7.0	5.2	21.3	21.2	0.1
1969	37.1	28.3	8.7	4.6	1.1	3.5	12.3	7.3	5.0	20.1	19.9	0.2
1970	35.9	27.5	8.3	4.4	1.0	3.4	12.0	7.2	4.8	19.4	19.3	0.1
1971	38.5	30.0	8.4	4.4	1.1	3.3	12.9	7.9	5.0	21.1	21.0	0.1
1972	39.5	31.0	8.5	4.4	1.1	3.3	13.0	8.0	5.0	22.1	21.9	0.2
1973	40.4	31.6	8.8	4.6	1.1	3.5	13.2	8.0	5.2	22.6	22.5	0.1
1974	36.2	27.7	8.4	4.4	1.1	3.3	11.9	7.0	4.9	19.8	19.6	0.2
1975	34.1	26.7	7.3	4.1	1.1	3.0	11.1	7.0	4.1	18.8	18.6	0.2
1976[Rd]	37.7	29.7	8.0	6.3	1.8	4.5	16.5	13.4	3.1	14.9	14.5	0.3
1977[Rd]	40.2	31.7	8.5	6.7	1.9	4.8	17.6	14.3	3.3	15.9	15.6	0.3
1978[Rd]	41.0	32.1	9.0	7.0	1.9	5.1	17.9	14.4	3.5	16.1	15.7	0.4
1979[Rd]	40.7	31.4	9.3	7.1	1.9	5.3	17.8	14.1	3.6	15.8	15.4	0.4
1980[Rd]	35.4	26.2	9.2	6.8	1.6	5.2	15.4	11.8	3.6	13.2	12.9	0.4
1981[d]	32.2	24.7	7.5	5.7	1.5	4.3	14.0	11.1	2.9	12.4	12.1	0.3
1982	31.8	23.8	8.0	3.9	1.1	2.8	13.5	8.8	4.7	14.4	14.1	0.3
1983	38.5	29.7	8.8	4.4	1.3	3.1	15.7	10.3	5.4	18.4	18.2	0.2
1984	41.3	31.2	10.1	4.6	1.2	3.4	17.1	10.7	6.4	19.6	19.4	0.2
1985	40.9	31.3	9.6	4.6	1.2	3.4	15.9	10.2	5.7	20.4	20.2	0.2
1986	45.8	35.3	10.5	5.0	1.4	3.6	18.8	11.7	7.1	22.0	21.8	0.2
1987	49.5	38.2	11.3	5.3	1.5	3.8	19.9	12.3	7.6	24.3	24.0	0.3
1988	49.9	38.1	11.7	5.3	1.4	3.9	20.7	12.7	8.0	23.9	23.6	0.3
1989	49.6	37.5	12.1	4.4	1.2	3.2	21.2	12.3	8.9	24.0	23.7	0.3
1990	48.1	35.8	12.3	3.9	1.5	2.4	22.5	12.6	9.9	21.7	21.3	0.4
1991	44.3	33.2	11.2	4.8	1.5	3.3	20.0	12.1	7.9	19.5	19.1	0.4
1992	45.9	34.5	11.4	4.7	1.6	3.1	21.1	13.0	8.1	20.1	19.7	0.4
1993	45.2	32.9	12.2	7.8	1.9	5.9	21.0	15.4	5.6	16.4	16.0	0.4
1994	46.5	34.1	12.4	8.0	1.9	6.1	21.8	16.0	5.8	16.7	16.3	0.4
1995	44.9	32.2	12.6	8.1	1.9	6.1	21.1	15.3	5.8	15.6	15.2	0.4
1996	45.8	33.3	12.5	7.9	2.0	5.9	22.0	15.7	6.3	15.8	15.4	0.4
1997	47.3	34.7	12.7	9.3	2.1	7.2	20.5	15.6	4.9	17.5	17.0	0.5
1998	47.4	34.7	12.7	9.3	2.1	7.3	20.6	15.6	5.0	17.5	17.0	0.5
1999	49.5	36.6	12.9	9.6	2.2	7.4	21.5	16.5	5.0	18.5	17.9	0.5
2000	48.6	36.0	12.6	9.3	2.2	7.2	21.1	16.2	4.9	18.1	17.6	0.5
2001	46.4	34.6	11.8	8.8	2.1	6.7	20.2	15.6	4.6	17.4	16.9	0.5
2002	47.6	35.8	11.8	8.8	2.1	6.7	20.7	16.1	4.6	18.0	17.6	0.5
2003	47.5	36.6	10.9	8.4	2.2	6.2	20.7	16.5	4.2	18.4	17.9	0.4
2004	50.8	39.1	11.7	9.0	2.3	6.7	22.1	17.6	4.6	19.7	19.2	0.5
2005	52.3	40.7	11.6	9.1	2.4	6.7	22.8	18.3	4.5	20.4	19.9	0.5

[a]The West includes: Alaska, Arizona, California, Colorado, Hawaii, Idaho, Montana, Nevada, New Mexico, Oregon, South Dakota, Utah, Washington, and Wyoming. The South includes: Alabama, Arkansas, Florida, Georgia, Louisiana, Mississippi, North Carolina, Oklahoma, South Carolina, Tennessee, Texas, and Virginia. The North includes: the remaining 24 states.

[b]U.S. Department of Commerce, Bureau of the Census (57); American Forest and Paper Association (4); Data may not add to totals because of rounding.

[c]Western Wood Products Association (82).

[d]Estimated based on current percentage by region

[R]Revised

Table 30—Lumber production in the U.S., 1965-2005 (million board feet)

	Softwood							Hardwood								
										USDC^c,r					Luppold and	
Year	Howard^a	89 RPA^b	USDC^c,r	AF&PA dr	WWPA^e	Adams^f	Final^g	Howard^a	89 RPA^b	Total	West	AF&PA^d	WWPA^e	Adams^f	Dempsey^h,r	Final^i,r
1965	29,295	29,295	29,295	29,240	28,230	28,149	29,295	9,440	9,431	7,467	161	7,655	7,467	9,447	9,279	9,440
1966	28,847	28,847	28,847	z	27,973	27,879	28,847	9,771	9,771	7,737	204	z	7,737	9,782	9,567	9,771
1967	28,172	28,172	28,172	z	27,069	26,978	28,172	9,311	9,311	7,430	197	z	7,430	9,320	9,114	9,311
1968	29,285	30,224	29,285	z	28,936	28,832	29,285	8,430	8,432	7,188	156	z	7,188	8,795	8,579	8,735
1969	28,342	28,342	28,342	z	27,900	28,193	28,342	7,844	7,849	7,482	157	z	7,482	8,739	8,570	8,727
1970	27,530	27,297	27,530	z	27,107	27,001	27,530	7,715	7,701	7,138	127	z	7,138	8,340	8,203	8,330
1971	30,039	30,040	30,039	z	29,432	29,327	30,039	8,107	8,106	6,949	142	z	6,949	8,454	8,305	8,447
1972	30,975	30,975	30,975	z	30,873	30,763	30,975	8,245	8,230	6,770	139	z	6,770	8,502	8,355	8,494
1973	31,586	31,586	31,586	z	31,289	31,149	31,586	8,792	8,792	7,009	151	z	7,008	8,802	8,641	8,792
1974	27,704	28,357	27,704	z	27,193	27,059	27,704	8,448	8,448	6,904	189	z	6,904	8,459	8,259	8,448
1975	26,747	26,148	26,747	z	25,711	25,602	26,747	7,304	7,304	5,872	146	z	5,872	7,309	7,158	7,304
1976	30,600	30,274	30,571	29,693	29,693	29,510	29,693	7,977	7,978	6,427	177	7,801	6,417	7,983	7,800	7,977
1977	32,700	32,159	32,661	31,737	31,737	31,496	31,737	8,500	8,500	6,701	184	8,317	6,680	8,506	8,316	8,500
1978	33,500	32,585	33,467	32,057	32,057	31,698	32,057	8,960	8,959	7,031	232	8,728	8,728	8,963	8,728	8,960
1979	33,300	31,942	33,255	31,432	31,432	31,044	31,432	9,308	9,305	7,314	238	9,069	9,069	9,313	9,070	9,308
1980	28,200	26,966	28,239	26,246	26,246	25,632	26,246	9,147	9,087	7,115	297	8,860	8,860	9,160	8,860	9,157
1981	25,400	24,956	25,432	24,676	24,676	24,518	24,676	8,046	8,018	6,252	334	7,147	7,147	7,378	7,146	7,480
1982	23,787	24,098	24,949	23,787	23,787	23,631	23,787	7,946	7,854	5,061	329	7,668	7,668	7,995	7,667	7,996
1983	29,726	29,991	28,926	29,726	29,726	29,547	29,726	8,767	8,822	5,627	211	8,556	8,556	8,768	8,556	8,767
1984	31,174	31,192	30,801	31,174	31,174	30,945	31,174	9,844	9,826	6,264	211	9,865	9,865	10,082	9,879	10,090
1985	31,321	30,853	30,479	31,321	31,321	31,092	31,321	9,537	9,474	5,966	204	8,866	8,866	9,597	9,394	9,597
1986	35,273	34,700	34,815	35,273	35,273	35,003	35,273	10,347	10,311	7,184	249	10,877	10,877	10,819	10,228	10,477
1987	38,325	z	37,410	38,235	38,235	38,039	38,235	11,263	z	7,476	253	11,695	11,695	11,465	11,010	11,263
1988	38,130	z	36,845	38,130	38,130	37,826	38,130	11,741	z	7,731	275	12,170	12,170	12,151	11,466	11,741
1989	37,545	z	36,040	37,545	37,225	37,225	37,545	11,944	z	7,536	313	12,415	12,415	12,236	11,743	12,056
1990	35,791	z	36,224	35,791	35,459	35,459	35,791	12,021	z	7,242	374	12,660	12,660	11,947	12,321
1991	33,161	z	33,064	33,161	32,800	32,800	33,161	11,046	z	6,766	363	11,633	11,633	11,383	10,805	11,168
1992	34,526	z	33,704	34,526	34,151	34,151	34,526	11,423	z	7,050	416	11,639	11,639	11,630	11,007	11,423
1993	32,947	z	34,725	32,947	32,517	32,517	32,947	11,732	z	10,631	438	11,914	11,914	12,170	11,781	12,219
1994	34,107	z	35,556	34,107	33,657	33,657	34,107	11,108	z	10,910	445	12,311	12,311	12,311	11,940	12,385
1995	32,233	z	33,043	32,233	31,782	31,782	32,233	11,307	z	10,928	441	12,434	12,434	12,434	12,203	12,644
1996	33,266	z	34,065	33,266	32,859	32,859	33,266	12,725	z	10,690	449	z	z	12,705	12,039	12,488
1997	34,667	z	35,457	34,667	34,663	34,662	34,667	12,921	z	11,103	468	z	z	z	12,205	12,673
1998	34,677	z	35,896	34,677	34,678	z	34,677	12,729	z	11,367	407	z	z	z	12,322	12,729
1999	36,605	z	38,033	36,605	36,816	z	36,605	12,927	z	12,523	508	z	z	z	12,419	12,927
2000	35,964	z	37,147	35,964	35,965	z	35,964	12,598	z	12,298	518	z	z	z	12,080	12,598
2001	34,581	z	35,479	34,581	34,579	z	34,581	11,834	z	11,109	475	z	z	z	11,359	11,834
2002	35,830	z	36,329	35,830	36,418	z	35,830	11,750	z	11,122	470	z	z	z	11,280	11,750
2003	36,607	z	36,687	36,607	36,608	z	36,607	10,880	z	10,494	386	z	z	z	10,494	10,880
2004	39,075	z	38,502	39,075	39,112	z	39,075	11,679	z	10,954	391	z	z	z	11,288	11,679
2005	40,698	z	38,502	40,698	40,785	z	40,698	11,591	z	10,900	391	z	z	z	11,200	11,591

^a Data derived from Table 28.

^b U.S. Department of Agriculture, Forest Service (49).

^c U.S. Department of Commerce, Bureau of the Census (57).

^d 1950-1965: National Forest Products Association. 1966. Forest Industry facts 1966. Washington, DC: National Forest Products Association. 31 p.
 1986-Present: American Forest & Paper Association (4).

^e Western Wood Products Associaton (83).

^f Adams, Luppold, and Dempsy (1).

^g Final estimated Forest Service softwood lumber production series: 1950-1975: USDC Bureau of the Census. 1998. 1976-present AF&PA 1998 (7).

^h Forest Service (24). Estimated Eastern hardwood lumber production.

^i Final estimated Forest Service hardwood lumber production series: 1965-1998: Luppold and Dempsey (24) plus USDC Bureau of the Census 1998 - West (57).

^r 1996-1999 numbers revised.

^z Not available.

Table 31—United States lumber imports, by softwoods and hardwoods and country of origin, 1965–2005 (million board feet)[a]

Year	All species				Softwoods				Hardwoods			
	Total	Canada	Mexico	Other[b]	Total[c]	Canada	Mexico	Other[b]	Total	Canada	Mexico	Other[b]
1965	5,232.4	5,016.6	10.1	205.7	4,898.1	4,855.7	8.1	34.3	334.3	160.9	2.0	171.4
1966	5,200.0	4,920.9	5.2	273.9	4,779.2	4,730.4	3.7	45.1	420.8	190.5	1.5	228.8
1967	5,140.8	4,902.5	5.6	232.7	4,798.1	4,747.1	3.1	47.9	342.7	155.4	2.5	184.8
1968	6,154.2	5,899.2	4.0	251.0	5,809.1	5,750.0	3.2	55.9	345.1	149.2	0.8	195.1
1969	6,300.6	5,963.4	6.6	330.6	5,854.0	5,784.4	5.8	63.8	446.6	179.0	0.8	266.8
1970	6,114.4	5,867.6	7.5	239.3	5,777.7	5,722.5	5.5	49.7	336.7	145.1	2.0	189.6
1971	7,589.4	7,314.5	6.5	268.4	7,231.7	7,172.0	4.9	54.8	357.7	142.5	1.6	213.6
1972	9,433.6	9,029.2	20.5	383.9	8,984.8	8,877.8	18.6	88.4	448.8	151.4	1.9	295.5
1973	9,568.6	8,999.3	20.4	548.9	9,019.9	8,843.9	17.5	158.5	548.7	155.4	2.9	390.4
1974	7,270.8	6,847.3	6.1	417.4	6,821.1	6,732.2	2.4	86.5	449.7	115.1	3.7	330.9
1975	5,975.8	5,738.8	28.5	208.5	5,723.8	5,677.0	0.4	46.4	252.0	61.8	28.1	162.1
1976	8,246.8	7,995.3	1.0	250.5	7,958.5	7,912.6	0.8	45.1	288.3	82.7	0.2	205.4
1977	10,713.3	10,408.0	7.0	298.3	10,369.6	10,327.0	1.2	41.4	343.7	81.0	5.8	256.9
1978	12,214.6	11,879.4	11.9	323.3	11,853.2	11,776.7	11.3	65.2	361.4	102.7	0.6	258.1
1979	11,529.5	11,187.6	4.7	337.2	11,153.3	11,100.9	3.1	49.3	376.2	86.7	1.6	287.9
1980	9,866.1	9,618.7	2.9	244.5	9,572.9	9,546.3	2.5	24.1	293.2	72.4	0.4	220.4
1981	9,523.2	9,285.4	1.8	236.0	9,232.1	9,208.1	1.5	22.5	291.1	77.3	0.3	213.5
1982	9,360.5	9,191.8	6.5	162.2	9,149.5	9,114.9	1.1	33.5	211.0	76.9	5.4	128.7
1983	12,253.5	12,039.6	13.6	200.3	11,993.0	11,962.7	12.0	18.3	260.5	76.9	1.6	182.0
1984	13,632.1	13,342.8	14.6	274.7	13,304.4	13,252.3	11.8	40.3	327.7	90.5	2.8	234.4
1985	14,995.6	14,636.1	12.2	347.3	14,632.0	14,531.7	11.8	88.5	363.6	104.4	0.4	258.8
1986	14,585.1	14,250.0	32.8	302.3	14,238.2	14,142.3	31.9	64.0	346.9	107.7	0.9	238.3
1987	15,191.5	14,763.3	55.1	373.1	14,680.4	14,600.8	54.1	25.5	511.1	162.5	1.0	347.6
1988	13,777.8	12,999.2	72.9	705.7	13,473.0	12,855.2	72.5	545.2	304.8	144.0	0.3	160.5
1989	15,258.4	13,964.2	193.4	1,100.8	14,909.0	13,761.2	193.0	954.8	349.4	202.9	0.4	146.0
1990	13,106.7	11,918.4	360.4	827.8	12,875.0	11,804.7	360.3	710.0	231.7	113.6	0.2	117.8
1991	11,725.2	11,517.6	48.0	159.6	11,515.0	11,410.8	47.8	56.4	210.2	106.8	0.2	103.2
1992	13,449.9	13,207.9	53.3	188.7	13,190.0	13,055.1	53.1	81.9	259.9	152.8	0.2	106.8
1993	15,399.5	15,059.7	51.7	288.1	15,086.0	14,856.2	51.6	178.3	313.5	203.5	0.2	109.8
1994	16,593.3	16,103.5	51.6	438.1	16,224.0	15,871.6	51.4	301.0	369.3	231.9	0.2	137.1
1995	17,556.3	16,989.5	108.8	458.0	17,202.0	16,780.5	106.2	315.3	354.3	209.0	2.7	142.7
1996	18,397.8	17,823.6	120.9	453.3	18,021.0	17,593.2	117.6	310.2	376.8	230.4	3.3	143.1
1997	18,451.2	17,535.7	124.4	791.1	18,000.0	17,235.5	120.0	644.5	451.2	300.2	4.4	146.6
1998	19,234.5	18,227.8	70.1	936.7	18,685.7	17,838.0	66.5	781.2	548.8	389.8	3.5	155.5
1999	19,854.2	18,486.5	58.3	1,309.4	19,178.0	18,021.2	56.9	1,099.9	676.2	465.4	1.4	209.5
2000	20,243.3	18,615.6	31.3	1,596.4	19,448.6	18,104.8	30.5	1,313.4	794.7	510.8	0.8	283.0
2001	20,720.1	18,930.3	27.7	1,762.1	20,074.5	18,503.0	27.2	1,544.3	645.6	427.3	0.5	217.8
2002	21,724.1	19,397.3	19.6	2,307.2	20,985.6	18,922.8	19.2	2,043.7	738.5	474.5	0.4	263.6
2003	21,981.2	19,709.0	15.3	2,256.9	21,187.7	19,257.8	15.0	1,914.9	793.5	451.2	0.3	342.0
2004	25,492.9	21,330.7	20.0	4,142.3	24,498.3	20,844.3	19.2	3,634.8	994.6	486.4	0.7	507.5
2005	25,701.3	21,840.7	16.0	3,844.6	24,626.2	21,367.6	15.0	3,243.6	1,075.1	473.1	1.0	601.0

[a] U.S. International Trade Commission (80); U.S. Department of Commerce, Bureau of the Census (57)
Data may not add to totals because of rounding.
[b] For the years 1974 to 1977, all imports with a value of less than $500 are included in Other.
[c] Includes small volumes of hardwoods.

Table 32—United States lumber exports, by softwoods and hardwoods and country or region of destination, 1965–2005 (million board feet)[a]

	All species						Softwoods						Hardwoods					
Year	Total	Canada	European Union[b]	Central and South America[c]	Japan	Other	Total	Canada	European Union	Central and South America	Japan	Other	Total	Canada	European Union	Central and South America	Japan	Other
1965	919.1	285.1	249.4	1.1	105.7	277.8	778.9	184.0	229.3	1.0	103.1	261.5	140.2	101.1	20.1	0.1	2.6	16.3
1966	1,022.6	309.0	250.2	1.3	174.4	287.7	867.9	186.5	230.3	1.2	171.3	278.6	154.7	122.5	19.9	0.1	3.1	9.1
1967	1,129.5	338.0	261.0	1.1	265.8	263.6	965.2	207.6	241.0	1.1	260.7	254.8	164.3	130.4	20.0	0.0	5.1	8.8
1968	1,161.7	295.4	304.3	1.2	288.6	272.2	1,048.1	210.4	288.9	1.1	284.8	262.9	113.6	85.0	15.4	0.1	3.8	9.3
1969	1,142.2	285.0	278.3	1.1	317.3	260.5	1,023.8	198.3	264.6	1.0	309.6	250.3	118.4	86.7	13.7	0.1	7.7	10.2
1970	1,243.4	269.9	299.3	1.3	383.5	289.4	1,115.5	202.6	281.8	1.1	359.6	270.4	127.9	67.3	17.5	0.2	23.9	19.0
1971	1,093.6	289.3	239.0	1.0	323.1	241.2	933.3	206.3	213.8	0.9	287.4	224.9	160.3	83.0	25.2	0.1	35.7	16.3
1972	1,428.3	419.5	286.0	1.0	478.7	243.1	1,191.1	290.1	267.9	0.9	407.2	225.0	237.2	129.4	18.1	0.1	71.5	18.1
1973	1,965.9	548.4	517.0	1.2	569.1	330.2	1,752.7	388.5	488.3	1.0	564.4	310.5	213.2	159.9	28.7	0.2	4.7	19.7
1974	1,765.4	522.3	347.4	1.1	573.9	320.7	1,566.5	382.2	311.3	1.0	570.5	301.5	198.9	140.1	36.1	0.1	3.4	19.2
1975	1,618.1	549.4	244.9	1.3	516.8	305.7	1,405.4	397.5	218.7	1.1	515.3	272.8	212.7	151.9	26.2	0.2	1.5	32.9
1976	1,846.0	619.7	354.5	1.4	478.0	392.4	1,605.5	437.9	316.3	1.3	475.1	374.9	240.5	181.8	38.2	0.1	2.9	17.5
1977	1,665.6	537.4	336.6	1.5	439.6	350.5	1,427.7	365.5	288.6	1.4	436.7	335.5	237.9	171.9	48.0	0.1	2.9	15.0
1978	1,740.9	648.4	347.4	1.3	411.3	332.5	1,353.9	374.4	257.6	1.3	407.6	313.0	387.0	274.0	89.8	0.0	3.7	19.5
1979	2,186.5	651.5	456.1	2.0	647.6	429.3	1,781.3	427.6	345.6	1.9	640.5	365.7	361.1	223.9	110.5	0.1	7.1	19.5
1980	2,506.8	631.3	594.7	3.6	648.9	628.3	2,006.5	388.3	429.2	3.2	633.9	551.9	487.5	243.0	165.5	0.4	15.0	63.6
1981	2,379.0	729.1	398.3	4.0	524.3	723.3	1,927.8	509.1	234.4	3.6	506.5	674.2	478.5	220.0	163.9	0.4	17.8	76.4
1982	2,050.3	418.9	410.6	3.1	627.9	589.8	1,634.9	261.9	248.2	2.9	610.7	511.2	385.9	157.0	162.4	0.2	17.2	49.1
1983	2,319.1	664.1	458.8	2.3	631.6	562.3	1,755.6	433.2	290.6	2.0	595.3	434.5	514.3	230.9	168.2	0.3	36.3	78.6
1984	2,121.0	555.7	345.0	2.7	602.4	615.2	1,623.6	347.7	212.0	2.1	545.0	516.8	526.8	208.0	133.0	0.6	57.4	127.8
1985	1,840.9	431.3	277.0	5.3	617.6	509.7	1,420.1	300.7	177.3	4.7	574.2	363.2	372.7	130.6	99.7	0.6	43.4	98.4
1986	2,422.0	510.1	395.3	10.6	888.3	617.7	1,888.4	361.2	253.3	10.0	827.0	436.9	499.3	148.9	142.0	0.6	61.3	146.5
1987	3,241.0	648.0	528.1	9.0	1,200.5	855.4	2,447.0	445.8	309.5	8.1	1,077.2	606.4	725.8	202.2	218.6	0.9	123.3	180.8
1988	4,347.8	753.7	891.0	5.0	1,532.4	1,165.7	3,227.5	493.9	490.5	3.5	1,280.0	959.6	1,163.2	259.8	400.5	1.5	252.4	249.0
1989	4,136.9	642.7	673.1	7.7	1,614.2	1,199.1	3,339.6	457.1	397.0	6.7	1,457.8	1,021.0	825.3	185.6	276.1	1.0	156.4	206.1
1990	4,614.4	657.6	685.8	6.7	1,270.3	1,994.0	3,752.9	422.7	412.0	6.0	1,145.1	1,767.1	812.8	234.9	273.8	0.7	125.2	178.1
1991	3,880.1	564.8	753.7	10.7	1,215.7	1,335.2	2,999.5	365.4	429.2	10.2	1,086.1	1,108.6	880.9	199.4	324.5	0.5	129.6	226.9
1992	3,512.5	571.7	735.1	9.3	1,112.9	1,083.5	2,567.3	313.8	399.2	8.3	1,003.6	842.5	930.8	258.0	335.9	1.0	109.3	226.6
1993	3,280.3	566.0	548.1	4.7	1,180.5	980.9	2,291.5	267.0	242.8	3.7	1,063.2	714.8	963.7	299.0	305.3	1.0	117.4	241.0
1994	3,115.4	610.7	543.8	7.2	1,056.6	897.0	2,078.0	285.5	230.5	6.4	958.4	597.2	1,003.5	325.1	313.3	0.8	98.2	266.1
1995	2,957.8	650.3	513.4	5.9	978.2	810.0	1,872.1	312.5	201.5	4.7	871.6	481.8	1,057.3	337.8	311.9	1.2	106.6	299.8
1996	2,897.9	664.3	485.3	7.2	961.3	779.8	1,788.7	312.3	178.2	5.3	860.7	432.2	1,089.8	352.0	307.1	1.9	100.6	328.2
1997	2,933.4	713.3	592.3	15.9	796.6	815.3	1,709.4	329.3	206.2	14.0	692.2	467.7	1,224.0	384.0	386.1	1.9	104.4	347.6
1998	2,189.4	576.3	560.8	15.3	355.4	681.5	1,129.2	230.6	207.0	10.8	297.5	383.3	1,060.2	345.7	353.8	4.5	57.9	298.2
1999	2,548.6	659.3	555.8	11.1	353.2	969.1	1,366.5	255.4	214.2	7.3	288.7	600.9	1,182.1	404.0	341.6	3.9	64.5	368.1
2000	2,700.0	700.7	506.5	12.7	325.4	1,154.7	1,400.0	265.2	151.8	10.6	274.8	697.6	1,300.0	435.6	354.7	2.1	50.6	457.1
2001	2,190.3	571.3	391.3	5.1	226.6	996.0	968.8	186.4	86.3	2.4	180.2	513.4	1,221.5	384.9	304.9	2.7	46.4	482.6
2002[r]	2,185.7	585.0	357.7	4.1	154.8	1,084.1	966.4	174.4	73.2	2.3	115.2	601.3	1,219.3	410.6	284.5	1.8	39.6	482.7
2003	2,117.6	633.4	347.8	2.9	149.0	984.5	957.0	201.5	76.0	1.4	111.5	566.6	1,160.6	431.9	271.8	1.5	37.5	417.9
2004	2,097.7	629.3	339.6	7.4	119.3	1,002.2	821.0	189.9	53.9	2.1	82.5	492.6	1,276.7	439.4	285.7	5.2	36.8	509.6
2005	2,347.8	649.0	345.7	10.0	79.5	1,263.5	897.0	226.8	65.8	5.6	49.2	549.7	1,450.8	422.3	280.0	4.4	30.3	713.8

[a]U.S. International Trade Commission (80); Data may not add to totals because of rounding.
[b]Includes Belgium–Luxembourg, Denmark, France, Germany, Greece, Ireland, Italy, the Netherlands, Portugal, Spain, Trieste, and the United Kingdom.
[c]Includes Mexico.
[r]Revised.

Table 33—Lumber[a] production in Canada, by softwoods and hardwoods and region, 1965–2005 (billion board feet)[b]

Year	All species	Softwoods					Hardwoods		
		Total	British Columbia[c]			Other Canada	Total	British Columbia	Other Canada
			Total	Coast	Interior				
1965	10.8	10.3	7.4	3.6	3.8	2.9	0.5	z	0.5
1966	10.6	10.0	7.3	3.7	3.6	2.7	0.6	z	0.6
1967	10.3	9.7	7.1	3.9	3.2	2.6	0.6	z	0.6
1968	11.4	10.8	7.8	4.1	3.7	3.0	0.6	d	0.6
1969	11.5	11.0	7.7	3.8	3.9	3.3	0.5	d	0.5
1970	11.3	10.8	7.7	3.8	3.9	3.1	0.5	d	0.5
1971	12.8	12.3	9.0	4.2	4.8	3.3	0.5	d	0.5
1972	13.9	13.4	9.5	4.0	5.5	3.9	0.5	d	0.5
1973	15.5	14.9	10.4	4.4	6.0	4.5	0.6	d	0.6
1974	13.6	13.0	8.7	3.4	5.3	4.3	0.6	d	0.6
1975	11.5	11.1	7.4	2.5	4.9	3.7	0.4	d	0.4
1976	15.6	15.1	10.6	4.0	6.6	4.5	0.5	d	0.5
1977	17.6	17.2	12.0	4.5	7.5	5.2	0.4	d	0.4
1978	19.0	18.4	12.5	4.8	7.7	5.9	0.6	d	0.6
1979	19.8	19.3	12.9	4.7	8.2	6.4	0.5	d	0.5
1980	19.0	18.4	11.9	4.2	7.7	6.5	0.6	d	0.6
1981	17.0	16.6	10.4	3.5	6.9	6.2	0.4	d	0.4
1982	15.6	15.2	9.9	3.0	6.9	5.3	0.4	d	0.4
1983	20.5	20.1	13.0	4.1	8.9	7.1	0.4	d	0.4
1984	20.7	20.2	13.1	3.9	9.2	7.1	0.5	d	0.5
1985	22.0	21.6	13.6	3.6	10.0	8.0	0.4	d	0.4
1986	22.4	21.9	13.1	3.7	9.4	8.8	0.5	d	0.5
1987	26.2	25.6	15.9	4.7	11.2	9.7	0.6	d	0.6
1988	25.7	25.1	15.6	4.6	11.0	9.5	0.6	d	0.6
1989	25.0	24.5	15.2	4.1	11.1	9.3	0.5	d	0.5
1990	23.1	22.7	14.2	3.8	10.4	8.5	0.4	d	0.4
1991	21.9	21.5	13.3	3.5	9.8	8.2	0.4	d	0.4
1992	23.6	23.1	14.1	3.5	10.6	9.0	0.5	d	0.5
1993	25.3	24.8	14.4	3.6	10.8	10.4	0.5	d	0.5
1994	26.1	25.6	14.3	3.7	10.6	11.3	0.5	d	0.5
1995	26.0	25.5	13.8	3.5	10.4	11.7	0.5	d	0.5
1996	27.0	26.6	13.8	3.5	10.4	12.7	0.4	d	0.4
1997	27.4	27.1	13.4	3.3	10.0	13.7	0.4	d	0.4
1998	27.5	27.2	12.8	2.7	10.1	14.4	0.4	d	0.4
1999	29.5	29.2	13.5	2.8	10.7	15.7	0.4	d	0.4
2000	29.8	29.4	13.6	2.9	10.8	15.8	0.4	d	0.4
2001	28.2	27.8	12.8	2.2	10.5	15.0	0.4	d	0.4
2002	30.9	29.5	13.7	2.2	11.5	15.8	1.4	d	1.4
2003	29.8	29.4	13.7	2.2	11.6	15.7	0.4	d	0.4
2004	30.3	29.9	13.9	2.2	11.8	16.0	0.4	d	0.4
2005	26.3	25.9	13.1	z	z	12.8	0.4	d	0.4

[a]Does not include sawn ties.
[b]Natural Resources Canada (28); Statistics Canada (33,34,35);
Wood Markets (84) Bilateral Trade-Canada (2)
Data may not add to totals because of rounding.
[c]Includes small volumes of hardwoods.
[d]Fewer than 50 million board feet.
[z]Not Available

Table 34—Lumber and competing engineered wood products production, by type of product, 1970-2005

Year	Wood laminated veneer lumber[a]	Wood glulam[a]	Wood I-joists[a]	Structural panels[a]		Lumber[b]	
				Oriented strandboard	Softwood plywood	Hardwood	Softwood
	Million cubic feet	Million board feet	Million linear feet	Million square feet (3/8-in. basis)	Million square feet (3/8-in. basis)	Billion board feet	Billion board feet
1970	z	z	z	z	14,340	8.3	27.5
1971	z	z	z	z	16,635	8.4	30.0
1972	z	z	z	z	18,324	8.5	31.0
1973	z	z	z	z	18,305	8.8	31.6
1974	z	z	z	z	15,878	8.4	27.7
1975	z	z	z	z	16,050	7.3	26.7
1976	z	z	z	z	18,440	8.0	29.7
1977	z	z	z	z	19,376	8.5	31.7
1978	z	z	z	z	19,964	9.0	32.1
1979	z	z	z	z	19,653	9.3	31.4
1980	3	204	45	135	16,333	9.2	26.2
1981	4	190	45	271	16,752	7.5	24.7
1982	4	164	54	557	15,846	8.0	23.8
1983	5	192	63	1,341	19,480	8.8	29.7
1984	5	229	72	2,042	19,926	10.1	31.2
1985	7	246	90	2,669	20,169	9.6	31.3
1986	8	330	99	3,513	22,118	10.5	35.3
1987	9	279	108	4,076	22,899	11.3	38.2
1988	11	298	108	4,604	22,599	11.7	38.1
1989	12	322	117	5,105	21,385	12.1	37.5
1990	16	324	122	5,418	20,919	12.3	35.8
1991	16	265	158	5,613	18,652	11.2	33.2
1992	17	258	252	6,653	19,332	11.4	34.5
1993	21	239	358	7,002	19,315	12.2	32.9
1994	23	264	380	7,486	19,638	12.4	34.1
1995	28	282	358	7,903	19,367	12.6	32.2
1996	32	309	444	9,314	19,181	12.5	33.3
1997	38	300	547	10,534	17,963	12.7	34.7
1998	41	287	619	11,227	17,776	12.7	34.7
1999	48	316	733	11,612	17,816	12.9	36.6
2000	48	356	693	11,906	17,475	12.6	36.0
2001	53	335	746	12,532	15,121	11.8	34.6
2002	56	321	756	13,426	15,200	11.8	35.8
2003	68	344	1,075	13,615	14,706	10.9	36.6
2004	86	402	1,282	14,271	14,665	11.7	39.1
2005	91	491	1,263	14,985	14,330	11.6	40.7

[a]APA–The Engineered Wood Association (11,13).

[b]U.S. Department of Commerce, Bureau of the Census (57); American Forest & Paper Association (4); Luppold and Dempsey (24).

[z]Data not available.

[p]Preliminary

Table 35—Producer price indexes for lumber and selected nonwood competing materials, 1965–2005 (1997 = 100)[a]

Year	All commodities	Lumber and wood products		All lumber		Softwood lumber						All hardwood lumber	
						All		Douglas-fir*		Southern pine*			
		Actual	Relative[b]	Actual	Relative	Actual	Relative	Actual	Relative	Actual	Relative	Actual	Relative
1965	25.3	18.3	72.5	15.5	61.3	14.0	55.4	15.7	62.1	17.1	67.6	21.3	84.2
1966	26.1	19.1	73.4	16.6	63.5	14.7	56.4	16.5	63.1	18.8	72.0	23.8	91.2
1967	26.2	19.1	72.8	16.6	63.3	15.1	57.7	17.0	65.0	18.8	71.8	21.9	83.6
1968	26.8	21.6	80.7	19.4	72.3	18.2	67.8	20.5	76.3	21.4	79.8	22.8	85.2
1969	27.9	23.9	85.8	21.8	78.0	20.3	72.6	22.5	80.5	23.7	85.0	26.3	94.3
1970	28.9	21.7	75.0	18.8	65.0	17.0	58.9	18.5	63.9	21.5	74.5	25.1	86.8
1971	29.9	24.3	81.5	22.5	75.4	21.3	71.2	23.8	79.8	25.2	84.3	24.8	83.0
1972	31.2	27.6	88.5	26.4	84.6	25.2	80.9	27.4	88.0	28.5	91.3	27.6	88.5
1973	35.3	33.8	95.9	33.9	96.1	32.3	91.5	35.6	101.0	35.3	100.0	37.0	104.8
1974	41.9	35.1	83.7	34.2	81.7	31.8	75.9	36.4	86.8	34.6	82.6	41.5	99.0
1975	45.8	33.8	73.9	31.8	69.5	30.2	65.9	36.0	78.7	33.0	72.0	35.1	76.7
1976	47.9	39.2	82.0	38.6	80.5	37.4	78.0	42.7	89.1	40.8	85.2	38.6	80.6
1977	50.9	45.1	88.8	45.7	89.8	44.8	88.0	49.6	97.5	49.3	96.9	43.8	86.2
1978	54.8	52.7	96.2	53.3	97.2	52.1	95.1	57.8	105.5	57.2	104.5	51.7	94.3
1979	61.7	57.4	93.1	58.5	94.9	57.2	92.7	65.3	105.9	60.9	98.8	56.9	92.3
1980	70.4	55.2	78.4	53.9	76.5	52.0	73.8	60.1	85.4	55.9	79.4	55.1	78.3
1981	76.8	55.9	72.8	53.7	69.9	51.6	67.2	53.0	69.1	54.8	71.4	55.9	72.8
1982	78.4	54.4	69.4	51.4	65.6	48.4	61.8	45.3	57.8	53.7	68.5	57.5	73.3
1983	79.4	58.7	73.9	58.3	73.5	55.7	70.2	61.5	77.5	60.1	75.7	62.1	78.2
1984	81.3	58.8	72.3	57.8	71.1	53.2	65.5	55.8	68.6	60.1	74.0	70.0	86.1
1985	80.9	58.0	71.7	56.3	69.6	52.0	64.3	57.3	70.9	56.5	69.9	67.2	83.1
1986	78.5	58.3	74.3	56.8	72.3	52.5	66.8	56.4	71.8	56.4	71.8	67.9	86.4
1987	80.6	61.3	76.1	60.7	75.3	56.2	69.8	56.6	70.3	61.3	76.1	72.8	90.4
1988	83.8	64.7	77.2	62.7	74.8	58.1	69.4	61.5	73.4	60.4	72.1	75.2	89.8
1989	87.9	68.9	78.4	64.6	73.4	61.5	70.0	68.7	78.1	58.1	66.0	73.6	83.7
1990	91.1	70.6	77.5	64.0	70.3	59.9	65.8	62.7	68.8	59.8	65.6	75.2	82.5
1991	91.3	71.9	78.7	64.2	70.3	60.9	66.7	63.2	69.2	59.7	68.6	73.9	80.9
1992	91.8	79.8	86.8	74.3	80.9	71.9	78.2	76.6	83.4	70.1	76.4	80.7	87.9
1993	93.2	94.7	101.6	94.2	101.1	93.5	100.3	107.6	115.5	90.7	97.3	93.8	100.7
1994	94.4	98.0	103.9	97.0	102.8	95.9	101.7	107.1	113.5	98.0	103.9	96.7	102.5
1995	97.7	96.9	99.2	89.1	91.1	86.5	88.5	90.0	92.1	89.7	91.8	96.0	98.2
1996	100.1	95.9	95.8	92.4	92.3	91.9	91.8	103.8	103.8	95.4	95.4	94.2	94.1
1997	100.0	100.0	100.0	100.0	100.0	100.0	100.0	100.0	100.0	100.0	100.0	100.0	100.0
1998	97.5	97.4	100.0	90.9	93.3	88.4	90.7	84.2	86.4	95.1	97.5	102.7	105.3
1999	98.4	99.9	101.6	95.4	97.0	94.9	96.5	96.1	97.7	99.8	101.5	101.9	103.6
2000	104.0	97.0	93.2	90.6	87.1	86.5	83.2	83.9	80.7	86.5	83.2	106.8	102.7
2001	105.2	94.9	90.2	87.0	82.7	82.4	78.3	80.7	76.7	82.0	77.9	104.2	99.0
2002	102.7	94.3	91.8	86.5	84.1	82.7	80.5	80.8	78.7	78.0	75.9	102.4	99.7
2003	108.2	96.5	89.2	88.3	81.6	82.7	76.4	80.0	73.9	78.1	72.2	108.5	100.2
2004	115.0	106.4	92.6	103.2	89.7	101.6	88.4	z	z	z	z	114.5	99.6
2005	123.4	106.9	86.7	100.6	81.6	98.6	79.9	z	z	z	z	112.9	91.6

Table 35—Producer price indexes for lumber and selected nonwood competing materials, 1965–2005 (1997 = 100)[a]—Con.

Year	Metals and metal products		Metal doors, sash, and trim		Flat glass		Concrete products		Ready mixed concrete	
	Actual	Relative	Actual	Relative	Actual	Relative	Actual	Relative	Actual	Relative
1965	24.3	95.9	20.4	80.5	z	z	23.8	93.8	23.3	92.1
1966	24.9	95.4	20.9	79.9	z	z	24.1	92.4	23.6	90.4
1967	25.2	96.2	21.4	81.6	41.7	159.5	24.7	94.4	24.1	92.1
1968	25.8	96.3	22.2	82.9	43.5	162.3	25.4	94.6	24.8	92.5
1969	27.3	97.9	23.2	83.0	45.7	163.8	26.3	94.4	25.9	92.8
1970	29.4	101.5	24.2	83.5	48.2	166.7	27.7	95.9	27.4	94.6
1971	29.9	100.1	25.1	84.2	51.3	171.9	29.8	99.7	29.6	99.1
1972	31.0	99.5	25.8	82.6	51.1	163.7	31.0	99.5	30.8	98.8
1973	33.4	94.7	26.6	75.5	50.6	143.5	32.5	92.2	32.2	91.2
1974	43.3	103.2	31.5	75.1	53.7	128.2	37.4	89.3	37.0	88.1
1975	46.7	102.0	34.7	75.8	58.0	126.7	42.1	92.1	41.5	90.6
1976	49.3	103.0	36.6	76.5	62.5	130.6	44.5	92.9	44.4	92.7
1977	52.6	103.4	40.3	79.2	67.0	131.8	47.4	93.1	47.4	93.2
1978	57.1	104.3	44.4	81.0	72.0	131.5	52.9	96.5	52.8	96.4
1979	65.3	105.8	49.1	79.5	76.6	124.3	60.3	97.8	60.2	97.6
1980	72.1	102.4	54.5	77.5	81.9	116.4	67.6	96.1	67.9	96.4
1981	75.6	98.4	59.6	77.6	88.6	115.4	71.9	93.6	72.4	94.2
1982	75.9	96.8	62.1	79.2	92.3	117.8	73.5	93.8	73.8	94.1
1983	77.2	97.3	63.8	80.4	95.8	120.6	74.6	93.9	74.7	94.1
1984	79.5	97.9	66.2	81.4	93.6	115.2	764.0	940.1	76.9	94.7
1985	79.2	97.9	66.6	82.4	93.9	116.1	79.0	97.7	79.0	97.7
1986	78.3	99.7	67.6	86.1	96.5	122.9	80.3	102.3	79.4	101.2
1987	81.3	100.9	69.5	86.3	99.0	122.9	80.4	99.8	79.1	98.2
1988	90.1	107.5	76.0	90.7	101.3	120.9	80.9	96.5	79.6	95.0
1989	94.2	107.1	80.7	91.8	101.3	115.2	81.8	93.0	80.6	91.7
1990	93.3	102.3	81.6	89.5	99.3	108.9	83.5	91.6	82.5	90.6
1991	91.2	99.9	83.6	91.5	97.8	107.1	85.7	93.9	84.6	92.7
1992	90.4	98.5	83.8	91.2	98.4	107.2	86.2	93.8	85.0	92.5
1993	90.4	97.1	84.8	91.0	99.1	106.3	88.4	94.9	87.6	94.0
1994	94.7	100.4	88.2	93.4	101.9	108.0	91.5	97.0	91.2	96.7
1995	102.1	104.4	97.2	99.4	104.5	107.0	95.1	97.4	95.1	97.4
1996	99.4	99.3	98.9	98.8	101.6	101.5	97.9	97.9	98.2	98.1
1997	100.0	100.0	100.0	100.0	100.0	100.0	100.0	100.0	100.0	100.0
1998	97.0	99.5	100.3	102.9	99.0	101.5	103.0	105.7	103.1	105.8
1999	94.5	96.1	100.7	102.4	98.2	99.9	105.6	107.4	105.7	107.4
2000	97.2	93.5	102.5	98.6	101.3	97.4	108.6	104.5	108.5	104.4
2001	95.2	90.5	103.7	98.6	103.4	98.3	111.5	106.0	110.9	105.4
2002	95.5	93.0	104.3	101.5	102.7	99.9	112.2	109.2	110.8	107.9
2003	98.0	90.6	105.5	97.5	102.5	94.7	112.9	104.3	111.3	102.8
2004	113.5	98.7	109.1	94.9	100.3	87.2	118.5	103.1	117.1	101.8
2005	122.0	98.9	114.8	93.1	102.5	83.1	130.2	105.6	131.1	106.3

Table 35—Producer price indexes for lumber and selected nonwood competing materials, 1965–2005 (1997 = 100)[a]—Con.

Year	Ceramic tile[c] Actual	Relative	Prepared asphalt roofing[d] Actual	Relative	Gypsum products Actual	Relative	Soft surface floor covering Actual	Relative	Hard surface floor covering Actual	Relative
1965	33.7	133.3	28.7	113.4	23.1	91.4	53.7	212.3	26.9	106.3
1966	34.2	131.0	30.1	115.2	22.8	87.3	53.5	205.0	26.7	102.3
1967	34.9	133.3	29.3	112.1	22.9	87.5	51.0	194.8	26.5	101.3
1968	35.9	134.0	30.5	113.7	23.7	88.5	51.3	191.4	27.2	101.6
1969	37.1	132.9	30.4	108.8	23.7	85.0	51.3	183.9	26.5	95.0
1970	38.1	131.7	29.8	103.2	22.8	78.8	50.4	174.4	26.6	91.9
1971	39.8	133.3	37.1	124.3	25.0	83.7	49.3	165.1	27.6	92.3
1972	40.0	128.1	39.2	125.6	26.2	84.1	49.0	157.0	27.7	88.7
1973	41.5	117.8	40.6	115.2	27.6	78.4	51.5	146.0	27.9	79.0
1974	45.4	108.2	55.8	133.0	31.4	75.0	56.5	134.8	33.3	79.5
1975	50.7	110.8	63.9	139.7	32.9	71.9	58.4	127.5	39.3	86.0
1976	54.5	113.8	67.9	141.8	35.3	73.7	60.1	125.4	43.2	90.3
1977	55.4	109.0	72.3	142.2	42.0	82.5	62.2	122.2	45.6	89.6
1978	55.1	100.6	84.7	154.6	52.4	95.7	64.4	117.5	47.8	87.3
1979	59.8	96.9	92.4	149.9	57.7	93.5	66.2	107.4	52.8	85.6
1980	63.2	89.8	109.3	155.4	58.6	83.3	72.1	102.5	60.5	85.9
1981	68.6	89.4	105.3	137.1	58.6	76.3	80.1	104.3	63.7	82.9
1982	72.3	92.2	103.6	132.2	58.6	74.7	81.1	103.4	64.8	82.7
1983	75.0	94.5	97.5	122.8	65.4	82.4	82.8	104.4	66.6	83.9
1984	77.8	95.8	101.3	124.6	79.3	97.6	85.4	105.0	68.7	84.6
1985	81.9	101.2	104.2	128.8	77.5	95.8	84.5	104.5	71.6	88.6
1986	86.0	109.5	100.3	127.8	80.2	102.2	86.7	110.5	73.5	93.6
1987	88.9	110.4	95.2	118.2	73.3	91.0	88.6	110.0	75.3	93.4
1988	91.9	109.7	97.8	116.8	66.1	78.9	91.5	109.2	79.4	94.8
1989	94.1	107.0	99.1	112.7	64.4	73.2	93.6	106.5	84.2	95.8
1990	95.7	105.0	99.3	108.9	61.6	67.6	94.8	104.1	86.2	94.6
1991	94.7	103.8	99.7	109.2	58.1	63.7	95.4	104.5	90.2	98.8
1992	95.8	104.3	97.7	106.4	58.7	63.9	94.9	103.3	92.1	100.2
1993	96.5	103.5	98.4	105.6	63.4	68.1	94.6	101.5	94.1	101.0
1994	98.0	103.8	96.3	102.0	79.6	84.4	95.6	101.3	95.5	101.2
1995	99.7	102.0	101.4	103.7	90.5	92.6	97.1	99.4	99.3	101.6
1996	99.9	99.9	100.9	100.9	90.2	90.1	99.1	99.0	99.7	99.6
1997	100.0	100.0	100.0	100.0	100.0	100.0	100.0	100.0	100.0	100.0
1998	97.0	99.5	100.1	102.7	104.0	106.7	100.5	103.1	99.8	102.3
1999	97.5	99.1	99.6	101.3	121.8	123.9	99.3	100.9	99.1	100.8
2000	95.0	91.4	104.6	100.6	118.0	113.4	101.4	97.5	99.6	95.8
2001	87.9	83.6	108.1	102.8	91.6	87.1	102.3	97.3	98.2	93.4
2002	76.7	74.7	111.6	108.6	98.9	96.3	102.5	99.8	99.1	96.4
2003	76.7	70.9	115.7	106.9	100.4	92.8	105.2	97.2	101.2	93.5
2004	77.1	67.1	116.5	101.3	116.4	101.3	107.8	93.7	103.4	89.9
2005	79.0	64.1	130.8	106.0	134.5	109.0	116.0	94.0	109.6	88.8

[a]U.S. Department of Labor, Bureau of Labor Statistics (74).
[b]Derived by dividing the actual price index by the all commodities price index.
[c]Ceramic floor and wall tile.
[d]Prepared asphalt and tar roofing and siding products.
[z]Not available.

Table 36—Relative[a] producer price index for lumber, 1800–2005 (1997 = 100)[b]

Year	All lumber	Year	All lumber	Year	All lumber	Year	All lumber	Year	All lumber	Year	All Lumber
1800	5.0	1840	12.6	1881	20.7	1922	40.3	1963	75.1	2004	101.6
1801	5.2	1841	13.0	1882	21.1	1923	43.7	1964	76.7	2005	98.6
1802	6.2	1842	12.9	1883	20.9	1924	39.8	1965	61.3		
1803	5.3	1843	12.6	1884	22.4	1925	38.3	1966	63.5		
1804	5.3	1844	13.3	1885	22.9	1926	38.2	1967	63.3		
1805	5.4	1845	14.7	1886	23.7	1927	37.4	1968	72.3		
1806	5.5	1846	13.9	1887	23.7	1928	35.4	1969	78.0		
1807	5.9	1847	13.4	1888	23.1	1929	37.5	1970	65.0		
1808	5.8	1848	13.9	1889	23.1	1930	37.5	1971	75.4		
1809	5.4	1849	14.1	1890	23.6	1931	36.0	1972	84.6		
1810	5.1	1850	14.8	1891	23.2	1932	34.8	1973	96.1		
1811	5.1	1851	14.3	1892	24.1	1933	40.5	1974	81.7		
1812	4.8	1852	15.7	1893	23.8	1934	42.7	1975	69.5		
1813	4.3	1853	15.2	1894	26.3	1935	38.7	1976	80.5		
1814	3.6	1854	14.8	1895	24.6	1936	40.8	1977	89.8		
1815	6.4	1855	15.6	1896	25.9	1937	44.1	1978	97.2		
1816	7.1	1856	16.0	1897	25.1	1938	42.6	1979	94.9		
1817	6.2	1857	16.5	1898	25.4	1939	45.7	1980	76.5		
1818	5.8	1858	16.4	1899	26.0	1940	49.8	1981	69.9		
1819	6.7	1859	16.0	1900	26.8	1941	53.2	1982	65.6		
1820	7.5	1860	16.0	1901	27.3	1942	51.0	1983	73.5		
1821	7.5	1861	15.6	1902	26.7	1943	51.9	1984	71.1		
1822	7.1	1862	14.2	1903	28.4	1944	56.2	1985	69.6		
1823	7.5	1863	13.6	1904	26.5	1945	55.7	1986	72.3		
1824	7.6	1864	13.6	1905	28.1	1946	56.1	1987	75.3		
1825	7.9	1865	12.6	1906	33.2	1947	72.8	1988	74.8		
1826	8.5	1866	15.9	1907	31.7	1948	76.3	1989	73.4		
1827	8.6	1867	16.9	1908	30.4	1949	73.7	1990	70.3		
1828	9.0	1868	17.4	1909	28.3	1950	82.8	1991	70.3		
1829	8.9	1869	17.0	1910	26.8	1951	80.5	1992	80.9		
1830	8.8	1870	17.4	1911	28.8	1952	80.5	1993	101.1		
1831	8.8	1871	18.4	1912	29.1	1953	80.8	1994	102.8		
1832	8.7	1872	18.7	1913	30.4	1954	79.1	1995	91.1		
1833	9.1	1873	19.0	1914	28.8	1955	84.1	1996	92.3		
1834	10.0	1874	18.8	1915	27.6	1956	83.1	1997	100.0		
1835	8.8	1875	18.0	1916	25.3	1957	75.9	1998	93.3		
1836	8.0	1876	18.4	1917	24.1	1958	73.8	1999	97.0		
1837	11.5	1877	18.6	1918	25.0	1959	79.3	2000	87.1		
1838	12.0	1878	18.6	1919	32.0	1960	75.7	2001	82.7		
1839	11.4	1879	19.9	1920	42.0	1961	72.0	2002	84.1		
1840	12.6	1880	19.4	1921	35.9	1962	73.1	2003	81.6		

[a]Derived by dividing the actual price index by the all commodities price index.

[b]1800 to 1914, Cornell University Agricultural Experiment Station (17);
1915 to present, U.S. Department of Labor, Bureau of Labor Statistics (74);
1800-1964 (1992=100) 1965-present (1997=100).

Table 37—Plywood production, imports, exports, and consumption, by softwoods and hardwoods,1965–2005 (3/8-in. basis)[a]

Year	Production Total	Soft-woods	Hard-woods	Imports Total	Soft-woods	Hard-woods	Exports Total	Soft-woods	Hard-woods [b]	Consumption Total	Soft-woods	Hard-woods	Per capita Total	Soft-woods	Hard-woods
	Million square feet	Million square feet	Million square feet	Million square feet	Million square feet	Million square feet	Million square feet	Million square feet	Million square feet	Million square feet	Million square feet	Million square feet	Square feet	Square feet	Square feet
1965	14,496	12,447	2,049	1,052	5	1,047	36	30	6	15,512	12,422	3,090	80	64	16
1966	15,132	13,056	2,076	1,257	3	1,254	56	48	8	16,333	13,011	3,322	83	66	17
1967	14,874	12,958	1,916	1,247	3	1,244	93	85	8	16,028	12,876	3,152	81	65	16
1968	16,704	14,695	2,009	1,896	10	1,886	78	64	14	18,522	14,641	3,881	92	73	19
1969	15,563	13,694	1,869	2,122	15	2,107	215	199	16	17,470	13,510	3,960	86	67	20
1970	16,136	14,340	1,796	2,049	2	2,047	172	114	58	18,013	14,228	3,785	88	69	18
1971	18,559	16,635	1,924	2,545	3	2,542	114	99	15	20,990	16,539	4,451	101	80	21
1972	20,354	18,324	2,030	3,162	6	3,156	247	221	26	23,269	18,109	5,160	111	86	25
1973	20,112	18,305	1,807	2,536	9	2,527	451	411	40	22,197	17,903	4,294	105	84	20
1974	17,279	15,878	1,401	1,648	4	1,644	610	542	68	18,317	15,340	2,977	86	72	14
1975	17,102	16,050	1,052	1,925	7	1,918	859	791	68	18,168	15,266	2,902	84	71	13
1976	19,523	18,440	1,083	2,368	12	2,356	795	716	79	21,096	17,736	3,360	97	81	15
1977	20,563	19,376	1,187	2,272	18	2,254	357	287	70	22,478	19,107	3,371	102	87	15
1978	21,149	19,964	1,185	2,555	63	2,492	329	298	31	23,375	19,729	3,646	105	89	16
1979	20,803	19,653	1,150	2,097	27	2,070	431	402	29	22,469	19,278	3,191	100	86	14
1980	17,371	16,333	1,038	1,235	37	1,198	413	373	40	18,193	15,997	2,196	80	70	10
1981	17,728	16,752	976	1,512	30	1,482	733	686	47	18,507	16,096	2,411	80	70	10
1982	17,231	15,846	1,385	1,878	9	1,869	493	452	41	18,616	15,403	3,213	80	66	14
1983	20,960	19,480	1,480	2,747	18	2,729	615	574	41	23,092	18,924	4,168	99	81	18
1984	21,431	19,926	1,505	2,527	48	2,480	408	371	37	23,550	19,603	3,948	100	83	17
1985	21,511	20,169	1,342	3,112	54	3,058	365	321	44	24,259	19,903	4,356	102	83	18
1986	23,508	22,118	1,390	3,234	63	3,171	676	614	61	26,067	21,567	4,500	108	90	19
1987	24,423	22,899	1,524	3,932	129	3,803	855	796	60	27,500	22,232	5,268	113	92	22
1988	24,151	22,599	1,552	3,358	96	3,262	1,108	1,004	104	26,401	21,691	4,711	108	89	19
1989	22,926	21,385	1,541	1,983	49	1,935	1,562	1,442	119	23,348	19,991	3,356	94	81	14
1990	22,456	20,919	1,537	1,687	38	1,649	1,766	1,613	153	22,377	19,344	3,033	90	77	12
1991	20,148	18,652	1,496	1,457	28	1,429	1,553	1,322	231	20,052	17,358	2,695	79	69	11
1992	20,755	19,332	1,423	1,776	47	1,729	1,760	1,442	318	20,771	17,937	2,834	81	70	11
1993	20,826	19,315	1,511	1,786	41	1,745	1,677	1,409	268	20,935	17,946	2,989	81	70	12
1994	21,439	19,638	1,801	1,693	47	1,646	1,455	1,211	244	21,677	18,474	3,203	83	71	12
1995	21,209	19,367	1,842	1,951	60	1,892	1,517	1,267	250	21,643	18,160	3,483	82	69	13
1996	20,965	19,181	1,784	1,780	85	1,695	1,499	1,248	251	21,246	18,018	3,228	80	68	12
1997	19,835	17,963	1,872	2,111	104	2,007	1,802	1,548	254	20,143	16,519	3,625	75	62	14
1998	19,738	17,776	1,962	2,429	179	2,250	969	764	205	21,198	17,191	4,007	78	64	15
1999[r]	19,832	17,816	2,016	2,827	309	2,518	984	781	203	21,675	17,344	4,331	79	63	16
2000	19,741	17,475	2,266	2,902	408	2,494	916	735	181	21,727	17,148	4,579	77	61	16
2001	17,225	15,121	2,104	3,220	665	2,555	676	514	162	19,768	15,272	4,496	69	54	16
2002[r]	17,296	15,200	2,096	4,115	907	3,208	619	439	180	20,792	15,668	5,124	72	55	18
2003[r]	16,753	14,706	2,047	4,489	1,306	3,183	640	410	230	20,603	15,602	5,001	71	54	17
2004	16,687	14,665	2,022	6,629	2,023	4,606	783	492	291	22,532	16,196	6,336	77	55	22
2005	16,327	14,330	1,997	6,964	2,421	4,543	686	411	275	22,604	16,340	6,264	76	55	21

[a]U.S. Department of Commerce, Bureau of the Census (53,64); APA–The Engineered Wood Association (13);
 U.S. International Trade Commission (80); Data may not add to totals because of rounding.
[b]Includes mixed species (not classified as hardwoods or softwoods).
[r]Revised.

Table 38—Production, imports, exports, and consumption of structural panel products, by type, 1980–2005 (million square feet, 3/8-in. basis)[a]

Year	Production			Imports			Exports			Consumption		
	Total	Softwood plywood	Other structural panels[b]	Total	Softwood plywood	Other structural panels[b,c]	Total	Softwood plywood	Other structural panels[b]	Total	Softwood plywood	Other structural panels[b]
1980	16,468	16,333	135	360	37	323	373	373	z	16,455	15,997	458
1981	17,023	16,752	271	349	30	319	686	686	z	16,686	16,096	590
1982	16,403	15,846	557	268	9	259	452	452	z	16,219	15,403	816
1983	20,821	19,480	1,341	423	18	405	574	574	z	20,670	18,924	1,746
1984	21,968	19,926	2,042	727	48	679	371	371	z	22,324	19,603	2,721
1985	22,838	20,169	2,669	848	54	794	321	321	z	23,366	19,903	3,463
1986	25,631	22,118	3,513	723	63	660	614	614	z	25,740	21,567	4,173
1987	26,975	22,899	4,076	889	129	760	796	796	z	27,068	22,232	4,836
1988	27,203	22,599	4,604	911	96	815	1,004	1,004	z	27,110	21,691	5,419
1989	26,490	21,385	5,105	1,160	49	1,111	1,442	1,442	z	26,207	19,991	6,216
1990	26,337	20,919	5,418	1,351	38	1,313	1,613	1,613	z	26,075	19,344	6,731
1991	24,265	18,652	5,613	1,016	28	988	1,379	1,322	57	23,901	17,358	6,544
1992	25,985	19,332	6,653	1,619	47	1,572	1,491	1,442	49	26,113	17,937	8,176
1993	26,317	19,315	7,002	2,203	41	2,163	1,470	1,409	60	27,051	17,946	9,105
1994	27,124	19,638	7,486	2,635	47	2,588	1,289	1,211	78	28,469	18,474	9,995
1995	27,270	19,367	7,903	3,274	60	3,214	1,348	1,267	82	29,196	18,160	11,036
1996	28,495	19,181	9,314	4,500	85	4,414	1,405	1,248	157	31,590	18,018	13,572
1997	28,497	17,963	10,534	5,376	104	5,272	1,715	1,548	167	32,158	16,519	15,639
1998	29,003	17,776	11,227	6,671	179	6,492	864	764	100	34,810	17,191	17,619
1999[r]	29,428	17,816	11,612	7,659	309	7,350	960	781	179	36,127	17,344	18,783
2000	29,381	17,475	11,906	8,030	408	7,622	914	735	179	36,498	17,148	19,350
2001	27,653	15,121	12,532	8,755	665	8,090	681	514	167	35,727	15,272	20,455
2002	28,626	15,200	13,426	9,368	907	8,461	634	439	195	37,360	15,668	21,692
2003	28,321	14,706	13,615	10,386	1,306	9,080	567	410	157	38,140	15,602	22,538
2004	28,936	14,665	14,271	11,870	2,023	9,847	685	492	193	40,120	16,196	23,924
2005	29,315	14,330	14,985	12,965	2,421	10,544	580	411	169	41,700	16,340	25,360

[a] APA– The Engineered Wood Association (11,13); U.S. International Trade Commission (80); Data may not add to totals because of rounding.

[b] Oriented strandboard and waferboard.

[c] Based on Canadian export data. Industry sources estimate that about 95% of Canadian exports are to U.S. markets.

[r] Revised.

[z] Not available.

69

Table 39—Hardwood plywood imports, by country or region of origin, 1965–2005 (million square feet, surface measured)[a]

			Latin America					Asia									Europe				
Year[b]	Total	Canada	Total	Mexico	Central America and West Indies	Brazil	Other[c] South America	Total	Japan	Philip-pines	China[d]	Taiwan	Korea	Indo-nesia	Malaysia	Other Asia	Total	Russian Federation	Other	Africa	Other[e]
1965	2,032.8	64.5	10.8	[f]	[f]	[z]	10.8	1,832.4	768.0	307.8	368.2	[z]	336.7	[z]	[z]	51.7	118.3	[z]	[z]	6.8	[z]
1966	2,553.7	64.1	8.7	[z]	[z]	[z]	8.7	2,328.9	783.4	397.9	528.8	[z]	573.6	[z]	[z]	45.2	145.1	[z]	[z]	6.6	0.3
1967	2,532.7	48.0	8.1	[f]	[z]	[z]	8.1	2,356.0	632.3	471.5	485.4	[z]	702.0	[z]	[z]	64.8	118.2	[z]	[z]	2.4	[f]
1968	3,841.3	53.0	12.2	[z]	1.0	[z]	11.2	3,619.1	921.3	602.2	829.6	[z]	1,167.2	[z]	[z]	98.8	156.0	[z]	[z]	1.0	[f]
1969	4,290.2	40.6	11.7	0.1	4.0	[z]	7.6	4,043.8	802.3	572.1	936.0	[z]	1,589.8	[z]	[z]	143.6	192.3	[z]	[z]	1.8	[f]
1970	4,168.1	24.9	10.2	[f]	1.9	[z]	8.3	3,996.3	623.5	570.9	939.6	[z]	1,787.3	[z]	[z]	75.0	136.1	[z]	[z]	0.5	0.1
1971	5,176.7	45.8	13.8	[z]	1.3	[z]	12.5	4,989.7	598.3	592.2	1,395.5	[z]	2,251.3	0.1	[z]	152.3	127.3	[z]	[z]	[f]	0.1
1972	6,427.5	69.5	20.5	[z]	8.7	[z]	11.8	6,216.0	519.1	644.2	2,021.9	[z]	2,865.6	[z]	[z]	165.2	121.3	[z]	[z]	0.1	0.1
1973	5,146.7	74.4	18.0	[z]	4.5	[z]	13.5	4,959.6	341.0	695.3	1,367.2	[z]	2,443.0	[z]	[z]	113.1	94.0	[z]	[z]	0.5	0.2
1974	3,349.1	46.8	18.8	[z]	1.0	[z]	17.8	3,229.0	244.3	279.3	937.2	[z]	1,694.7	[z]	[z]	73.5	48.2	[z]	[z]	[z]	6.3
1975	3,906.4	50.4	15.8	[z]	7.5	[z]	8.3	3,805.1	240.5	224.1	1,011.8	[z]	2,290.0	[z]	[z]	38.7	30.8	[z]	[z]	[z]	4.3
1976	4,797.8	53.6	18.3	[z]	6.8	[z]	11.5	4,668.7	312.5	352.9	1,189.4	[z]	2,785.7	[z]	[z]	28.2	47.6	[z]	[z]	0.5	9.1
1977	4,590.7	69.3	24.8	[z]	5.1	[z]	19.7	4,445.3	356.1	231.0	1,149.1	[z]	2,676.9	[z]	[z]	32.2	44.2	[z]	[z]	[z]	7.1
1978	5,076.0	75.3	29.6	0.1	5.9	[z]	23.6	4,922.2	255.6	312.4	1,752.8	[z]	2,493.0	64.3	[z]	44.1	48.1	[z]	[z]	0.7	0.1
1979	4,216.3	82.2	53.7	[f]	2.4	[z]	51.3	4,039.6	192.7	367.3	1,523.1	[z]	1,836.7	95.5	[z]	24.3	40.8	[z]	[z]	[f]	[f]
1980	2,440.5	72.8	46.1	[z]	3.7	[z]	42.4	2,290.5	150.4	246.7	859.8	[z]	902.1	120.8	[z]	10.7	30.6	[z]	[z]	[f]	0.5
1981	3,017.5	64.7	30.4	[z]	4.4	[z]	26.0	2,884.4	139.8	436.7	1,080.9	[z]	943.7	271.7	[z]	11.6	37.9	[z]	[z]	0.1	[z]
1982	2,249.4	54.5	24.3	[z]	2.5	[z]	21.8	2,146.4	95.8	161.3	850.6	[z]	559.6	473.9	[z]	5.2	24.1	[z]	[z]	[z]	0.1
1983	3,346.6	57.5	44.1	0.3	1.3	[z]	42.5	3,205.6	119.9	182.4	1,124.6	[z]	414.8	1,352.2	[z]	11.7	39.4	[z]	[z]	[z]	[f]
1984	2,982.3	73.4	90.0	0.1	1.4	[z]	88.5	2,767.9	109.7	94.9	904.8	[z]	78.1	1,568.8	[z]	11.6	50.9	[z]	[z]	[f]	0.1
1985	3,522.1	69.4	75.1	[f]	2.9	[z]	72.2	3,294.6	106.7	212.6	780.3	[z]	28.2	2,147.2	[z]	19.6	82.3	[z]	[z]	0.4	0.3
1986	3,809.2	55.8	120.8	0.2	1.8	[z]	118.8	3,556.4	74.0	110.9	723.5	[z]	61.8	2,551.1	[z]	35.1	71.5	[z]	[z]	4.7	[f]
1987	3,950.2	87.4	105.9	0.2	0.9	[z]	104.8	3,670.7	41.6	126.1	665.6	[z]	48.7	2,721.4	[z]	67.3	85.1	[z]	[z]	0.5	0.6
1988	3,262.3	81.7	118.5	[f]	0.5	[z]	118.0	3,022.0	19.8	51.8	523.8	[z]	6.7	2,345.4	[z]	74.5	39.6	[z]	[z]	[z]	0.5
1989	3,938.9	249.1	232.1	0.6	2.2	186.9	42.3	3,271.2	11.5	59.5	0.4	770.2	9.5	2,341.2	40.3	38.5	158.7	0.0	158.7	0.2	27.5
1990	3,356.4	211.1	306.3	0.0	4.2	248.9	53.3	2,700.6	3.9	35.7	0.4	255.9	7.9	2,209.4	159.1	28.3	90.6	0.0	90.6	0.0	47.9
1991	2,910.3	215.8	297.2	0.1	1.3	237.6	58.2	2,268.6	3.2	16.5	1.4	141.9	0.6	1,798.0	289.0	18.0	82.0	0.0	82.0	0.0	46.7
1992	3,520.5	268.4	455.6	1.8	1.4	397.6	54.7	2,706.1	1.8	23.2	2.1	109.5	0.0	2,084.1	471.3	13.9	87.7	25.6	62.1	0.1	2.8
1993	3,553.3	310.0	686.5	0.2	3.8	594.8	87.8	2,430.9	0.6	8.6	14.5	90.5	0.4	1,858.5	443.7	14.2	122.8	60.0	62.8	0.6	2.5
1994	3,351.3	372.9	847.1	5.7	8.2	687.2	146.0	1,922.3	1.5	0.8	20.4	45.9	0.1	1,456.4	379.1	18.1	205.6	141.9	63.6	0.9	2.4
1995	3,851.4	422.6	832.6	10.1	8.7	554.0	259.8	2,282.7	0.2	0.2	12.4	29.3	0.0	1,858.4	373.9	8.3	311.9	252.1	59.8	0.0	1.6
1996	3,451.0	339.4	826.7	21.0	9.8	496.5	299.4	1,931.6	1.2	0.4	14.3	38.4	0.0	1,575.1	300.4	1.7	351.6	330.3	21.3	0.2	1.6
1997	4,086.1	606.1	856.4	16.4	6.2	569.1	264.7	2,200.7	2.0	0.0	47.3	33.4	0.0	1,786.2	326.8	5.0	422.3	306.8	115.6	0.3	0.2
1998	4,581.7	654.6	490.1	7.2	6.2	271.3	205.4	2,948.5	1.2	0.0	104.1	36.7	1.2	2,074.2	723.3	7.8	480.8	388.1	92.8	2.0	5.6
1999[r]	5,126.8	713.9	720.4	16.3	2.4	463.3	238.5	3,010.1	0.8	0.0	149.3	45.2	1.3	1,839.3	962.7	11.5	637.8	535.3	102.5	3.8	40.8
2000	5,078.0	819.6	874.4	18.0	2.5	602.7	251.2	2,558.8	2.2	0.0	162.0	49.2	0.1	1,510.6	813.0	21.8	784.6	668.4	116.2	28.7	11.9
2001	5,201.6	813.6	858.9	18.4	3.1	642.3	195.1	2,486.0	0.2	0.0	276.4	39.0	1.2	1,368.2	762.4	38.7	978.6	794.8	183.8	38.6	25.9
2002[r]	6,531.5	840.5	1011.0	19.9	6.3	789.1	195.7	3,320.8	0.5	0.0	662.1	53.6	4.2	1,515.2	1049.9	35.3	1312.6	972.2	340.4	42.5	4.1
2003	6,480.9	796.4	1181.5	17.1	3.7	941.9	218.7	3,382.3	0.9	0.0	1,017.3	49.3	14.1	1,241.7	972.4	86.6	1079.0	893.1	185.9	35.9	5.9
2004	9,377.2	825.3	1305.1	10.9	3.6	1,055.8	234.8	5,781.0	3.2	0.0	2,954.1	80.5	1.7	1,177.8	1433.3	130.5	1425.8	1188.8	237.0	27.4	12.5
2005	9,249.0	969.5	799.0	1.2	10.9	596.9	190.0	6,176.0	0.9	0.0	3,891.3	67.3	0.3	984.2	1137.0	95.1	1259.8	986.1	273.8	18.3	26.4

[a]U.S. International Trade Commission (80). Data may not add to totals because of rounding.
Conversion of 2.036 used from square feet 3/8 inch basis.

[b]For the years 1974 to 1977, all imports with a value of less than $500 are included in Other.

[c]Includes Brazil from 1965-1988.

[d]Includes Taiwan from 1965-1988.

[e]Includes mixed species (not classified as hardwoods or softwoods).

[f]Fewer than 100 ft^2.

[z]Not Available

[r]Revised

Table 40—Veneer imports and exports, by species, 1965–2005 (million square feet, surface measured)[a]

| | Imports | | | | | Exports | | | | | |
| | | Hardwoods | | | | | Hardwoods | | | | |
Year	Total	Total	Birch and maple	Other	Soft-woods	Total	Total	Walnut	Red and white oak	Other	Soft-woods
1965	1,958.2	1,871.2	817.4	1,053.8	87.0	169.8	143.7	80.6	[b]	63.1	26.1
1966	2,043.0	1,843.7	766.4	1,077.3	199.3	153 9	110.5	54.2	[b]	56.3	43.4
1967	1,990.9	1,796.7	754.9	1,041.8	194.2	192.8	105.8	44.8	[b]	61.0	87.0
1968	2,340.1	2,178.7	820.8	1,357.9	161.4	306.3	173.6	71.9	[b]	101.7	132.7
1969	2,054.6	1,855.7	698.2	1,157.5	198.9	360.6	194.2	92.4	[b]	101.8	166.4
1970	1,876.6	1,605.8	650.0	955.8	270.8	327.1	183.8	111.3	[b]	72.5	143.3
1971	2,302.1	2,035.2	812.0	1,223.2	266.9	571.5	172.7	97.7	[b]	75.0	398.8
1972	3,151.4	2,786.0	997.9	1,788.1	365.4	491.7	204.3	84.9	[b]	119.4	287.4
1973	2,967.7	2,582.9	890.5	1,692.4	384.8	660.5	346.0	90.9	[b]	255.1	314.5
1974	2,281.6	1,965.9	679.6	1,286.3	315.7	599.4	380.8	77.4	[b]	303.4	218.6
1975	1,497.7	1,145.6	552.2	593.4	352.1	736.8	390.3	63.6	[b]	326.7	346.5
1976	1,993.5	1,595.6	760.3	835.3	397.9	768 2	505.8	91.8	[b]	414.0	262.4
1977	2,261.0	1,718.5	721.3	997.2	542.5	687 0	516.5	93.1	[b]	423.4	170.5
1978	2,143.3	1,632.5	722.8	909.7	510.8	1,541.6	1,353.3	128.9	476.1	748.3	188.3
1979	2,076.6	1,560.1	713.4	846.7	516.5	1,072.5	886.0	80.6	522.0	283.4	186.5
1980	1,666.8	1,213.2	584.2	629.0	453.6	1,333.1	1,077.3	117.8	631.2	328.3	255.8
1981	1,729.3	1,406.3	605.1	801.2	323.0	1,378.1	919.6	107.9	509.2	302.5	458.5
1982	1,665.9	1,231.9	506.8	725.1	434.0	1,140.3	803.6	78.6	512.9	212.1	336.7
1983	2,072.5	1,607.2	637.8	969.4	465.3	1,438.8	1,023.8	106.0	624.4	293.4	415.0
1984	1,886.8	1,502.9	537.2	965.7	383.9	1,370.5	1,002.7	84.4	636.0	282.3	367.8
1985	1,753.4	1,398.0	501.5	896.5	355.4	1,100 2	792.6	85.6	481.5	225.5	307.6
1986	1,997.4	1,603.9	557.3	1,046.6	393.5	1,466.1	995.8	72.6	639.3	283.9	470.3
1987	2,106.6	1,682.2	563.4	1,118.8	424.4	1,775.9	1,384.7	90.7	857.4	436.6	391.2
1988	2,226.7	1,713.8	588.0	1,125.8	512.9	1,830.1	1,574.2	69.9	1,058.7	445.6	255.9
1989	1,163.9	719.7	239.9	479.8	444.1	1,712.2	1,599.6	35.8	431.0	1,132.7	112.6
1990	2,109.3	1,600.7	559.2	1,041.5	508.6	1,820.2	1,681.4	103.4	1,135.5	442.5	138.9
1991	1,917.4	1,383.7	523.5	860.2	533.7	1,896.1	1,725.5	85.9	1,084.3	555.4	170.6
1992	2,422.3	1,674.4	599.1	1,075.3	747.9	2,072.2	1,884.8	69.7	1,094.0	721.2	187.4
1993	2,870.0	1,904.1	619.2	1,284.9	965.9	2,209.9	1,977.4	60.7	958.1	958.6	232.5
1994	3,036.6	1,946.6	713.0	1,233.7	1,090.0	2,459.3	2,310.0	68.4	1,086.1	1,155.5	149.3
1995	3,223.2	2,283.2	739.4	1,543.8	940.0	2,800.0	2,613.3	73.6	1,109.9	1,429.8	186.7
1996	3,011.4	2,093.4	718.2	1,375.1	918.0	2,792.7	2,613.3	49.1	1,080.1	1,484.1	179.4
1997	2,926.9	1,994.9	767.9	1,227.0	932.0	3,068.6	2,875.4	60.2	1,070.3	1,744.8	193.2
1998	3,435.1	2,210.7	789.2	1,421.6	1,224.3	2,946.1	2,722.2	58.6	1,041.5	1,622.0	223.9
1999	3,933.3	2,350.6	947.9	1,402.7	1,582.7	3,293.3	2,986.8	78.6	1,008.7	1,899.4	306.5
2000	4,339.0	2,479.8	1,085.4	1,394.4	1,859.1	3,527.8	3,200.2	83.7	1,022.0	2,094.5	327.6
2001	4,263.7	2,166.5	897.0	1,269.5	2,097.2	3,372 2	3,148.8	102.6	936.9	2,109.3	223.4
2002[r]	4,714.0	2,328.7	954.4	1,374.3	2,385.3	3,720.7	3,460.4	92.8	836.8	2,530.9	260.3
2003	4,487.5	2,073.1	712.9	1,360.2	2,414.4	3,681.4	3,283.3	74.9	763.7	2,444.7	398.1
2004	5,491.5	2,310.4	706.6	1,603.8	3,181.1	4,280.4	3,707.5	104.2	880.7	2,722.6	572.9
2005	5,751.8	2,239.4	827.1	1,412.3	3,512.4	4,130 2	3,540.0	115.5	764.0	2,660.5	590.3

[a]American Forest & Paper Association (4); U.S. International Trade Commission (80). Data may not add to totals because of rounding.
[b]Red and white oak are included in Other for 1965 to 1977.
[r]Revised.

Table 41—Hardwood veneer imports, by country or region of origin, 1965–2005 (million square feet, surface measured)[a]

Year	Total	Canada	Latin America				Asia				Africa	Europe	Other[b]
			Total	Mexico	West Indies	South America	Total	Japan	Philippines	Other Asia			
1965	1,871.2	852.0	67.1	0.1	19.2	47.8	687.0	4.8	527.0	155.2	219.8	44.3	0.9
1966	1,843.7	792.8	96.4	0.3	21.2	74.9	714.1	3.8	522.7	187.6	209.7	29.6	1.0
1967	1,796.7	775.8	140.9	0.1	8.0	132.8	580.9	3.8	451.8	125.3	271.2	27.7	0.2
1968	2,178.7	837.7	200.5	1.5	16.8	182.2	837.7	4.3	609.8	223.6	276.5	26.3	0.1
1969	1,855.7	713.9	152.7	0.6	13.1	139.0	838.6	5.3	671.4	161.9	128.1	22.2	0.3
1970	1,605.8	672.4	191.0	0.6	5.0	185.4	569.1	3.3	460.0	105.8	147.0	26.1	0.2
1971	2,035.2	842.4	216.1	0.5	15.1	200.5	809.4	4.5	590.9	214.0	143.1	24.0	0.2
1972	2,786.0	1,051.8	303.8	c	28.8	275.0	1226.5	0.9	822.5	403.1	153.9	30.2	19.7
1973	2,582.9	944.4	288.4	c	43.2	245.2	1126.1	2.3	850.8	273.0	167.2	27.8	29.0
1974	1,965.9	709.2	243.8	z	43.9	199.9	874.0	0.9	660.8	212.3	78.6	39.4	20.8
1975	1,145.6	570.7	132.5	z	22.2	110.3	331.5	3.8	294.3	33.4	74.3	23.1	13.5
1976	1,595.6	804.6	210.8	z	8.3	202.5	520.6	4.5	452.4	63.7	15.0	30.1	14.5
1977	1,718.5	801.4	159.1	0.9	13.0	145.2	689.3	5.5	580.5	103.3	19.6	30.5	18.7
1978	1,632.5	817.4	213.1	3.6	21.8	187.7	536.8	7.1	442.6	87.1	19.1	44.7	1.5
1979	1,560.1	834.0	149.4	2.0	28.2	119.2	482.5	1.3	448.2	33.0	35.4	56.4	2.4
1980	1,213.2	700.4	156.0	z	27.3	130.7	301.6	2.0	261.5	38.1	21.9	31.4	1.5
1981	1,406.3	753.6	165.0	0.2	27.3	137.5	398.2	0.9	330.7	66.6	36.3	41.6	11.4
1982	1,231.9	705.9	161.2	0.8	24.4	136.0	149.9	0.7	120.0	29.2	19.2	193.2	2.6
1983	1,607.2	908.3	192.2	3.0	23.1	166.1	366.0	2.8	318.3	44.9	27.1	100.9	12.8
1984	1,502.9	828.1	227.5	0.8	31.6	195.1	287.2	8.5	180.7	98.0	13.7	127.6	19.0
1985	1,398.0	728.7	233.1	0.2	26.5	206.4	240.5	6.5	110.7	123.3	26.1	150.8	18.8
1986	1,603.9	831.8	233.9	0.2	20.8	212.9	310.4	5.1	112.7	192.6	57.4	139.0	31.3
1987	1,682.2	910.8	245.0	z	18.0	227.0	331.3	6.3	122.8	202.2	40.9	127.0	27.2
1988	1,713.8	944.3	312.8	0.8	33.2	278.8	279.5	2.0	182.4	95.1	41.6	92.8	42.8
1989	719.7	366.9	143.1	0.0	6.4	136.7	116.4	2.5	72.5	41.4	23.9	53.9	15.6
1990	1,600.7	904.2	320.6	0.0	28.4	292.2	221.2	5.8	111.6	103.8	31.8	93.6	29.4
1991	1,383.7	832.1	254.4	0.0	25.5	228.9	167.3	4.8	73.3	89.1	26.7	75.0	28.2
1992	1,674.4	997.9	364.5	1.0	109.0	254.5	182.9	2.9	64.2	115.8	21.8	80.9	26.4
1993	1,904.1	1,158.4	452.8	2.9	7.8	442.0	120.5	2.5	11.6	106.3	39.2	95.7	37.5
1994	1,946.6	1,220.8	414.5	1.4	6.5	406.5	71.7	3.0	5.7	63.1	41.5	151.5	46.6
1995	2,283.2	1,186.4	575.4	9.1	14.8	551.5	213.0	3.5	47.9	161.6	114.4	137.8	56.1
1996	2,093.4	1,190.2	508.8	13.6	6.1	489.1	58.1	4.3	0.1	53.7	171.4	112.0	52.9
1997	1,994.9	1,247.4	374.4	17.0	1.6	355.7	61.9	6.1	0.0	55.8	137.2	139.8	34.2
1998	2,210.7	1,316.2	351.8	22.3	1.9	327.6	99.2	3.2	0.0	96.0	218.4	176.1	49.0
1999	2,350.6	1,440.5	340.8	22.6	0.7	317.5	94.0	5.6	0.0	88.4	282.7	167.5	25.2
2000	2,479.8	1,503.9	309.4	41.6	0.8	267.0	96.4	6.8	0.0	89.6	269.3	279.6	21.2
2001	2,166.5	1,277.2	295.3	35.7	2.0	257.7	96.1	2.9	0.0	93.2	262.4	210.6	24.9
2002	2,328.7	1,322.6	314.7	24.4	0.2	290.0	99.4	3.3	0.0	96.1	314.9	254.0	23.1
2003	2,073.1	1,168.7	259.3	13.7	0.2	245.4	158.3	3.4	0.0	154.9	283.3	187.2	16.4
2004	2,310.4	1,400.6	212.1	17.7	3.3	191.0	149.6	3.7	0.0	145.9	289.8	228.6	29.6
2005	2,239.4	1,196.5	308.6	20.7	0.0	289.8	177.6	4.9	0.0	172.8	295.3	235.5	25.9

[a]U.S. International Trade Commission (80). Data may not add to totals because of rounding.

[b]For the years 1974 to 1977, all imports with a value of less than $500 are included in Other.

[c]Fewer than 50,000 ft^2.

[z]Not available.

Table 42—Producer price indexes for plywood, 1965–2005 (1997 = 100)[a]

			Softwood plywood						All hardwood plywood[b]	
	All plywood		All softwood plywood		Western		Southern			
Year	Actual	Relative[c]	Actual	Relative	Actual	Relative	Actual	Relative	Actual	Relative
1965	28.0	110.7	21.4	84.5	z	z	z	z	43.7	172.5
1966	28.2	108.0	21.5	82.3	z	z	z	z	44.1	168.9
1967	27.1	103.5	20.2	77.2	z	z	z	z	43.4	165.8
1968	31.3	116.7	26.2	97.6	z	z	z	z	43.7	162.9
1969	33.2	119.0	28.1	100.7	26.9	96.2	32.1	115.0	45.3	162.2
1970	29.4	101.5	23.0	79.5	21.9	75.5	27.2	93.8	44.5	153.9
1971	31.0	103.9	25.7	85.9	24.4	81.6	31.0	103.9	43.7	146.5
1972	35.4	113.4	31.3	100.3	29.8	95.3	37.1	118.6	45.3	145.4
1973	42.1	119.3	39.2	111.3	37.7	106.9	42.9	121.5	49.0	139.1
1974	43.6	103.9	37.7	90.0	36.5	87.0	40.6	96.9	56.6	135.0
1975	43.6	95.2	40.6	88.7	39.2	85.7	42.6	93.0	51.9	113.4
1976	50.7	105.8	50.1	104.6	47.3	98.8	55.9	116.8	53.2	111.2
1977	57.4	113.0	59.9	117.7	56.2	110.3	68.1	133.7	55.4	109.0
1978	63.8	116.5	66.0	120.5	62.7	114.4	72.9	133.1	60.9	111.2
1979	67.8	110.0	65.2	105.6	63.5	102.8	66.7	107.9	73.5	119.2
1980	66.7	94.8	62.5	88.8	60.1	85.3	66.4	94.3	76.7	109.0
1981	66.6	86.7	62.0	80.7	60.7	79.0	63.1	82.1	78.1	101.7
1982	62.8	80.1	57.0	72.8	54.6	69.6	61.3	78.2	78.6	100.4
1983	66.1	83.2	62.7	79.0	59.4	74.8	69.1	87.0	78.1	98.4
1984	65.4	80.5	61.4	75.5	58.8	72.3	65.3	80.3	78.4	96.5
1985	62.6	77.3	61.3	75.8	58.8	72.7	64.9	80.1	70.7	87.5
1986	63.7	81.1	62.4	79.5	60.0	76.4	66.0	84.0	71.6	91.2
1987	64.5	80.0	62.6	77.8	60.8	75.4	65.1	80.7	73.1	90.7
1988	65.0	77.6	62.2	74.3	61.7	73.6	62.4	74.5	74.1	88.5
1989	72.8	82.8	70.9	80.6	70.6	80.3	70.1	79.6	78.6	89.3
1990	71.7	78.7	68.3	74.9	68.4	75.1	66.7	73.1	80.8	88.7
1991	71.8	78.7	68.9	75.5	69.2	75.7	67.1	73.4	80.9	88.6
1992	83.6	91.0	83.9	91.3	83.5	90.8	84.6	92.0	84.1	91.6
1993	96.0	103.0	96.8	103.9	97.3	104.3	95.6	102.5	90.8	97.5
1994	99.7	105.6	100.9	106.9	101.0	107.0	102.6	108.7	96.2	102.0
1995	103.9	106.3	107.3	109.8	105.0	107.4	112.4	115.0	96.1	98.4
1996	98.4	98.3	99.2	99.1	98.3	98.1	96.6	96.4	98.3	98.3
1997	100.0	100.0	100.0	100.0	100.0	100.0	100.0	100.0	100.0	100.0
1998	99.0	101.5	99.9	102.5	98.0	96.6	106.2	104.7	99.9	102.4
1999	110.8	112.6	118.1	120.1	116.7	105.7	125.4	113.5	101.2	102.9
2000	99.0	95.2	98.9	95.1	97.9	80.3	101.7	83.4	102.4	98.5
2001	96.9	92.2	95.7	91.0	94.3	76.4	100.2	81.2	102.6	97.6
2002	95.3	92.8	93.6	91.1	93.0	77.2	94.9	78.7	103.5	100.7
2003	104.9	96.9	111.8	103.3	111.1	87.5	123.5	97.3	101.5	93.8
2004	124.7	108.5	143.1	124.5	d	d	d	d	105.8	92.0
2005	117.4	95.1	127.5	103.4	d	d	d	d	78.7	63.8

[a]U.S. Department of Labor, Bureau of Labor Statistics (74).
[b]Hardwood plywood and related products.
[c]Derived by dividing the actual price index by the all commodities index.
[d]Discontinued series after 2003.
[z]Not available.

Table 43—Paper and board[a] production, imports, exports, and consumption, 1965–2005[b]

Year	Production	Imports[c]		Exports[c]		Consumption	
						Total	Per capita
	Thousand tons	Thousand tons	Percent of consumption	Thousand tons	Percent of production	Thousand tons	Pounds
1965	40,489	6,536	14.4	1,530	3.8	45,495	468
1966	43,904	7,178	14.5	1,696	3.9	49,386	502
1967	43,745	6,818	14.0	1,835	4.2	48,728	490
1968	47,085	6,643	12.9	2,125	4.5	51,602	514
1969	49,824	7,051	12.9	2,377	4.8	54,498	538
1970	48,719	6,845	12.9	2,433	5.0	53,131	518
1971	49,741	6,932	12.8	2,665	5.4	54,008	520
1972	53,842	7,245	12.4	2,790	5.2	58,297	555
1973	56,346	7,865	12.8	2,616	4.6	61,595	581
1974	55,756	8,128	13.4	3,058	5.5	60,827	569
1975	47,997	5,961	11.6	2,400	5.0	51,557	477
1976	54,993	6,879	11.6	2,637	4.8	59,235	543
1977	56,656	7,190	11.7	2,546	4.5	61,301	557
1978	58,571	8,311	12.9	2,583	4.4	64,299	578
1979	61,070	8,462	12.7	2,864	4.7	66,668	592
1980	61,042	8,013	12.4	4,241	6.9	64,814	569
1981	62,109	7,779	11.7	3,630	5.8	66,258	576
1982	59,290	7,321	11.6	3,494	5.9	63,117	544
1983	64,947	8,357	12.0	3,786	5.8	69,519	593
1984	68,449	10,148	13.5	3,542	5.2	75,055	635
1985	66,983	10,444	14.1	3,290	4.9	74,137	622
1986	70,905	10,922	14.0	3,972	5.6	77,855	647
1987	74,361	11,855	14.4	4,111	5.5	82,105	676
1988	76,587	12,184	14.4	4,239	5.5	84,532	690
1989	76,786	12,027	14.3	4,713	6.1	84,100	680
1990	78,679	12,195	14.2	5,163	6.6	85,711	686
1991	79,427	11,086	13.2	6,435	8.1	84,078	665
1992	82,868	11,731	13.4	7,021	8.5	87,578	686
1993	84,857	12,990	14.3	6,835	8.1	91,013	705
1994	89,080	13,651	14.3	7,536	8.5	95,195	730
1995	89,509	14,238	14.8	7,621	8.5	96,126	731
1996	90,381	13,023	13.8	9,118	10.1	94,287	710
1997	95,029	14,513	14.6	10,367	10.9	99,175	740
1998	94,510	15,571	15.4	9,103	9.6	100,978	747
1999	97,020	16,678	15.9	8,824	9.1	104,873	768
2000	94,491	17,356	16.8	8,701	9.2	103,147	731
2001	88,913	16,449	16.9	8,059	9.1	97,303	683
2002	89,636	16,567	17.0	8,976	10.0	97,227	676
2003	88,385	18,109	18.1	6,238	7.1	100,256	689
2004	91,899	19,036	18.3	6,742	7.3	104,193	709
2005	91,031	17,958	17.6	7,125	7.8	101,864	687

[a]Excludes hardboard, wet machine board, and construction grades.

[b]Numbers are the sum of Table 44 & Table 45.

[c]Excludes converted products.

Table 44—Paper shipments, imports, exports, and consumption, 1965–2005[a]

Year	Shipments[b,c]	Imports[b,c,d]		Exports[b,c]		Consumption	
						Total[e]	Per capita[f]
	Thousand tons	Thousand tons	Percent of consumption	Thousand tons	Percent of production	Thousand tons	Pounds
1965	19,157	6,528	25.9	491	2.6	25,194	259
1966	20,725	7,128	26.1	530	2.6	27,323	278
1967	20,926	6,805	25.0	501	2.4	27,230	274
1968	22,181	6,625	23.4	529	2.4	28,277	282
1969	23,449	7,040	23.5	517	2.2	29,972	296
1970	23,351	6,835	23.1	534	2.3	29,652	289
1971	23,722	6,915	23.0	550	2.3	30,087	290
1972	25,359	7,237	22.6	559	2.2	32,037	305
1973	26,797	7,832	23.0	601	2.2	34,028	321
1974	26,863	8,094	23.8	909	3.4	34,049	318
1975	23,260	5,953	21.1	947	4.1	28,266	262
1976	26,577	6,866	21.1	928	3.5	32,515	298
1977	27,722	7,162	21.0	716	2.6	34,168	310
1978	28,320	8,211	22.8	543	1.9	35,988	323
1979	29,666	8,380	22.4	601	2.0	37,445	333
1980	30,116	7,915	21.3	907	3.0	37,124	326
1981	30,901	7,649	20.4	1,008	3.3	37,542	326
1982	30,245	7,206	19.7	840	2.8	36,611	315
1983	32,802	8,189	20.4	774	2.4	40,217	343
1984	34,446	9,905	22.7	811	2.4	43,540	369
1985	34,061	10,260	23.6	779	2.3	43,542	365
1986	35,550	10,641	23.5	884	2.5	45,307	376
1987	36,919	11,494	24.2	921	2.5	47,492	391
1988	38,353	11,843	24.1	1,102	2.9	49,094	401
1989	38,266	11,494	23.8	1,466	3.8	48,295	391
1990	39,361	11,569	23.4	1,519	3.9	49,411	395
1991	39,084	10,313	21.8	2,072	5.3	47,325	375
1992	40,973	10,787	22.0	2,635	6.4	49,125	385
1993	41,745	11,905	23.3	2,587	6.2	51,063	396
1994	43,356	12,384	23.5	2,980	6.9	52,760	405
1995	42,868	12,820	24.3	3,011	7.0	52,677	401
1996	42,481	11,694	23.1	3,500	8.2	50,676	382
1997	44,697	13,016	24.1	3,599	8.1	54,114	404
1998	44,761	13,905	25.1	3,288	7.3	55,378	410
1999[r]	45,979	14,707	25.7	3,405	7.4	57,281	419
2000	45,519	15,373	26.9	3,767	8.3	57,125	405
2001[r]	42,104	14,502	27.3	3,389	8.0	53,217	374
2002[r]	41,510	14,502	27.4	3,111	7.5	52,901	368
2003[r]	40,367	16,224	30.3	3,107	7.7	53,484	367
2004	41,814	16,938	30.6	3,464	8.3	55,288	376
2005	41,321	15,995	29.9	3,739	9.0	53,578	361

[a]Excludes building paper and converted products.

[b]American Forest & Paper Association (5).

[c]American Forest & Paper Association (3).

[d]This import series incorporates data on Canadian exports of newsprint & uncoated groundwood to the U.S. rather than US Dept. of Commerce import data for these commodities. Such data for 1998 obtained from the Canadian Pulp & Paper Association (CPPA), in Ottawa, Canada, by fax communication.

[e]Consumption = Production + Imports − Exports.

[f]Based upon population data given in Table 1.

[r]Revised.

Table 45—Paperboard[a] production,[b] imports, exports, and consumption, 1965–2005

Year	Production[c,d]	Imports[c,d]		Exports[c,d,e]		Consumption	
						Total[f]	Per capita[g]
	Thousand tons	Thousand tons	Percent of consumption	Thousand tons	Percent of production	Thousand tons	Pounds
1965	21,332	8	0.0	1,039	4.9	20,301	209
1966	23,179	50	0.2	1,166	5.0	22,063	224
1967	22,819	13	0.1	1,334	5.8	21,498	216
1968	24,904	18	0.1	1,596	6.4	23,326	232
1969	26,376	11	0.0	1,860	7.1	24,527	242
1970	25,368	10	0.0	1,899	7.5	23,479	229
1971	26,019	17	0.1	2,115	8.1	23,921	230
1972	28,483	8	0.0	2,231	7.8	26,260	250
1973	29,549	33	0.1	2,015	6.8	27,567	260
1974	28,894	34	0.1	2,149	7.4	26,779	250
1975	24,736	8	0.0	1,453	5.9	23,291	216
1976	28,416	13	0.0	1,709	6.0	26,720	245
1977	28,935	28	0.1	1,830	6.3	27,133	246
1978	30,251	100	0.4	2,040	6.7	28,311	254
1979	31,404	82	0.3	2,263	7.2	29,223	260
1980	30,926	98	0.4	3,334	10.8	27,690	243
1981	31,208	130	0.5	2,622	8.4	28,716	250
1982	29,045	115	0.4	2,654	9.1	26,506	228
1983	32,146	168	0.6	3,012	9.4	29,302	250
1984	34,002	243	0.8	2,731	8.0	31,514	267
1985	32,922	184	0.6	2,511	7.6	30,595	257
1986	35,355	281	0.9	3,088	8.7	32,548	270
1987	37,442	361	1.0	3,190	8.5	34,613	285
1988	38,234	341	1.0	3,137	8.2	35,438	289
1989	38,519	533	1.5	3,247	8.4	35,805	290
1990	39,318	626	1.7	3,644	9.3	36,300	291
1991	40,343	773	2.1	4,363	10.8	36,753	291
1992	41,895	944	2.5	4,386	10.5	38,453	301
1993	43,113	1,085	2.7	4,248	9.9	39,950	310
1994	45,724	1,267	3.0	4,556	10.0	42,435	326
1995	46,641	1,418	3.3	4,610	9.9	43,449	330
1996	47,900	1,329	3.0	5,618	11.7	43,611	329
1997	50,332	1,497	3.3	6,768	13.4	45,061	336
1998	49,749	1,666	3.7	5,815	11.7	45,600	337
1999[r]	51,041	1,971	4.1	5,419	10.6	47,593	348
2000	48,972	1,983	4.3	4,934	10.1	46,021	326
2001	46,809	1,948	4.4	4,670	10.0	44,087	310
2002	48,126	2,065	4.7	5,865	12.2	44,326	308
2003	48,018	1,884	4.0	3,131	6.5	46,771	321
2004	50,085	2,098	4.3	3,278	6.5	48,905	333
2005	49,710	1,963	4.1	3,387	6.8	48,287	326

[a]Does not include wet machine board, hard pressed board nor insulation board. Does not include converted products.
[b]By end use.
[c]American Forest & Paper Association (5).
[d]American Forest & Paper Association (3).
[e]This export series represents production for export; numbers may differ from exports reported by U.S. Dept. of Commerce.
[f]Based upon population data given in Table 1.
[g]Consumption = Production + Imports - Exports.
[r]Revised.

Table 46—Paper and board production and fibrous materials consumed in the manufacture of paper and board, 1965–2005

Year	Paper and board[a] production[b,c] Thousand tons	Consumption of fibrous materials				Consumption of fibrous materials per ton of paper and board produced				Recovered Paper Utilization Rate Percent[g]
		Total Thousand tons	Wood pulp[c] Thousand tons	Recovered Paper[d] Thousand Tons	Other[e] Thousand tons	Total Tons	Wood pulp Tons	Recovered paper[f] Tons	Other Tons	
1965	40,489	46,838	35,728	10,231	879	1.157	0 882	0.253	0.022	25.3
1966	43,904	49,958	38,414	10,564	980	1.138	0 875	0.241	0.022	24.1
1967	43,745	48,846	38,122	9,888	836	1.117	0 871	0.226	0.019	22.6
1968	47,085	53,635	42,508	10,222	905	1.139	0 903	0.217	0.019	21.7
1969	49,824	57,597	44,750	11,969	878	1.156	0 898	0.240	0.018	24.0
1970	48,719	56,595	43,964	11,803	828	1.162	0 902	0.242	0.017	24.2
1971	49,741	58,224	45,243	12,106	875	1.171	0 910	0.243	0.018	24.3
1972	53,842	62,059	48,242	12,925	892	1.153	0 896	0.240	0.017	24.0
1973	56,346	64,953	49,976	14,094	883	1.153	0 887	0.250	0.016	25.0
1974	55,756	64,490	49,670	13,982	838	1.157	0 891	0.251	0.015	25.1
1975	47,997	55,970	43,597	11,748	625	1.166	0 908	0.245	0.013	24.5
1976	54,993	63,294	48,930	13,622	742	1.151	0 890	0.248	0.013	24.8
1977	56,656	65,240	50,356	14,058	826	1.152	0 889	0.248	0.015	24.8
1978	58,571	67,059	51,445	14,760	854	1.145	0 878	0.252	0.015	25.2
1979	61,070	68,648	52,560	15,361	727	1.124	0 861	0.252	0.012	25.2
1980	61,042	68,727	53,203	14,922	602	1.126	0 872	0.244	0.010	24.4
1981	62,109	68,828	53,199	15,037	592	1.108	0 857	0.242	0.010	24.2
1982	59,290	66,611	51,729	14,433	449	1.123	0 872	0.243	0.008	24.3
1983	64,947	70,573	54,504	15,638	431	1.087	0 839	0.241	0.007	24.1
1984	68,449	75,732	58,643	16,724	365	1.106	0 857	0.244	0.005	24.4
1985	66,983	71,482	54,816	16,371	295	1.067	0 818	0.244	0.004	24.4
1986	70,905	75,368	57,121	17,934	313	1.063	0 806	0.253	0.004	25.3
1987	74,361	78,522	59,508	18,694	320	1.056	0 800	0.251	0.004	25.1
1988	76,587	80,730	60,668	19,685	377	1.054	0.792	0.257	0.005	25.7
1989	76,786	81,772	61,234	20,220	318	1.065	0.797	0.263	0.004	26.3
1990	78,679	84,040	62,036	21,736	268	1.068	0.788	0.276	0.003	27.6
1991	79,427	86,143	62,294	23,662	187	1.085	0.784	0.298	0.002	29.8
1992	82,868	89,507	63,145	26,185	177	1.080	0.762	0.316	0.002	31.6
1993	84,857	91,471	63,227	28,011	233	1.078	0.745	0.330	0.003	33.0
1994	89,080	95,771	64,842	30,670	259	1.075	0.728	0.344	0.003	34.4
1995	89,509	96,529	64,811	31,389	329	1.078	0.724	0.351	0.004	35.1
1996	90,381	98,410	64,025	33,979	406	1.089	0.708	0.376	0.004	37.6
1997	95,029	101,591	66,057	35,209	298	1.069	0.695	0.371	0.003	37.1
1998[r]	94,510	101,218	65,122	35,771	249	1.071	0.689	0.378	0.003	37.8
1999[r]	97,020	100,690	63,638	36,727	255	1.038	0.656	0.379	0.003	37.9
2000	94,491	99,348	63,576	35,447	254	1.051	0.673	0.375	0.003	37.5
2001[r]	88,913	94,232	59,380	34,527	268	1.060	0.668	0.388	0.003	38.8
2002	89,636	93,967	59,063	34,579	261	1.048	0.659	0.386	0.003	38.6
2003	88,385	92,478	58,503	33,650	236	1.046	0.662	0.381	0.003	38.1
2004	91,899	94,627	59,566	34,736	212	1.030	0.648	0.378	0.002	37.8
2005	91,031	94,891	60,616	33,950	214	1.042	0.666	0.373	0.002	37.3

[a]Excludes wet machine board and construction grades.

[b]Production numbers = totals in Table 43. Source: see (e) below.

[c]American Forest & Paper Association (5); American Forest & Paper Association, Paper Recycling Group (7)

[d]Wood pulp consumption numbers from Table 49.

[e]Wastepaper consumption numbers from Table 47 (1985-1999 numbers were revised on Table 47).

[f]When given in percents, referred to as "Recovered Paper Utilization Rate".

[g]Recovery Rate is the ratio of paper and board production to recovered paper consumption.

[r]Revised.

Table 47—Paper and board new supply and recyclable paper consumption, exports, imports, and total recovered, 1965–2005[a,b,c]

Year	Paper and board— new supply[d]	Consumed at paper and board mills	For molded pulp, insulation, and o her uses	Exports	Imports	Total recovered[e]	Recovery rate[f]
	Thousand tons	Thousand tons	Thousand tons	Thousand tons	Thousand tons	Thousand tons	Percent
1965	48,270	10,231	z	292	108	z	z
1966	52,118	10,564	z	246	113	z	z
1967	51,435	9,888	z	262	86	z	z
1968	54,351	10,222	z	253	93	z	z
1969	57,423	11,969	z	289	75	z	z
1970	55,969	11,803	418	408	67	12,562	22.4
1971	57,450	12,106	442	419	68	12,899	22.4
1972	62,040	12,925	447	415	88	13,699	22.1
1973	65,004	14,094	499	683	87	15,189	23.4
1974	63,308	13,982	489	1,307	89	15,689	24 8
1975	54,113	11,748	535	861	72	13,072	24 2
1976	62,014	13,622	630	1,273	106	15,419	24 9
1977	64,243	14,058	870	1,512	92	16,348	25.4
1978	67,787	14,760	502	1,613	70	16,805	24 8
1979	69,796	15,361	509	2,127	78	17,919	25.7
1980	67,166	14,922	472	2,636	87	17,943	26.7
1981	67,957	15,037	480	2,282	79	17,720	26.1
1982	64,730	14,433	487	2,233	74	17,078	26.4
1983	71,166	15,638	474	2,705	100	18,727	26 3
1984	76,937	16,724	459	3,456	110	20,530	26.7
1985[r]	76,133	16,371	529	3,556	88	20,369	26 8
1986[r]	79,752	17,934	594	4,093	99	22,521	28 2
1987[r]	83,484	18,694	657	4,809	127	24,033	28 8
1988[r]	85,720	19,685	703	5,953	161	26,179	30 5
1989[r]	85,370	20,220	722	6,307	173	27,077	31.7
1990[r]	86,901	21,736	994	6,505	123	29,112	33 5
1991[r]	85,145	23,662	1,063	6,598	122	31,201	36.6
1992[r]	88,369	26,185	1,137	6,782	150	33,955	38.4
1993[r]	91,639	28,011	1,216	6,371	138	35,460	38.7
1994[r]	95,717	30,670	1,300	7,974	253	39,691	41 5
1995[r]	95,971	31,389	1,390	9,908	498	42,189	44 0
1996[r]	94,529	33,979	1,487	8,084	474	43,077	45.6
1997[r]	99,556	35,209	1,590	7,882	693	43,989	44 2
1998[r]	101,183	35,771	1,700	8,117	511	45,077	44.6
1999[r]	105,316	36,727	2,000	8,517	426	46,818	44 5
2000	102,811	35,447	2,200	10,272	608	47,311	46 0
2001	97,394	34,527	2,200	10,597	328	46,996	48 3
2002	98,976	34,579	2,200	11,267	411	47,635	48.1
2003	98,016	33,650	2,200	13,805	399	49,256	50 3
2004	101,882	34,736	2,200	13,910	558	50,288	49 5
2005	99,565	33,950	2,000	15,906	545	51,311	51 5

[a]Includes paper, paperboard, wet machine board and construction paper and board.
[b]American Forest and Paper Association, Paper Recycling Group (7).
[c]Data may not add to totals because of rounding.
[d]Production plus imports less exports. Includes imports and exports of products.
[e]Total recovered paper = total recyclable paper consumption plus exports less imports.
[f]Recovery rate is the ratio of total recovered paper collected to new supply of paper and paperboard.
[r]Revised
[z]Not available.
[p]Preliminary

Table 48—Recovered paper consumption, by major grade, in paper and paperboard manufacture[a], 1970–2005 (thousand short tons)[b]

Year	Mixed grades	Old newspapers	Old corrugated	Pulp substitutes[c]	High grade deinking	Total all grades	Total recovery rate (%)[d,r]
			Recovered paper consumption				
1970	2,639.0	2,235.0	4,080.0	3,067.0	z	12,021.0	22.4
1971	2,776.0	2,174.0	4,277.0	3,096.0	z	12,323.0	22.4
1972	3,054.0	2,317.0	4,722.0	3,039.0	z	13,132.0	22.1
1973	3,371.0	2,456.0	5,292.0	3,199.0	z	14,318.0	23.4
1974	3,118.0	2,408.0	5,716.0	2,954.0	z	14,196.0	24.8
1975	2,606.0	2,040.0	4,743.0	2,594.0	z	11,983.0	24.2
1976	2,798.0	2,278.0	5,696.0	2,117.0	933.0	13,822.0	24.9
1977	2,773.0	2,287.0	6,205.0	2,079.0	944.0	14,288.0	25.4
1978	2,729.0	2,212.0	6,721.0	2,242.0	1,068.0	14,972.0	24.8
1979	2,648.0	2,480.0	6,967.0	2,308.0	1,117.0	15,520.0	25.7
1980	2,268.0	2,564.0	6,866.0	2,254.0	1,142.0	15,094.0	26.7
1981	2,233.0	2,552.0	6,910.0	2,307.0	1,215.0	15,217.0	26.1
1982	1,707.0	2,673.0	6,770.0	2,247.0	1,223.0	14,620.0	26.4
1983	1,908.0	2,692.0	7,443.0	2,456.0	1,323.0	15,822.0	26.3
1984	1,974.5	2,894.8	7,971.7	2,673.4	1,368.6	16,883.0	26.7
1985	1,901.5	2,875.0	7,899.5	2,493.7	1,380.4	16,550.1	26.8
1986	2,044.5	3,117.8	8,633.6	2,761.5	1,570.3	18,127.7	28.2
1987	2,116.0	3,142.6	9,176.7	2,902.2	1,563.5	18,901.0	28.8
1988	2,182.2	3,215.6	9,909.1	2,889.5	1,691.1	19,887.5	30.5
1989	2,355.8	3,638.1	9,993.5	2,642.4	1,812.4	20,442.2	31.7
1990	2,504.9	4,084.5	10,686.5	2,731.8	1,999.8	22,007.5	33.5
1991	2,890.6	4,572.4	11,247.0	2,988.5	2,239.5	23,938.0	36.6
1992	3,463.8	4,816.9	12,532.3	2,997.7	2,669.1	26,479.8	38.4
1993	4,110.1	5,000.3	13,566.8	2,802.1	2,856.8	28,336.1	38.7
1994	4,786.0	5,368.0	15,009.6	2,696.0	3,090.0	30,949.6	41.5
1995	4,529.4	5,157.3	16,513.5	2,459.1	3,004.0	31,663.3	44.0
1996	4,801.7	5,238.4	18,733.3	2,428.8	3,039.9	34,242.1	45.6
1997	4,698.6	5,561.5	19,640.8	2,640.3	2,954.6	35,495.8	44.2
1998	5,440.8	5,611.3	19,530.1	2,341.8	3,147.8	36,071.8	44.6
1999[r]	5,592.1	5,539.9	20,457.8	2,431.7	3,003.2	37,024.7	44.5
2000	4,948.0	5,809.0	19,968.0	1,890.0	3,129.0	35,744.0	46.0
2001	4,800.0	6,077.0	19,348.0	1,845.0	2,750.0	34,820.0	48.3
2002	4,877.0	5,957.0	19,627.0	1,705.0	2,695.0	34,861.0	48.1
2003	4,591.0	5,756.0	19,294.0	1,818.0	2,473.0	33,932.0	50.3
2004	4,976.0	5,867.0	19,926.0	1,701.0	2,537.0	35,007.0	49.5
2005	4,519.0	5,700.0	20,024.0	1,438.0	2,523.0	34,204.0	51.5

[a]Includes paper, paperboard, construction grades and molded pulp grades.

[b]American Forest & Paper Association, Paper Recycling Group (7).

[c]For years 1972-1975, high grade deinking is included with pulp substitutes.

[d]Recovery rate is the ratio of total recovered paper collected to new supply of paper and paperboard.

[r]Revised (1985-1999 Total recovery on Table 47).

[z]Not available separately; included with pulp substitutes.

[p]Preliminary

Table 49—Wood pulp production, imports, exports, and consumption, 1965–2005[a]

Year	Production[b,d]	Imports[c]		Exports[c]		Consumption[d]	
						Total	Per capita[c]
	Thousand tons	Thousand tons	Percent of consumption	Thousand tons	Percent of production	Thousand tons	Pounds
1965	33,993	3,137	8.8	1,402	4.1	35,728	368
1966	36,603	3,358	8.7	1,547	4.2	38,414	391
1967	36,677	3,166	8.3	1,721	4.7	38,122	384
1968	40,892	3,532	8.3	1,916	4.7	42,508	424
1969	42,813	4,040	9.0	2,103	4.9	44,750	442
1970	43,546	3,513	8.0	3,095	7.1	43,964	429
1971	43,903	3,515	7.8	2,175	5.0	45,243	436
1972	46,767	3,728	7.7	2,253	4.8	48,242	460
1973	48,327	3,993	8.0	2,344	4.9	49,976	472
1974	48,349	4,123	8.3	2,802	5.8	49,670	464
1975	43,084	3,078	7.1	2,565	6.0	43,597	404
1976	47,721	3,727	7.6	2,518	5.3	48,930	449
1977	49,132	3,864	7.7	2,640	5.4	50,356	457
1978	50,020	4,024	7.8	2,599	5.2	51,445	462
1979	51,177	4,318	8.2	2,935	5.7	52,560	467
1980	52,958	4,051	7.6	3,806	7.2	53,203	467
1981	52,790	4,087	7.7	3,678	7.0	53,199	463
1982	51,468	3,656	7.1	3,395	6.6	51,729	446
1983	54,055	4,093	7.5	3,644	6.7	54,504	465
1984	57,747	4,490	7.7	3,594	6.2	58,643	496
1985	54,145	4,466	8.1	3,795	7.0	54,816	460
1986	56,997	4,582	8.0	4,458	7.8	57,121	475
1987	59,547	4,850	8.2	4,889	8.2	59,508	490
1988	61,158	5,038	8.3	5,528	9.0	60,668	495
1989	61,996	5,004	8.2	5,766	9.3	61,234	495
1990	63,048	4,893	7.9	5,905	9.4	62,036	496
1991	63,635	4,997	8.0	6,338	10.0	62,294	493
1992	65,338	5,029	8.0	7,222	11.1	63,145	494
1993	64,313	5,413	8.6	6,499	10.1	63,227	490
1994	65,920	5,650	8.7	6,728	10.2	64,842	497
1995	67,103	5,969	9.2	8,261	12.3	64,811	493
1996	65,503	5,692	8.9	7,170	10.9	64,025	482
1997	66,650	6,398	9.7	6,990	10.5	66,057	493
1998	65,163	5,984	9.2	6,025	9.2	65,122	482
1999[r]	62,914	6,660	10.5	5,936	9.4	63,638	466
2000	62,758	7,227	11.4	6,409	10.2	63,576	451
2001	58,198	7,348	12.4	6,167	10.6	59,380	417
2002	58,069	7,247	12.3	6,254	10.8	59,063	411
2003	57,659	6,691	11.4	5,847	10.1	58,503	402
2004	59,065	6,726	11.3	6,225	10.5	59,566	405
2005	60,267	6,762	11.2	6,413	10.6	60,616	409

[a]Includes dissolving and special alpha pulps, excludes defibrated/exploded pulps and screenings.

[b]U.S. Department of Commerce, Bureau of the Census (62,66,67); United Nations,
Food and Agriculture Organization, Economic Commission for Europe (38); American Forest & Paper Association (5).

[c]Based on U.S. population data given in Table 1.

[d]Consumption = Production + Imports – Exports.

[r]Revised.

Table 50—Pulpwood consumed in the manufacture of wood pulp, 1965–2005[a]

| Year | Pulpwood consumption[b] | | Wood pulp production |
| | Total | Per ton of pulp produced | |
	Thousand cords	*Cords*	*Thousand tons*
1965	54,034	1.59	33,993
1966	57,399	1.57	36,603
1967	58,419	1.59	36,677
1968	60,969	1.49	40,892
1969	64,577	1.51	42,813
1970	66,732	1.53	43,546
1971	66,601	1.52	43,903
1972	68,068	1.46	46,767
1973	71,421	1.48	48,327
1974	75,787	1.57	48,349
1975	63,941	1.48	43,084
1976	71,094	1.49	47,721
1977	72,952	1.48	49,132
1978	75,073	1.50	50,020
1979	78,680	1.54	51,177
1980	81,921	1.55	52,958
1981	81,003	1.53	52,790
1982	76,912	1.49	51,468
1983	84,504	1.56	54,055
1984	86,282	1.49	57,747
1985	85,380	1.58	54,145
1986	91,187	1.60	56,997
1987	93,005	1.56	59,547
1988	93,000	1.52	61,158
1989	92,615	1.49	61,996
1990	92,561	1.47	63,048
1991	91,925	1.44	63,635
1992	93,642	1.43	65,338
1993	90,996	1.41	64,313
1994	93,259	1.41	65,920
1995	93,013	1.39	67,103
1996	88,246	1.35	65,503
1997	92,312	1.39	66,650
1998	90,591	1.39	65,163
1999	86,969	1.38	62,914
2000	87,453	1.39	62,758
2001	83,384	1.43	58,198
2002	82,715	1.42	58,069
2003	85,001	1.47	57,659
2004	86,903	1.47	59,065
2005	86,284	1.43	60,267

[a]U.S. Department of Commerce, Bureau of the Census (65); American Forest & Paper Association (3,5,6); American Pulpwood Association (14). Data may not add to totals because of rounding
[b]Includes changes in inventories.

Table 51—Producer price indexes for paper, board, and wood pulp, 1965–2005 (1997 = 100)[a]

Year	Pulp, paper, and allied products		Paper		Paperboard		Building paper and board		Wood pulp	
	Actual	Relative[b]	Actual	Relative	Actual	Relative	Actual	Relative	Actual	Relative
1965	19.8	78.3	22.9	90.7	27.5	108.6	32.3	127.7	20.5	81.1
1966	20.4	78.3	23.7	90.9	27.7	106.0	32.3	123.9	20.5	78.6
1967	20.6	78.7	24.3	92.9	27.1	103.6	32.1	122.5	20.5	78.4
1968	20.9	77.8	24.7	92.3	26.0	97.0	32.3	120.6	20.5	76.6
1969	21.5	76.9	25.6	91.8	26.9	96.5	33.9	121.5	20.5	73.6
1970	22.3	77.2	27.0	93.3	27.4	94.7	32.4	112.1	22.5	77.7
1971	22.7	75.9	27.7	92.9	27.8	93.0	33.0	110.4	23.0	77.2
1972	23.5	75.2	28.3	90.6	28.6	91.7	34.1	109.3	22.9	73.3
1973	25.2	71.4	29.5	83.5	31.2	88.5	36.2	102.6	26.3	74.6
1974	31.3	74.7	36.1	86.2	41.2	98.3	39.6	94.4	44.8	106.8
1975	35.1	76.8	42.0	91.9	46.1	100.8	40.8	89.1	58.2	127.2
1976	37.0	77.3	44.3	92.4	47.7	99.7	44.5	92.8	58.8	122.7
1977	38.5	75.7	47.2	92.8	47.7	93.8	50.3	99.0	57.7	113.5
1978	40.3	73.6	50.1	91.4	48.7	89.0	60.1	109.7	54.8	100.0
1979	45.3	73.4	55.8	90.5	54.8	88.8	58.5	94.9	64.6	104.7
1980	51.4	73.0	62.4	88.7	63.6	90.4	66.1	94.0	78.1	110.9
1981	56.5	73.6	68.0	88.5	69.9	91.0	74.3	96.8	81.6	106.3
1982	59.6	76.1	69.5	88.7	69.1	88.2	76.8	98.0	77.9	99.4
1983	61.5	77.5	68.5	86.3	68.0	85.6	80.2	101.0	71.3	89.8
1984	65.8	80.9	73.6	90.5	76.2	93.8	83.1	102.3	81.6	100.4
1985	67.5	83.5	73.7	91.2	74.4	92.0	82.5	102.0	71.2	88.0
1986	69.2	88.2	74.4	94.8	73.6	93.8	83.6	106.4	73.7	93.8
1987	72.6	90.1	77.6	96.3	81.6	101.3	85.4	106.0	86.8	107.8
1988	77.7	92.8	85.7	102.3	92.0	109.8	87.0	103.8	106.4	127.0
1989	82.1	93.4	90.2	102.5	96.8	110.0	88.8	101.0	122.6	139.4
1990	84.1	92.3	89.6	98.3	93.8	102.9	86.2	94.5	117.8	129.3
1991	85.1	93.3	88.3	96.7	90.0	98.5	85.9	94.1	92.8	101.7
1992	86.5	94.2	85.6	93.2	92.9	101.1	91.9	100.0	93.3	101.6
1993	87.7	94.2	86.1	92.4	89.8	96.4	102.0	109.4	81.2	87.1
1994	90.9	96.3	87.5	92.7	96.8	102.6	110.8	117.4	90.7	96.1
1995	102.6	105.0	110.6	113.2	126.5	129.4	111.3	113.9	142.6	145.9
1996	100.6	100.5	104.0	103.9	107.8	107.7	105.3	105.2	104.2	104.1
1997	100.0	100.0	100.0	100.0	100.0	100.0	100.0	100.0	100.0	100.0
1998	101.8	104.4	101.6	104.2	104.9	107.6	101.9	104.5	95.5	97.9
1999	103.8	105.5	98.6	100.2	105.8	107.6	108.7	110.6	93.2	94.8
2000	109.5	105.3	104.2	100.2	122.1	117.4	106.6	102.5	113.1	108.8
2001	110.2	104.8	104.8	99.6	118.9	113.1	99.3	94.4	98.0	93.1
2002	110.9	107.9	100.8	98.1	113.7	110.6	94.6	92.0	90.6	88.1
2003	113.3	104.7	101.6	93.9	112.4	103.9	116.7	107.8	94.5	87.3
2004	116.7	101.5	103.9	90.4	117.6	102.3	140.4	122.1	102.9	89.5
2005	120.8	97.9	111.0	90.0	121.3	98.3	134.9	109.4	107.5	87.1

[a]U.S. Department of Labor, Bureau of Labor Statistics (74).
[b]Derived by dividing the actual price index by the all commodities price index.

Table 52—Producer price indexes for wastepaper, by grade, 1965–2005(1997 = 100)[a]

Year	Wastepaper		Newspaper		Mixed papers		Corrugated		High grades[b]		Exports (all grades)	
	Actual	Relative[c]	Actual	Relative	Actual	Relative	Actual	Relative	Actual	Relative	Actual	Relative
1965	63.5	250.8	z	z	z	z	z	z	z	z	z	z
1966	67.0	256.9	z	z	z	z	z	z	z	z	z	z
1967	49.9	190.5	126.6	483.6	67.7	258.8	42.5	162.3	z	z	z	z
1968	64.8	241.9	173.6	647.8	103.3	385.4	54.6	203.8	z	z	z	z
1969	69.1	247.8	155.7	558.0	114.0	408.4	59.7	213.8	z	z	z	z
1970	62.4	215.7	136.8	473.1	88.2	304.9	57.6	199.2	z	z	z	z
1971	55.9	187.1	130.6	437.4	83.1	278.2	47.4	158.9	z	z	z	z
1972	66.6	213.6	151.0	484.0	105.1	337.0	55.9	179.2	z	z	z	z
1973	98.4	279.0	173.7	492.6	156.2	443.0	95.0	269.3	z	z	z	z
1974	132.5	315.9	255.3	608.8	224.0	534.2	106.9	255.0	z	z	z	z
1975	54.9	120.1	141.5	309.2	70.1	153.1	38.2	83.5	z	z	z	z
1976	92.1	192.4	252.7	527.6	105.9	221.1	83.2	173.7	z	z	z	z
1977	93.4	183.6	265.3	521.6	118.0	232.0	79.2	155.8	z	z	z	z
1978	95.4	174.1	253.8	463.2	151.7	276.8	85.9	156.8	z	z	z	z
1979	103.0	167.1	192.2	311.6	138.3	224.3	118.4	191.9	z	z	z	z
1980	104.1	147.9	212.0	301.3	150.1	213.2	81.6	116.0	z	z	z	z
1981	87.7	114.1	z	z	z	z	z	z	z	z	z	z
1982	60.4	77.1	91.3	116.5	51.3	65.5	40.2	51.3	z	z	z	z
1983	z	z	z	z	z	z	z	z	z	z	z	z
1984	119.8	147.4	244.4	300.8	165.7	203.9	127.7	157.1	z	z	z	z
1985	74.3	91.9	189.9	234.8	140.9	174.2	62.3	77.0	z	z	z	z
1986	86.1	109.7	174.6	222.4	123.5	157.3	95.6	121.8	z	z	z	z
1987	109.6	136.0	222.7	276.4	146.5	181.9	125.9	156.3	112.1	139.2	112.4	139.5
1988	110.9	132.4	219.0	261.4	161.6	192.8	100.7	120.2	134.8	160.9	115.1	137.4
1989	94.9	108.0	113.5	129.1	110.4	125.6	72.5	82.4	139.3	158.4	101.7	115.7
1990	83.9	92.1	95.1	104.3	83.2	91.3	66.5	73.0	122.6	134.6	90.4	99.2
1991	73.4	80.4	93.1	101.9	61.3	67.2	66.3	72.6	99.0	108.4	80.6	88.2
1992	70.2	76.4	83.6	91.0	51.3	55.9	58.6	63.8	101.7	110.7	79.8	86.9
1993	70.9	76.1	92.1	98.8	86.4	92.7	57.2	61.4	97.6	104.7	74.4	79.9
1994	126.8	134.4	185.9	197.0	202.8	214.9	129.6	137.3	114.1	120.9	111.0	117.7
1995	224.2	229.4	388.9	397.9	496.9	508.5	206.9	211.7	164.2	168.1	199.3	203.9
1996	84.5	84.5	100.3	100.2	106.5	106.4	85.5	85.4	83.5	83.5	80.6	80.6
1997	100.0	100.0	100.0	100.0	100.0	100.0	100.0	100.0	100.0	100.0	100.0	100.0
1998	88.1	90.3	110.1	113.0	164.6	168.9	72.5	74.3	94.1	96.5	76.2	78.2
1999	110.9	112.8	151.5	154.0	381.5	387.9	81.9	83.3	102.3	104.1	104.0	105.7
2000	170.7	164.1	227.5	218.8	790.6	760.2	98.2	94.5	165.1	158.8	140.5	135.1
2001	89.8	85.4	140.8	133.9	195.7	186.1	53.4	50.8	103.5	98.4	78.8	74.9
2002	104.5	101.7	172.2	167.6	396.6	386.0	79.0	76.9	106.2	103.4	106.6	103.7
2003	119.2	110.1	189.7	175.2	537.2	496.3	80.7	74.5	87.8	81.1	90.3	83.4
2004	139.8	121.6	221.8	192.9	722.0	628.0	106.6	92.7	95.7	83.2	116.9	101.7
2005	162.0	131.3	199.1	161.4	338.8	274.7	147.2	119.4	95.4	77.3	110.2	89.4

[a] U.S. Department of Labor, Bureau of Labor Statistics (74).
[b] Pulp substitutes and deinking; December 1986 = 100.
[c] Derived by dividing the actual price index by the all commodities price index.
[z] Not available.

Table 53—Particleboard and medium-density fiberboard production, imports, exports, and consumption, 1965–2005 (3/4-in. basis)[a]

Year	Production Total	Particleboard	Medium-density fiberboard	Imports[b]	Exports	Consumption Total	Per capita
	Million square feet	Million square feet	Million square feet	Million square feet	Million square feet	Million square feet	Square feet
1965	828	753	75	4	c	832	4
1966	1,031	948	83	1	c	1,032	5
1967	1,167	1,074	93	1	2	1,166	6
1968	1,494	1,391	103	1	6	1,489	7
1969	1,796	1,682	114	12	14	1,794	9
1970	1,858	1,731	127	3	10	1,851	9
1971	2,500	2,359	141	8	20	2,488	12
1972	3,236	3,079	157	14	45	3,205	15
1973	3,634	3,460	174	17	77	3,574	17
1974	3,269	3,075	194	7	113	3,163	15
1975	2,718	2,503	215	16	84	2,650	12
1976	3,469	3,189	280	60	80	3,449	16
1977	4,010	3,569	441	158	63	4,105	19
1978	4,228	3,720	508	193	61	4,360	20
1979	3,883	3,376	507	221	84	4,020	18
1980	3,443	2,950	493	264	106	3,601	16
1981	3,385	2,869	516	254	117	3,522	15
1982	2,839	2,393	446	766	41	3,564	15
1983	3,613	3,009	604	994	47	4,560	19
1984	3,830	3,196	634	1,331	54	5,107	22
1985	4,016	3,331	685	1,335	59	5,292	22
1986	4,384	3,603	781	1,395	86	5,693	24
1987	4,605	3,706	899	1,550	113	6,042	25
1988	4,768	3,829	939	1,634	163	6,239	25
1989	4,828	3,858	970	425	333	4,920	20
1990	4,756	3,806	950	363	373	4,746	19
1991	4,730	3,772	958	293	369	4,654	18
1992	5,046	3,980	1,066	405	394	5,057	20
1993	5,402	4,241	1,161	572	318	5,656	22
1994	5,793	4,542	1,251	775	297	6,271	24
1995	5,307	4,200	1,107	840	319	5,828	22
1996	5,705	4,459	1,246	814	154	6,365	24
1997	5,916	4,531	1,385	963	188	6,691	25
1998	5,994	4,593	1,401	2,461	135	8,320	31
1999[r]	6,229	4,816	1,413	2,526	135	8,619	32
2000	6,292	4,804	1,488	2,968	162	9,098	32
2001	5,480	4,096	1,384	3,743	192	9,030	32
2002	6,035	4,414	1,621	4,104	212	9,927	35
2003	5,592	3,984	1,608	5,985	194	11,383	39
2004	6,052	4,305	1,747	11,929	195	17,786	61
2005	5,951	4,111	1,840	11,309	199	17,061	58

[a]Composite Panel Association (15); U.S. International Trade Commission (80).
Data may not add to totals because of rounding.
[b]May contain significant volumes of waferboard and oriented strandboard products prior to 1989.
[c]Fewer than 500,000 ft^2.
[r]Revised

Table 54—Insulating board[a] production, imports, exports, and consumption, 1965–2005 (1/2-in. basis)[b]

Year	Production	Imports[c]	Exports	Consumption	
				Total	Per capita
	Million square feet	*Million square feet*	*Million square feet*	*Million square feet*	*Square feet*
1965	3,362	75	42	3,395	17
1966	3,079	67	48	3,098	16
1967	3,209	69	45	3,233	16
1968	3,476	94	45	3,525	18
1969	3,623	98	65	3,656	18
1970	3,194	103	51	3,246	16
1971	3,839	115	65	3,889	19
1972	3,918	121	66	3,973	19
1973	3,914	140	79	3,975	19
1974	3,282	72	102	3,252	15
1975	2,960	36	77	2,919	14
1976	3,407	45	77	3,375	15
1977	3,462	107	84	3,485	16
1978	3,437	139	106	3,470	16
1979	3,310	138	49	3,399	15
1980	2,780	100	62	2,818	12
1981	2,124	104	110	2,118	9
1982	1,790	118	67	1,841	8
1983	2,277	204	83	2,398	10
1984	2,545	286	89	2,742	12
1985	2,461	343	80	2,724	11
1986	2,194	338	117	2,415	10
1987	2,242	273	127	2,388	10
1988	2,340	320	203	2,457	10
1989	2,455	346	180	2,621	11
1990	2,365	290	175	2,480	10
1991	2,323	200	191	2,332	9
1992	2,363	310	215	2,458	10
1993	2,358	285	208	2,435	9
1994	2,335	305	170	2,470	9
1995	2,335	305	170	2,470	9
1996	2,335	305	170	2,470	9
1997	2,335	305	170	2,470	9
1998	2,335	305	170	2,470	9
1999	2,335	305	170	2,470	9
2000	2,335	305	170	2,470	9
2001	2,335	305	170	2,470	9
2002	2,335	305	170	2,470	9
2003	2,335	305	170	2,470	8
2004	2,335	305	170	2,470	8
2005	2,335	305	170	2,470	8

[a]Density equal to or less than 31 lb/ft^3.

[b]American Forest & Paper Association (3,5); U.S. Department of Commerce, Bureau of the Census (62,66,67); Data may not add to totals because of rounding.

[c]Includes other building board.

Table 55—Insulating board[a] production, imports, exports, and consumption, 1965–2005[b]

Year	Production Thousand tons	Imports[c] Thousand tons	Exports Thousand tons	Consumption	
				Total Thousand tons	Per capita pounds
1965	1,234	28	15	1,246	6
1966	1,130	25	18	1,137	6
1967	1,178	25	17	1,187	6
1968	1,276	34	17	1,294	6
1969	1,330	36	24	1,342	7
1970	1,172	38	19	1,191	6
1971	1,409	42	24	1,427	7
1972	1,438	44	24	1,458	7
1973	1,436	51	29	1,459	7
1974	1,204	26	37	1,193	6
1975	1,086	13	28	1,071	5
1976	1,250	17	28	1,239	6
1977	1,271	39	31	1,279	6
1978	1,261	51	39	1,273	6
1979	1,215	51	18	1,247	6
1980	1,020	37	23	1,034	5
1981	780	38	40	777	3
1982	657	43	25	676	3
1983	836	75	30	880	4
1984	934	105	33	1,006	4
1985	903	126	29	1,000	4
1986	805	124	43	886	4
1987	823	100	47	876	4
1988	859	117	75	902	4
1989	901	127	66	962	4
1990	868	106	64	910	4
1991	853	73	70	856	3
1992	867	114	79	902	4
1993	865	105	76	894	3
1994	857	112	62	906	3
1995	857	112	62	906	3
1996	857	112	62	906	3
1997	857	112	62	906	3
1998	857	112	62	906	3
1999	857	112	62	906	3
2000	857	112	62	906	3
2001	857	112	62	906	3
2002	857	112	62	906	3
2003	857	112	62	906	3
2004	857	112	62	906	3
2005	857	112	62	906	3

[a]Density equal to or less than 31 lb/ft^3.

[b]Product of table 54 using a conversion of .367.

[c]Includes other building board.

Table 56—Hardboard[a] production, imports, exports, and consumption, 1965–2005 (1/8-in. basis)[b]

Year	Production[c] Thousand cubic meters	Imports Thousand cubic meters	Exports Thousand cubic meters	Consumption	
				Total Thousand cubic meters	Per capita Cubic meters
1965	862	169	6	1025	0.0053
1966	910	135	9	1036	0.0053
1967	896	134	9	1022	0.0051
1968	1095	184	12	1267	0.0063
1969	1253	205	14	1443	0.0071
1970	1293	133	23	1404	0.0068
1971	1541	186	24	1703	0.0082
1972	1711	313	30	1993	0.0095
1973	1785	309	39	2055	0.0097
1974	1668	218	52	1834	0.0086
1975	1676	78	47	1707	0.0079
1976	2002	143	55	2090	0.0096
1977	2276	184	51	2409	0.0109
1978	2308	266	23	2552	0.0115
1979	2268	245	30	2483	0.0110
1980	1811	152	26	1938	0.0085
1981	1801	168	50	1918	0.0083
1982	1648	135	14	1769	0.0076
1983	2154	212	18	2348	0.0100
1984	2017	238	19	2236	0.0095
1985	1859	231	57	2033	0.0085
1986	1718	252	54	1916	0.0080
1987	1610	245	79	1776	0.0073
1988	1510	187	95	1602	0.0065
1989	1533	212	126	1619	0.0065
1990	1482	203	163	1523	0.0061
1991	1444	168	179	1434	0.0057
1992	1556	168	247	1477	0.0058
1993	1548	189	271	1466	0.0057
1994	1536	330	351	1515	0.0058
1995	1454	340	406	1388	0.0053
1996	1558	349	421	1486	0.0056
1997	1328	385	371	1342	0.0050
1998	1269	376	257	1387	0.0051
1999	1294	526	270	1550	0.0057
2000	1115	520	278	1358	0.0048
2001	980	678	232	1426	0.0050
2002	861	790	197	1453	0.0051
2003	1270	909	191	1987	0.0068
2004	1144	1236	296	2084	0.0071
2005	1282	1412	317	2377	0.0080

[a]Density greater than 31 lb/ft^3.

[b]U.S. Department of Commerce, Bureau of the Census (62,66,67); American Forest & Paper Association (3,4,5); U.S. International Trade Commission (80); Composite Panel Association (15); data may not add to totals because of rounding.

[c]Data for the years 1982 to present are for shipments. History numbers do not reflect entire industry.

Table 57—Producer price indexes for hardboard and particleboard, 1965–2005(1997 = 100)[a]

Year	Hardboard and particleboard[b]		Hardboard		Particleboard[c]	
	Actual	Relative[d]	Actual	Relative[d]	Actual	Relative[d]
1965	38.1	150.6	36.6	144.4	z	z
1966	37.9	145.4	36.5	139.8	z	z
1967	36.6	140.0	35.8	136.8	z	z
1968	36.3	135.3	35.0	130.8	z	z
1969	37.7	135.0	35.8	128.3	z	z
1970	34.1	118.1	36.6	126.4	z	z
1971	34.2	114.6	36.1	121.0	z	z
1972	35.3	113.3	36.6	117.2	z	z
1973	38.7	109.7	37.6	106.5	z	z
1974	42.2	100.6	42.1	100.4	z	z
1975	41.6	91.0	42.0	91.8	z	z
1976	45.3	94.7	47.1	98.3	z	z
1977	51.6	101.5	51.2	100.6	z	z
1978	62.5	114.0	56.1	102.5	z	z
1979	60.7	98.4	58.9	95.5	z	z
1980	69.9	99.4	67.1	95.3	z	z
1981	77.9	101.4	78.0	101.6	z	z
1982	80.5	102.7	81.8	104.3	z	z
1983	83.9	105.7	82.1	103.4	74.6	93.9
1984	87.2	107.2	83.5	102.8	81.8	100.6
1985	85.4	105.6	84.3	104.2	77.4	95.6
1986	86.2	109.8	84.9	108.1	78.9	100.5
1987	88.1	109.3	83.2	103.3	84.9	105.4
1988	89.5	106.8	84.7	101.1	88.0	105.0
1989	90.3	102.7	84.8	96.4	90.2	102.6
1990	86.5	94.9	82.9	90.9	82.3	90.3
1991	85.7	93.8	81.3	89.0	82.1	89.9
1992	92.5	100.7	84.0	91.5	85.1	92.7
1993	103.1	110.6	89.5	96.1	97.7	104.8
1994	111.9	118.5	91.7	97.2	109.4	115.9
1995	112.3	114.9	95.1	97.4	109.3	111.8
1996	105.8	105.7	97.3	97.3	104.9	104.8
1997	100.0	100.0	100.0	100.0	100.0	100.0
1998	102.3	105.0	97.9	100.4	97.6	100.1
1999	109.4	111.2	100.1	101.8	100.7	102.4
2000	106.8	102.7	101.8	97.9	104.0	100.0
2001	98.6	93.7	95.5	90.8	97.5	92.7
2002	98.6	96.0	93.8	91.3	94.8	92.3
2003	123.0	113.7	95.7	88.5	96.5	89.1
2004	148.9	129.5	99.6	86.6	123.0	107.0
2005	142.3	115.3	98.6	79.9	118.9	96.4

[a]U.S. Department of Labor, Bureau of Labor Statistics (74).
[b]Hardboard, particleboard, and fiberboard products.
[c]Platen-type (mat formed)
[d]Derived by dividing the actual price index by the all commodities index.
[z]Not available.

Table 58—Production of treated wood products by type of treatment, treatment plant, and product, 1984–2005 (thousands of board feet)[a]

Year	Total	Volume Treated with				Plants treating wi h[c]			
		Creosote solutions	Oilborne[b] pressure	Waterborne pressure	Fire retardants	Creosote	Oilborne	Waterborne	Fire retardants
1984	5,989,488	1,651,128	643,320	3,620,364	74,676	120	95	445	75
1985	6,231,780	1,542,852	630,420	3,944,124	114,384	123	97	449	77
1986	6,649,236	1,424,988	593,808	4,505,496	124,944	117	81	475	79
1987	6,911,796	1,173,888	582,684	5,027,808	127,416	109	71	479	81
1988	7,189,740	1,085,772	574,428	5,406,780	122,760	97	65	484	80
1989	6,683,316	1,078,440	592,632	4,883,292	128,952	90	60	473	71
1990	7,027,620	1,118,304	559,104	5,252,100	98,112	85	65	458	66
1991	6,781,128	1,051,320	521,880	5,092,440	115,488	83	63	445	60
1992	7,025,796	1,078,452	477,876	5,369,244	100,224	81	44	432	57
1993	7,270,452	1,105,584	433,860	5,646,048	84,960	76	49	404	48
1994	7,609,020	1,134,780	495,348	5,962,596	16,296	85	33	461	44
1995	6,946,488	1,101,012	393,168	5,407,152	45,156	71	28	384	39
1996	7,099,307	1,038,136	401,934	5,614,264	44,974	68	27	368	29
1997	8,772,963	1,168,768	468,270	6,977,434	158,491	70	46	381	35
1998	8,772,963	1,168,768	468,270	6,977,434	158,491	70	46	381	35
1999	8,772,963	1,168,768	468,270	6,977,434	158,491	70	46	381	35
2000	8,772,963	1,168,768	468,270	6,977,434	158,491	70	46	381	35
2001	8,772,963	1,168,768	468,270	6,977,434	158,491	70	46	381	35
2002	8,772,963	1,168,768	468,270	6,977,434	158,491	70	46	381	35
2003	8,772,963	1,168,768	468,270	6,977,434	158,491	70	46	381	35
2004	8,772,963	1,168,768	468,270	6,977,434	158,491	70	46	381	35
2005	8,772,963	1,168,768	468,270	6,977,434	158,491	70	46	381	35

Year	Total[d]	Volume by product								Other[e]
		Lumber	Timbers	Poles	Pilings	Fence posts	Crossties	Switch and bridge ies	Plywood (thousand sq.ft)	
1984	3,980,729	948,965	324,492	931,896	142,068	235,800	1,064,640	98,376	179,936	234,492
1985	4,032,820	1,025,956	350,496	921,972	126,348	149,232	1,030,728	97,608	267,072	330,480
1986	4,136,740	1,173,628	387,348	880,092	125,784	208,092	965,316	70,884	297,664	325,596
1987	4,118,679	1,290,567	542,376	903,288	97,440	135,024	715,128	111,672	408,064	323,184
1988	4,136,768	1,417,868	540,204	854,292	116,388	148,848	693,240	75,780	406,560	290,148
1989	4,054,037	1,207,913	527,412	887,700	116,136	172,524	696,264	75,612	422,048	370,476
1990	4,240,101	1,290,657	576,012	882,012	86,232	178,488	755,856	85,980	392,736	384,864
1991	4,129,285	1,220,053	630,372	860,808	81,240	166,020	731,664	74,760	415,936	364,368
1992	4,236,767	1,284,479	622,284	812,592	93,012	165,504	747,348	77,052	430,368	434,496
1993	4,344,226	1,348,906	614,196	764,376	104,772	164,988	763,032	79,332	444,800	504,624
1994	5,146,279	1,084,470	970,867	903,974	121,390	246,946	756,648	120,036	651,267	941,949
1995	4,698,187	990,043	886,332	825,264	110,820	225,444	690,768	109,584	594,560	859,932
1996	4,470,363	1,160,247	667,572	762,792	101,028	281,208	669,948	68,880	681,088	758,688
1997	5,287,364	1,543,748	1,032,313	774,235	108,062	181,375	911,537	72,042	772,963	664,053
1998	5,287,364	1,543,748	1,032,313	774,235	108,062	181,375	911,537	72,042	772,963	664,053
1999	5,287,364	1,543,748	1,032,313	774,235	108,062	181,375	911,537	72,042	772,963	664,053
2000	5,287,364	1,543,748	1,032,313	774,235	108,062	181,375	911,537	72,042	772,963	664,053
2001	5,287,364	1,543,748	1,032,313	774,235	108,062	181,375	911,537	72,042	772,963	664,053
2002	5,287,364	1,543,748	1,032,313	774,235	108,062	181,375	911,537	72,042	772,963	664,053
2003	5,287,364	1,543,748	1,032,313	774,235	108,062	181,375	911,537	72,042	772,963	664,053
2004	5,287,364	1,543,748	1,032,313	774,235	108,062	181,375	911,537	72,042	772,963	664,053
2005	5,287,364	1,543,748	1,032,313	774,235	108,062	181,375	911,537	72,042	772,963	664,053

[a]Wood Preservers Institute (85); American Plywood Association, The Engineered Wood Associa ion (11,13).

[b]Pentachlorophenol, Copper Napthenate, Zinc Napthenate, Copper-8-Quinolinolate, and TBTO (mostly pentachlorophenol).

[c]1984 was estimated.

[d]Excludes plywood.

[e]Crossarms, landscape timbers, highway posts and guardrails, mine ties and timbers, crossing planks, and other misc. products not listed above.
Lumber taken from General Technical Report GTR-199 update, table 11 Hardwood Recovery Factor.
Plywood taken from GTR-199 update, Hardwood Plywood Lumber Conversion table B-7. All O her taken from GTR-199 update, table B-10.

Table 59—Forest chemical products production in gallons and short tons, 1965–2005[a]

	Tall oil fatty acids				Turpentine[b]				Rosin[c]		
		Over 2%	Under 2%		Sulphate	Gum	Steam		Tall oil	Gum	Steam
Year	Total	rosin	rosin	Total	turpentine[d]	turpentine	distilled	Total	rosin	rosin	distilled rosin
	1000 Short tons	*1000 Short tons*	*1000 Short tons*	*1000 U.S. liters*	*1000 U.S. liters*	*1000 U.S. liters*	*1000 U.S. liters*	*1000 Short tons*	*1000 Short tons*	*1000 Short tons*	*1000 Short tons*
1965	164.0	z	z	35,033	21,033	5,569	8,432	591.2	179.2	103.3	308 8
1966	185.5	z	z	33,275	21,338	4,211	7,727	559.9	200.0	78.1	281 9
1967	183.2	z	z	31,397	20,987	3,387	7,024	534.5	194.6	63 9	275 9
1968	186.3	z	z	32,609	23,658	2,521	6,430	527.8	204.3	48 9	274.6
1969	203.9	z	z	30,869	23,975	1,750	5,144	498.1	226.8	34 0	237.4
1970	220.2	z	z	28,790	22,768	1,292	4,731	473.6	228.7	25.1	219 8
1971	223.9	z	z	28,433	22,745	1,418	4,270	466.3	230.3	26 3	209 8
1972	235.9	z	z	28,295	23,206	1,328	3,761	465.7	240.1	25 5	200.1
1973	226.8	z	z	27,308	22,629	1,143	3,536	418.4	222.2	20 2	176 0
1974	199.8	z	z	25,583	21,379	797	3,407	369.3	198.0	14 5	156 8
1975	161.3	z	z	21,471	18,575	1,006	1,890	264.0	160.7	17 8	85.5
1976	205.7	z	z	24,183	20,265	920	2,998	350.2	201.7	16 8	131.7
1977	197.6	98.0	99.6	23,646	20,297	731	2,618	341.1	202.4	13.4	125 3
1978	193.8	102.1	91.7	24,949	22,066	517	2,366	340.8	211.5	9.4	119 9
1979	210.8	107.1	103.6	26,257	23,449	369	2,439	354.4	231.7	7.0	115.7
1980	209.0	114.8	94 2	27,685	24,979	314	2,392	343.6	223.3	5.9	114.4
1981	210.7	102.1	108.6	25,765	23,310	270	2,185	331.3	221.8	5.1	104 5
1982	187.7	91.1	96.6	23,353	21,283	230	1,840	286.4	194.0	4.4	88.0
1983	214.0	103.4	110.6	23,808	22,193	235	1,380	303.9	211.6	4.3	88.0
1984	235.8	118.4	117.5	23,233	21,628	225	1,380	295.8	225.6	4.2	66.0
1985	204.6	106.8	97 8	22,191	21,096	175	920	261.9	214.5	3.4	44.0
1986	215.1	112.5	102.5	21,956	21,956	z	z	216.8	216.8	z	z
1987	231.0	114.1	116.9	23,196	23,196	z	z	252.1	252.1	z	z
1988	239.4	118.9	120.5	28,000	28,000	z	z	256.5	256.5	z	z
1989	241.2	114.7	126.5	29,749	29,749	z	z	262.1	262.1	z	z
1990	236.8	112.8	124.1	31,077	31,077	z	z	274.6	274.6	z	z
1991	264.8	125.7	139.0	25,767	25,767	z	z	262.9	262.9	z	z
1992	251.9	115.0	137.0	24,498	24,498	z	z	266.1	266.1	z	z
1993	255.2	107.4	147.8	27,114	27,114	z	z	285.6	285.6	z	z
1994	279.1	124.6	154.4	26,424	26,424	z	z	281.8	281.8	z	z
1995	249.8	109.0	140.8	25,328	25,328	z	z	272.6	272.6	z	z
1996	254.7	109.0	145.6	22,412	22,412	z	z	290.6	290.6	z	z
1997	273.7	112.8	160.9	25,564	25,564	z	z	308.4	308.4	z	z
1998	281.9	130.8	151.1	24,146	24,146	z	z	271.7	271.7	z	z
1999	290.2	133.7	156.5	20,733	20,733	z	z	231.1	231.1	z	z
2000	263.0	102.1	160.9	23,080	23,080	z	z	245.0	245.0	z	z
2001	232.2	95.4	136.8	22,454	22,454	z	z	206.7	206.7	z	z
2002	241.4	102.1	139.3	24,162	24,162	z	z	229.8	229.8	z	z
2003	281.4	117.7	163.7	23,063	23,063	z	z	241.5	241.5	z	z
2004	383.0	191.5	191.5	22,468	22,468	z	z	268.7	268.7	z	z
2005	373.8	182.3	191.5	22,077	22,077	z	z	261.3	261.3	z	z

[a]Naval Stores Review (29); Pine Chemicals Association, Inc. (31).
[b]1965-1972 numbers are converted from 50-liter bbls to 1,000 liters.
[c]1965-1972 numbers are converted from 520-lb drums to 1,000 short tons.
[d]1988-present represents crude turpentine produc ion.
[z]Not available.

Table 60—Wood energy use in the United States 1973-2005[a]

Year	Trillion BTU					Million cubic feet of wood equivalent				
	Total	Residential	Commercial	Industrial	Electric Utilities	Total	Residential	Commercial	Industrial	Electric Utilities
1973	1,527	354	7	1,165	1	6,108	1,416	27	4,659	5
1974	1,538	371	7	1,159	1	6,151	1,484	28	4,636	3
1975	1,497	425	8	1,063	0	5,988	1,702	32	4,253	1
1976	1,711	482	9	1,220	1	6,846	1,927	36	4,880	4
1977	1,837	542	10	1,281	3	7,346	2,167	41	5,125	13
1978	2,036	622	12	1,400	2	8,145	2,487	47	5,602	8
1979	2,150	728	14	1,405	3	8,599	2,912	55	5,619	12
1980	2,483	859	21	1,600	3	9,931	3,436	84	6,400	11
1981	2,495	869	21	1,602	3	9,978	3,476	84	6,408	10
1982	2,477	937	22	1,516	2	9,908	3,748	88	6,064	8
1983	2,639	925	22	1,690	2	10,557	3,700	88	6,760	9
1984	2,629	923	22	1,679	5	10,515	3,692	88	6,716	19
1985	2,576	899	24	1,645	8	10,303	3,596	96	6,580	31
1986	2,518	876	27	1,610	5	10,073	3,504	108	6,440	21
1987	2,465	852	29	1,576	8	9,861	3,408	116	6,304	33
1988	2,552	885	32	1,625	10	10,207	3,540	128	6,500	39
1989	2,637	918	36	1,584	100	10,548	3,672	144	6,334	398
1990	2,191	581	39	1,442	129	8,762	2,324	157	5,768	514
1991	2,190	613	41	1,410	126	8,759	2,452	164	5,639	503
1992	2,290	645	44	1,461	140	9,162	2,580	176	5,845	561
1993	2,227	548	46	1,483	150	8,907	2,192	183	5,933	599
1994	2,315	537	46	1,580	152	9,261	2,148	184	6,319	609
1995	2,420	596	46	1,652	125	9,678	2,384	184	6,608	502
1996	2,467	595	50	1,684	138	9,867	2,380	202	6,734	551
1997	2,350	433	49	1,731	137	9,398	1,732	196	6,922	548
1998	2,175	387	48	1,603	137	8,702	1,549	193	6,414	547
1999	2,224	414	52	1,620	138	8,895	1,655	209	6,478	552
2000	2,257	433	53	1,636	134	9,027	1,733	213	6,544	537
2001	1,980	370	40	1,443	126	7,918	1,480	162	5,770	506
2002	1,899	313	39	1,396	150	7,595	1,252	157	5,586	601
2003	1,929	359	40	1,363	167	7,717	1,436	159	5,453	669
2004	2,015	332	41	1,476	165	8,060	1,329	166	5,904	661
2005	1,826	332	41	1,284	168	7,302	1,329	166	5,137	670

[a]Note - wood equivalent is esimtated using one quadrillian btu's equal to 4 billion cubic feet of wood, actual wood fuel includes roundwood, bark, mill residue, and black liquor from pulp mills
Source: USDA Energy Information Administration (88)